PSYCHOTHERAPY BY
RECIPROCAL INHIBITION

PSYCHOTHERAPY BY RECIPROCAL INHIBITION

by JOSEPH WOLPE, M.D.

STANFORD UNIVERSITY PRESS

STANFORD, CALIFORNIA

Stanford University Press
Stanford, California
© 1958 by the Board of Trustees of the
Leland Stanford Junior University
Printed in the United States of America
ISBN 0-8047-0509-7
Original edition 1958
Last figure below indicates year of this printing:
80 79 78 77 76 75 74

To Stella, my wife

Preface

*It seems possible that a clearer understanding of
the condition will come from a simple analysis in
terms of habit formation than from any more
complicated psychological explanation.*

For the neurosis obeys the laws of habit.

NORMAN FENTON*

The theory of neurosis and the methods of psychotherapy described in
this book stem directly from modern learning theory. The chain of events
leading to the writing of it may be dated from the year 1944, when as a
military medical officer I had plenty of spare time for reading. Then a
staunch follower of Freud, I was one day surprised to find in Malinowski's
Sex and Repression in Savage Society persuasive evidence against the assumption that the Oedipus theory had *universal* application. The ripple
this roused in me soon subsided since the point did not seem vital; but a
month or so later I chanced to read in C. W. Valentine's *Psychology of
Early Childhood* an account of observations on young children that threw
doubt on the validity of the Oedipus theory even for Western society. This
time my faith in the "sure stronghold" of Freudianism was seriously
shaken, and a paragraph in a newspaper to the effect that the Russians do
not accept psychoanalysis was enough to motivate me to find out what they
do accept; the answer was Pavlov. This answer did not directly yield much
enlightenment, but Pavlov led to Hull, and Hull to the studies of experimental neurosis that suggested the new methods of psychotherapy.

Mainly for the sake of the many psychiatrists and clinical psychologists
who have little or no acquaintance with modern learning theory, I have
thought it necessary to include a brief chapter on the biological matrix of
modern learning theory and another on those aspects of the learning process
most relevant to neurotic behavior, viewed in a neurophysiological framework.

* *Shell Shock and Its Aftermath* (St. Louis: C. V. Mosby Company, 1926).

The writing of this book was made possible by a Fellowship at the Center for Advanced Study in the Behavioral Sciences, Stanford, California, during the year 1956–57. The Center provided every amenity for facilitating the work, including a unique environment of continual intellectual stimulation.

A number of people have influenced my thinking. I am particularly indebted to Dr. L. J. Reyna, who helped to plan the animal experiments in 1947 and, subsequently, through the years, contributed ideas and criticisms, often bringing to light unexpected aspects of problems. Some of my colleagues at the Center for Advanced Study in the Behavioral Sciences gave me direct assistance in the preparation of the manuscript. Dr. E. R. Hilgard spent many hours reading the chapters as they were written, and made detailed comments that improved both the substance of the book and its organization. Various chapters were read and beneficially criticized by Dr. Fred Attneave, Dr. D. E. Berlyne, Dr. David A. Hamburg, Dr. William Lambert, Dr. Charles Morris, and Dr. Theodore M. Newcomb. Dr. Richard Savage gave indispensable guidance regarding the treatment of the statistical data. Mrs. Edna Proschan assembled the data on the Willoughby questionnaire.

I am indebted to Mr. S. Rachman for compiling the Bibliography and assisting with the Index, and to my wife for improving the clarity and felicity of the language of long tracts of the manuscript, besides collaborating in many other tasks. I was fortunate to be within easy reach of Stanford University Press and their staff for many months. The integration of the book owes much to their insight and judgment.

JOSEPH WOLPE
Lecturer in the Department of Psychiatry
University of the Witwatersrand

Johannesburg, South Africa
February 1958

Introduction

The ideal of medical treatment is to achieve the greatest effects in the shortest time. Today's most widely accepted regime for treating neurosis—psychoanalysis—is distinguished for the great length of time it takes to produce results that are no better than those obtained by therapists using the simple traditional methods customary in the psychiatric clinics of general hospitals (Landis, 1937; Wilder, 1945). The central thesis of psychoanalysis—that the essence of psychotherapy is the uncovering and expression of "the repressed"—has received some very severe criticism (e.g., Wohlgemuth, 1923; Salter, 1952; Eysenck, 1953); but as long as there has been no satisfactory alternative, the repression theory has maintained its dominating hold upon psychotherapeutic practice. Its proponents have felt themselves supported by a characteristic achievement of their therapy—the emergence of insights that are often comforting and sometimes very striking (even if not always incontestable). However, as will be seen, this kind of achievement really has no special relevance to the curing of neuroses.

In this book a new theory of psychotherapy is presented: a serious alternative to the repression theory, one that is based on the growing body of knowledge of the processes by which change is wrought in the behavior of organisms—modern learning theory—the fruit of the efforts of Pavlov, Thorndike, Watson, Tolman, Hull, Skinner, and their followers. This book owes especially much to Pavlov and to Hull.

The logic of the present approach may be briefly stated. Only three kinds of processes are known that can bring about lasting changes in an organism's habit of response to a given stimulus situation: growth, lesions, and learning. Since neurotic behavior demonstrably originates in learning, it is only to be expected that its elimination will be a matter of "unlearning."

Accordingly, known laws of learning were applied to the special problems of neurosis, a step rewarded by the emergence of techniques of therapy apparently much more effective than any previously reported. Both experimental and clinical observations supported the conclusion that *fundamental psychotherapeutic effects follow reciprocal inhibition of neurotic responses.*

The experimental observations came first. They were made on cats in which lasting neurotic states had been induced by the administration of several punishing but nondamaging shocks in a small cage. The neurotic anxiety and other reactions were subsequently in every case entirely removed by getting the animals to eat in the presence of small, and at later sessions progressively larger, "doses" of anxiety-evoking stimuli.

These findings revealed an antagonism between feeding responses and anxiety responses. When anxiety was great, feeding was inhibited: when anxiety was less, so that feeding could occur in its presence, the evocation of anxiety in the situation was later seen to have been weakened. Apparently, at the moment of eating there was a transient inhibition of anxiety; and the ensuing reduction of the hunger drive "stamped this in" (see Chapter 2), creating a measure of conditioned inhibition of the anxiety response, a weakening of the habit of responding with anxiety to this environment.

The suggestion that arose from these experiments was that human neurotic anxieties might similarly be handled by opposing feeding behavior to them. Long ago, Jones (1924) succeeded in overcoming fears in young children by giving them attractive food to eat in association with the presentation of a feared object first at a distance and then progressively closer at hand. There is no reason why feeding should not be effective in overcoming fears in adults under certain circumstances. What is required is that in the presence of the anxiety-evoking stimulus food must be given under so intense a hunger drive that in the act of eating there will be an inhibition of anxiety. Probably, it is precisely this that is the explanation of the beneficial effects on neuroses of subcoma doses of insulin; and it is worth noting that the effects of this method have been greatest when the patient has eaten substantially more than usual and has put on weight. Presumably, in eating voraciously because of heightened hunger drive, the patient obtains a reciprocal inhibition of any anxiety responses that happen to be occurring within him at that particular time. This explanation, with its close parallel in animal experiments, gains credence when one takes into account the haziness of the explanations that have been offered in terms of gross physiology. However, from the results of a controlled experiment by Teitelbaum and his associates (1946), as reviewed by Sargant and Slater (1947), it is clear that only a small percentage of patients are favorably affected by subcoma insulin. This finding is not surprising, because any effects depend on the fortuitous occurrence of anxiety-producing stimuli at the time of the eating.

I have not myself explored the possibilities of feeding responses for overcoming human neuroses. Other responses that are in various ways more convenient have turned out also to be capable of inhibiting anxiety. The most widely useful of these have been assertive responses, relaxation responses, and sexual responses. In special contexts I have also successfully employed respiratory responses, conditioned motor responses, "anxiety relief" (electric shock cessation) responses, and conditioned avoidance responses. I deliberately have caused these responses to be evoked, inside the consulting room or outside it, aiming always at arranging conditions so that neurotic anxiety will be maximally inhibited by the antagonistic response selected.

Details will be found in the body of the book, but here is an outline of one of the more important techniques. In this, relaxation is used to counter the effects of anxiety-evoking stimuli; paralleling in an obvious way the method of therapy in animals, described above. The patient is given preliminary training in relaxation by Jacobson's method (1938). Meanwhile an "anxiety hierarchy" is constructed. This is a list of stimuli to which the patient reacts with unadaptive anxiety. The items are ranked according to the amount of disturbance they cause, the most disturbing items being placed at the top and the least at the bottom. The patient is hypnotized and made to relax as deeply as possible. Then he is told to imagine the weakest item in the anxiety hierarchy—the smallest "dose" of phobic stimulation. If the relaxation is unimpaired by this, a slightly greater "dose" is presented at the next session. The "dosage" is gradually increased from session to session, until at last the phobic stimulus can be presented at maximum intensity without impairing the calm, relaxed state. It will then be found that the patient has ceased to react with his previous anxiety to encounters in real life with even the strongest of the once phobic stimuli.

It must not be assumed that because this instance relates to a phobia it is only for "simple" cases that these methods are adequate. Leaving aside the consideration that history is crowded with "simple" phobias that nobody could cure, investigation from the present standpoint reveals that even the difficult "character neuroses" usually consist of intricate systems of phobias that can be organized and treated along the same lines as a "simple" phobia. This is not remarkable, if, as will be contended, most neuroses are basically unadaptive conditioned anxiety reactions.

An obvious question arises. Since nobody else tries to treat patients on the reciprocal inhibition principle, how are other therapists' favorable results to be explained? The answer appears to be that the responses that I deliberately employ are not the only ones that have the capacity to inhibit anxiety. Apparently, emotional responses that can also do this are evoked in patients by the psychotherapeutic situation itself, no matter what its content. This would account for the fact that methods ranging from traditional counseling to psychoanalysis all record much the same measure of success (about 50 per cent). Of course, my patients, too, profit from these nonspecific effects of the interview situation; but that *my* special methods *do* have an additional effect is suggested by a ratio of "apparently cured" and "much improved" patients that is consistently in the region of 90 per cent.

The pages that follow will present the case for the general orientation of this book, the principles of learning that appear to be most relevant to its thesis, a review of experimental work on neurosis, and an explication of human neurosis formation in terms of principles of learning. All these are the substrate for the main substance of the book—an exposition of psychotherapy based on the reciprocal inhibition principle.

Contents

PART II: PSYCHOTHERAPY

*PART I: **BACKGROUND***

1 | *Relationships Between Some Anatomical*

Structures and Behavior

Basic Definitions

Everything in this book rests on the fundamental assumption that the behavior of organisms, including human beings, conforms to causal laws just as other phenomena do. It is an assumption that is justified by the history of the last two centuries, during which scientific investigation has lighted up, one by one, areas of experience whose elucidation has been held by mystics and others to be beyond the scope of the human mind.

Broadly, when one speaks of an organism "behaving" one is using the word just as one would use it in other contexts—to mean a change of state or of spatial relations to other things. The special properties of living matter have led to the development of a special terminology for referring to organismal behavior. The meaning of the terms must be clearly stated, for though they all have extensive current usage, variations of meaning are in some cases very considerable.

1. An *organism* is an individual living plant or animal.

2. *Organismal behavior* refers to each and every change that can be predicated of an organism or any part of it.

3. A *behavioral event* is a particular change or complex of changes occurring in an organism at a given time.

4. A *response* (or reaction) is a behavioral event that is thought of as standing in the relation of consequent to an antecedent event or events which may be either behavioral or extraorganismal. Thus vibration of the tympanum would be the first organismal response to the impingement of the sound of a bell on the ear. This would be followed in series by movement of the ossicles, disturbance in the organ of Corti, the passage of nerve impulses along sensory, central, and motor neurones, and finally contraction of muscles turning the head toward the sound. Each event in this series could be called a response relative not only to the immediately antecedent event but also to every antecedent event in the series. Because the muscle contraction is usually the only behavioral event in the series open to the view of an outside observer, it is usually called "the" response to

the bell. It is well to realize that no response has a solitary immediate antecedent, but, in the words of J. S. Mill (1898), ". . . several antecedents, the concurrence of all of them being requisite to produce, that is, to be certain of being followed by, the consequent."

It is useful to distinguish between *molecular* and *molar* aspects of responses. A response is called molecular when the change being observed takes place in a relatively small physiologically differentiated unit of the organism, such as a cell or group of cells. A molar response is the gross resultant of a number of molecular events occurring at more or less the same time. Since in this book we are essentially concerned with the nervous system, the relevant molecular responses will have their main location in neural, muscular, and secretory tissues. Their molar resultants—such responses as swallowing, jumping, sweating, and thinking (see below) — will form a very much greater part of our subject matter than the molecular events.

Although Tolman (1932, pp. 7–8) was the first to make use in psychology of the distinction between molecular and molar, he took a further step which we must reject: he tied up *molar* behavior with the notion of "behavior of the organism as a whole" (pp. 17–19). Every organism *is* a whole that is clearly distinguished from the "not-organism." In a sense *every* change in an organism implies alteration of the organism as a whole, but this is not what Tolman means. In another sense, since the character of molar behavior is always determined by changes in *particular* active parts, "behavior of the organism as a whole" would imply change in every single part. That is certainly not true in the actual examples of behavior that Tolman himself calls molar, and may well never be true.

5. An *act* is a sequence of molar responses. Examples are walking, talking, and breathing. Almost all molar responses are parts of acts.

6. A *stimulus* is the antecedent of a response. In a series of molecular behavioral events such as the example given in the discussion of "response," each response stands in the relation of stimulus to the response that follows it. In this usage, even the impulse in a motor nerve is, in relation to the subsequent muscle contraction, a stimulus. Similarly, an increase in circulating sex hormone is a stimulus to sexual activity. A *sensory* stimulus is anything that has as a consequence the passage of a nervous impulse centripetally along an afferent nerve. This usually occurs through the intermediary of a response in the end organ of the afferent nerve, but a centripetal impulse can also be initiated anywhere along the course of the nerve, by applying an electric current for example.

The sensory stimuli which we shall mention in this book will nearly always be relatively gross and complex, in keeping with the molar aspects of behavior that constitute our main subject matter. This corresponds with what organisms encounter in the ordinary course of life. It will be convenient to label as sensory stimuli not only such simple examples as a tone or a point of light, but also unitary objects such as a horse, a chair, or an elevator. But where sensory stimulation has a more complex origin we shall speak of *stimulus constellation* and, if it is very complex, of a *stimulus situation*. It will often be an arbitrary decision which of these two terms to use. Sometimes "stimulus" will be loosely used in their stead.

7. *Environment* is a collective term referring to everything to which the organism is responding at a given time. This accords with Lundberg's definition of environment as "that to which response is made" (1939, p. 223). This means that objects in physical proximity to an organism are "environment" only as far as they are sources of stimulation. To designate collectively the objects that are more or less in the immediate vicinity of an organism, the term *surroundings* may be used. In short, an organism *is in* its surroundings and *reacts to* its environment.

An organism's surroundings do not provide its only sources of stimulation—do not make up its whole environment. For many stimulations arise from within its own body. A few of these have correlates in consciousness, ranging from relatively simple sensations (such as feelings of tension in muscles, gastric hunger contractions, and hormone-induced sexual agitation) to the sequences of complex images that constitute a train of thought. At a particular moment a man may be responding much more strongly to the image of a girl a thousand miles away than to anything in his surroundings. Although the differentiation between external and internal environment has its uses, from the standpoint of the reacting entity, in Lundberg's words, "that which excites it to reaction, whether it be a glandular pressure or a symbolic mechanism, is environment as 'external' as any other" (1939, p. 221).

8. A *habit* is a recurring manner of response to a given stimulus situation. We shall use the word almost exclusively to mean habits that are learned. An example is applying the brakes when the traffic light is red. The repeatability of habitual responses implies that underlying them there is a *persisting state of the organism*—to use Hull's expression (1943, p. 102). This does not mean that habits have an all-or-nothing character. Each of them has a possible range of strength from a minimum where its very existence is in doubt to a maximum that is unsteady because of physiological variations that Hull has grouped under the phrase "behavioral oscillation" (1943, pp. 304–21). The strength of a habit may be estimated in several ways—by amplitude or intensity of response, by response velocity (Taylor, 1950), by the frequency of occurrence of the response in the given stimulus conditions, and by the measure of its persistence in the face of efforts to eliminate it.

Often the organism has a "repertoire" of two or more habits for the same stimulus conditions. These are then said to belong to a *habit family*. To indicate differences in their strength the expression *habit family hierarchy* is used (Hull, 1943).

When responses that differ in detail display a common feature this will be referred to as a *behavior pattern*. For example, after observing a man's behavior toward children in a variety of contexts, it may be noted that all of his acts are characterized by gentleness. Gentleness with children will then be stated to be a behavior pattern of that man. Another somewhat different example would be punctuality in keeping appointments; another would be deliberateness of movement. Behavior patterns are thus more or less generalized habits that modify the form of individual responses in defined ways.

Needs and Drives

In a vague way "everybody knows" what needs and drives are. Yet the words *need* and *drive* are often used in ways that are ambiguous or confused. Their area of reference is so important that considerable attention must be paid to giving them clear definition.

Let us ask what it is that the various states which are called *states of need* have in common that enables them to be classed together under a common heading. In common usage the word *need* derives its application from human feelings involving "wanting" or "unsatisfaction." Probably because allusion to extraorganismal referents aids communication, it is common to refer to each different need feeling in terms of whatever has come to be associated with reduction of the particular need. Thus we speak of the needs for oxygen, food, water, urination, defecation, sexual satisfaction, rest, and relief from pain. It is convenient to have such terms of reference, but in order to determine what is common to all needs we have to know what goes on *within the organism* in the case of each need.

Now by no means everything is known about the physiological states underlying the primary needs, but there is no doubt that they manifest great diversity. The need for food is correlated with the occurrence of rhythmic gastric contractions among other things (Cannon, 1929, pp. 289–98); the need for water with dryness of the mouth and throat as a result of reduced salivary secretion owing to diminished body fluid (Cannon, 1929, pp. 299–333); the need for physical rest with metabolic changes in muscles, and notably the accumulation of lactic acid (Wilhelmi, 1946); the need to micturate with fullness of the bladder producing tension on its walls; and the need to copulate with (*inter alia*) increases in the amount of circulating sex hormone (Beach, 1941, 1942; Moehlig, 1940; Shapiro, 1937).

If the physiological correlates of the various needs are compared, there seems to be no characteristic that is common to all of them—that is, if the physiological correlates of each need are surveyed in isolation from their consequents. Examination of their consequents shows that they *do* have something in common: they are one and all antecedents of neuro-effector responses. In a number of instances it has been shown that there is a correlation between the magnitude of some physiological aspect of the need state and the amount of motor activity displayed by the organism. This has been found in relation to the food need by Skinner (1938, pp. 396–97) and Richter (1927); and in relation to sexual needs by Richter (1927), and Wang, Richter, and Guttmacher (1925). The studies of Beach (1941, 1942), Miller, Hubert, and Hamilton (1938), and Shapiro (1937) indicate the same sort of correlation.*

That needs produce effector responses through central neural excitation was demonstrated by Pack (1923) in the case of physiological lack of water. He showed that if the oral mucous membrane of a water-deprived animal is kept moist by the injection of pilocarpine, the animal does not drink water placed before it. On the other hand, as a number of facts mustered by Cannon (1929, pp. 299–333) show, drying of the mouth results in drinking even when there is no physiological lack of water. Evidently, the motor activity associated with lack of water does not occur unless the lack of water results in excitation of the central nervous system as a consequent of the stimulation of those oral afferent nerves that are stimulable by dryness (see Fig. 1). A correlation between thirst and central neural excitation has been demonstrated by the excessive water drinking which follows the injection of hypertonic saline into certain parts of the hypothalamus (Andersson, 1953).

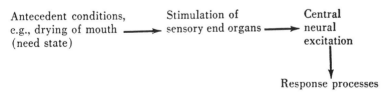

Fig. 1. Many physiological need states produce central neural excitation (drive) as a consequent of stimulation of peripheral nerves. Need reduction then subserves reinforcement only because it is followed by reduction of central neural excitation.

If being antecedents of neuro-effector responses is the only thing need conditions have in common, by what are they to be distinguished from "ordinary" sensory stimuli which are also antecedents of neuro-effector responses? The answer seems to be that no absolute difference exists; and

---

* For a review of recent work see Beach (1947).

if the stimulating effects of "primary needs" stand out in any way from those of other stimuli, it is only in that they tend more often to be *strong* as measured by strength and extent of effector responses. Every sensory stimulus, therefore, has the essential characteristic of a need.*

The converse, however, is not true, for not every need condition functions as a *sensory* stimulus. For instance, when, as in the experiments mentioned above, an increase in circulating sex hormone is correlated with increased molar activity, the increase in activity seems to be due to the hormone lowering the resistance of certain nervous pathways, without any increase in the number of *afferent* impulses taking place (as far as can be judged). This was well shown by an experiment by Beach (1942), who compared the behavior of testosterone-injected with that of nontestosterone-injected male rats in the presence of a variety of animals of different sexual "stimulus value," and in each case he noted greater activity in the injected animals.

Whatever the mechanisms involved, need conditions, being antecedents of neuro-effector responses, are stimulus conditions to these responses. But between the stimulus conditions and the effector responses *there intervenes excitation of neurones in the central nervous system;*† and to this excitation the term *drive* may usefully be applied.‡

The conception of drive employed by Miller and Dollard (1941) must be distinguished from that arrived at here. For them, notably, the word refers, not to the neural excitation, but to the antecedent sensory stimulus. They state (p. 18):

A drive is a strong stimulus that impels action. Any stimulus can become a drive if it is made strong enough. The stronger the stimulus, the more drive function it possesses. The faint murmur of distant music has but little primary drive function; the infernal blare of the neighbor's radio has considerably more.

* This, of course, does not make it desirable to call every sensory stimulus a need. The term is useful for distinguishing stronger stimulations, however ill-defined their limen. Thus, besides the primary needs, we have the need to explore (Berlyne, 1950) conditioned needs, such as a need for prestige, and needs for subgoals, e.g., money.

† "Central nervous system" is used in the present context not in opposition to "autonomic nervous system," but in Sherrington's sense, as that part of the nervous system in which "afferent paths from receptor-organs become connected with the efferent paths of effector-organs, not only those adjacent to their own receptors, but through 'internuncial' (J. Hunter, 1778) paths, with efferent paths to effector-organs remote" (Sherrington, 1906, pp. 312–13).

‡ This use of the word "drive" has affinities with the popular use which has its origin in the *feelings* people have of an impulse to action. Such feelings presumably have correlates of strong central neural excitation.

A weakness of their formulation is that it seems to imply that only excitations that result in *overt* activity qualify as drive. From the point of view of the learning process, as will be seen later, it is operationally more useful to say that all central excitation is drive, and when it reaches a certain intensity and if other conditions are present that enable the excitation to reach and excite effector neurones, overt motor activity results.

The Neural Substrate of Behavior

Nerve impulses are not vaguely diffused through various zones of the nervous system but course along definite neurones, any one of which (unless it is a peripheral afferent neurone) becomes activated only if another neurone transmits excitation to it. Much remains unknown concerning the intimate details of the conditions that determine the stimulability of one neurone by an impulse from another, but certain relationships have become quite firmly established in recent years and brief mention will be made of some of the more important. These relationships, multiplied many times, in intricately arranged units, form the basis of neural organization.

IMPULSES IN NERVE

When a neurone is stimulated, a feature of its response is the passage along its course of an impulse which is detectable by a sensitive galvanometer. This impulse is due to changes of potential associated with movement of sodium and potassium ions through the membranous casing of the nerve fibers (Eccles, 1953, pp. 30–64). It is sometimes disputed whether or not this electrical impulse is the "real" carrier of "nervous energy"; but the question is quite unimportant, since the electrical impulse seems to be an invariable correlate of neural activity; so that if it is not itself the "real" impulse it is at any rate a sign of its presence. Adrian (1928, p. 15) has said, "In every case so far investigated whenever there has been reason to suppose that a nerve is in action, the usual potential changes have been detected, provided that the conditions for recording them were favorable."

The amplitude of the electrical impulse passing along a given nerve fiber is independent of the strength of the stimulus of which it is a consequent, so that the electrical response evoked by the weakest physical energy strong enough to evoke a response will not be less in amplitude than that evoked by a much stronger physical energy. This is the "all-or-nothing relation between the stimulus and the propagated disturbance," first demonstrated by Lucas in 1909 and repeatedly confirmed since then. Increasing the strength of a stimulus energy does, however, have another effect. It is correlated with increased *frequency* of impulses conducted along the fiber. This was shown to be the case with peripheral afferent neurones by

Adrian (1928, pp. 144–47); and with peripheral efferent neurones by Adrian and Bronk (1928, 1929). There is no reason to suppose that central neurones behave differently, and the work of Grundfest and Campbell (1939) favors the assumption that they, too, respond to greater strength of stimulation with increased frequency of impulses.

It may now be stated, having regard to the terms of our definition of drive, that frequency of impulses is a quantitative correlate of strength of drive. Also, the greater the *number* of central neurones in a state of excitation at a given time, the greater will the strength of drive be. Hence, the two quantitative correlates of strength of drive are the *number* of neurones in a state of excitation and the *frequency* of the impulses in each.

SYNAPTIC CONDUCTION

In the central nervous system almost every presynaptic fiber has many branches and establishes anatomical contact with numerous nerve cells (Lorente de No, 1938). When conditions at a point of contact are such that neural excitation may be transmitted across it, the conjunction is a functional one and is called a *synapse*. Nonfunctional conjunctions that have the potentiality of becoming functional are the anatomical basis for learning.

One-way transmission across a synapse is the rule. Several presynaptic neurones may converge to form synapses with one postsynaptic neurone, and the various synapses may then be said to make up a synaptic zone. A number of factors are known to determine whether or not a synapse will transmit an impulse from a presynaptic neurone to a postsynaptic neurone. Chemical agents like strychnine increase synaptic excitability (Sollman, 1942), and agents like nembutal reduce it (Eccles, 1946). Excitability is also reduced immediately after an impulse has been conducted by the postsynaptic neurone, when for a short period, which varies in length from 0.5 to 3.0 milliseconds, the neurone is absolutely refractory and will not respond to any further impulse (Eccles, 1931, 1936; Lorente de No, 1935a). For a period of about 15 milliseconds after this absolutely refractory period, there is a relatively refractory period or period of subnormality (Eccles, 1931, 1936; Lorente de No, 1935b). During subnormality the neurone is refractory to weak stimulus energies only, and will transmit an impulse if the stimulus energy at the synapse is sufficiently strengthened. The impulse that is then transmitted is of normal amplitude, in accordance with the all-or-none principle.

If, at any time other than the absolutely refractory period, an impulse too weak to evoke a response in the postsynaptic neurone is followed after 0.1 to 0.5 millisecond by a second inadequate impulse along the same neurone, the effects of the two impulses may summate so as to excite the postsynaptic neurone (Eccles and Sherrington, 1931a). This is known as *temporal summation*. In like manner, the summation of the effects of impulses reaching a synaptic knob from two or more neurones may result in excitation of the postsynaptic neurone, though the separate impulses would have been ineffective. This phenomenon, known as *spatial summation*, has been demonstrated by Denny-Brown and Sherrington (1928), Eccles and Sherrington (1930), Bremer (1930), and Lorente de No (1935, 1938a). Lorente de No (1935) has found, in eye muscle nuclei, that for spatial summation to occur the interval between the impulses must not exceed 0.1 to 0.2 millisecond; and that it is maximal when the impulses arrive simultaneously. Eccles (1953) has shown that in other neurones summation is possible decreasingly over several milliseconds and that in the autonomic nervous system the interval may amount to 15 milliseconds or more (1937).

Summation of the effects of impulses more widely spaced in time seems to be due to the activity of those chains of internuncial neurones that are arranged in circular formations in such a way that if one part of a chain is stimulated, a circus movement is set up in the chain. And since at least some of the neurones comprising the chain also give off impulses at synapses *outside* the chain, impulses will be delivered at these synapses for as long as the circus movement continues. Impulses that are supraliminal will evoke responses in the contiguous neurone at the synapse. But if the impulses are subliminal and any one of them reaches the synapse synchronously with a subliminal impulse from elsewhere, a supraliminal effect may result from their spatial summation. The evidence in support of the above statement regarding the activity of internuncial neurones has been reviewed in two lucid articles by Lorente de No (1938b, 1939).

Apparently, some spatial summation is necessary for any synaptic transmission (Eccles, 1953, p. 113). But summation is *not the invariable result* when impulses arrive at a synaptic zone simultaneously from different neurones. Impulses delivered by certain neurones appear to have an inhibitory effect at the synaptic zone on the impulses that other neurones deliver. Indications of this were obtained by Eccles and Sherrington (1931b) some years ago. More direct demonstrations of this kind of inhibition (which is known as *direct inhibition*) have been provided by Lloyd (1941, 1946) and Renshaw (1941, 1942). It is now known that impulses from inhibitory fibers have electrical effects at the synaptic zone which are opposite to those of excitatory impulses (Brooks and Eccles, 1948).

THE NEURAL BASIS OF PRIMARY STIMULUS GENERALIZATION

When an organism has been conditioned to make a response to a clearly defined stimulus, it tends to make a similar response to a similar stimulus.

Hull (1943, pp. 186–87) has called this *primary stimulus generalization*, for it is a direct result of "the partial physical identity of the stimulation compounds." The physical similarity between two stimulus compounds may be discernible in any number of "dimensions"—for example, frequency of vibrations, shape, position, or identity of parts. The greater the resemblance of the generalized stimulus to the conditioned stimulus, the greater will the similarity of response be.

Primary stimulus generalization can be accounted for by the fact that similar stimuli excite a certain number of afferent neurones in common, this number decreasing as the two stimuli diverge from each other in any dimension. In the two examples given below there is evidence of such a relationship.

Pavlov (1927, p. 13), Anrep (1923), and Bass and Hull (1934) have found that if a response is conditioned to a stimulus to a given spot on the skin, application of the stimulus to other spots will also elicit the response, but with a strength that decreases with increasing distance from the spot where conditioning was established. This inverse relationship fits in neatly with the fact first noted by Sherrington (1906, pp. 126–29) that nerves supplying closely adjacent cutaneous spots give off impulses to more spinal afferent neurones in common than is the case when the spots are more widely spaced.

With regard to auditory stimuli, Pavlov (1927, pp. 118–27), Hovland (1937), and Humphreys (1939) have each reported that the responses to a stimulus differing in pitch from a conditioned auditory stimulus diminish in magnitude as the difference in pitch becomes wider. (Humphreys, having established a conditioned galvanic response to a tone of 1967 cycles, found a significantly greater generalized response to 984 cycles than to 1000 cycles. This, however, is easily understood, since 984 cycles, being an octave below 1967 cycles, would produce a harmonic of the latter frequency.) That such auditory generalization also depends on the number of neurones that are activated in common by different frequencies is indicated by the findings of Stevens, Davis, and Lurie (1935) that the lower the frequency of a tone acting on the ear, the nearer to the apex is the responding part of the organ of Corti; and the greater the similarity between the tones, the greater the overlap between the respective responding parts. It has further been demonstrated that adjacent parts of the organ of Corti are connected with adjacent areas of the primary acoustic nucleus and the medial geniculate body (Ades *et al.*, 1939) and with adjacent areas of the cerebral cortex (Woolsey and Walze, 1942).

The correlations noted in the above two examples support the suggestion that primary stimulus generalization is accounted for by similar stimuli exciting a certain number of neurones in common. Of course, experiments are needed which would demonstrate this directly. Also desirable is information which would make possible correlations involving other dimensions of difference and other sensory modalities. Nevertheless, we already seem to have fairly satisfactory grounds for the following general hypothesis: *Primary stimulus generalization occurs when a stimulus* S_2, *not previously conditioned to a response, evokes that response in some measure by activating some of the afferent neurones that are also activated by a stimulus* S_1 *that has been conditioned to the response; and the strength of the response to* S_2 *will depend upon the number of neurones whose activation is common to both stimuli* (see Fig. 2).

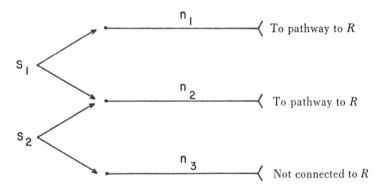

Fig. 2. Diagram illustrating the mechanism of primary stimulus generalization. Response R has been conditioned to stimulus S_1 which activates neurones n_1 and n_2. S_2, also activating n_2, also elicits R, but less strongly than S_1 does.

It follows from this hypothesis that the generalized effects of response-eliminating procedures (see below) will also be determined by the pathways that are common to different stimuli. For example, if a response has been conditioned to a tone of 1000 cycles, and then extinction is accomplished to the generalized stimulus of 950 cycles, the response to 1000 cycles will subsequently be diminished in strength by a measure that depends on the number of pathways also responding to 950 cycles—for this is the number of inactivated pathways. It follows also that no matter how many stimuli deriving their response-evoking potential from generalization have this potential extinguished, the original conditioned stimulus will still command a stronger response than *any* generalized stimulus; for its effects will be transmitted through *all surviving pathways*. Any "generalized" stimulus will have fewer pathways at its disposal. Although this was stated several years ago (Wolpe, 1952e), the very simple experiment that would confirm or deny this hypothesis still remains to be done.

THE NEURAL BASIS OF THE SPECIAL EFFECTS
OF COMPOUND STIMULATION*

When two stimuli in spatial or temporal juxtaposition (i.e., in a "pattern") act upon an organism, their combined effect is not the arithmetical sum of the effect that the individual stimuli would have if presented singly. If the separate stimuli evoke the *same* reaction, though perhaps in unequal strength, the combination will evoke that reaction in a strength that is usually less than the arithmetical sum of that of the separate reactions (see Hull, 1943, pp. 204–25). If the separate stimuli evoke *different* reactions, these too may be modified in strength when the stimuli are presented together; but, in addition, the reaction to the combination may include elements that are not to be found in the reactions to the separate stimuli. Thus, a gray patch surrounded by blue looks yellowish, and surrounded by red it looks greenish. Similarly, as Koffka (1930) points out, if the two bidimensional figures illustrated in Fig. 3 are placed appropriately in apposition, the combination gives the tridimensional impression of a cube.

Fig. 3. Koffka's cube.

Another kind of demonstration of the occurrence of interactive effects that are distinct from the effects of the component stimuli is provided by certain experiments on conditioned responses. In Woodbury's famous experiments (1943), dogs learned to make the same response to *either* a high-pitched buzzer or a low-pitched buzzer and a different response to the presentation of both buzzers in combination.

Spatial summation (see p. 15) provides us with a ready-made explanation of the emergence of these interactive effects. We may illustrate this with reference to Woodbury's experiment. When the high buzzer produces an impulse in an afferent neurone, responses follow in neurones which are contiguous with this afferent neurone and stimulable by impulses from it. Each responding neurone in turn stimulates stimulable neurones contiguous with it. But *in many contiguous neurones no response occurs;* they are not stimulable by these impulses. The same situation exists for the separate responses to the low buzzer. Now, suppose that certain of the non-

* A fuller discussion of this topic, with a criticism of the Gestalt position, was presented some years ago (Wolpe, 1949).

responding neurones are contiguous with both high-buzzer-stimulated and low-buzzer-stimulated neurones. Then it is easy to see that if impulses arrive from both sources simultaneously, the threshold of some of the neurones previously not responding will be exceeded, *so that they will now respond* (owing to spatial summation; see Fig. 4). So rich is the mosaic of neural interconnections that it is not difficult to believe that in the combination of almost any two stimuli at least some neurones will be stimulated that would not be stimulated consequent to either of the stimuli singly.

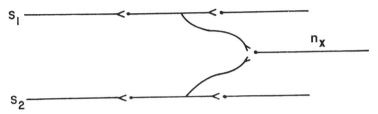

Fig. 4. Spatial summation as the basis of the special effects of compound stimulation. The neurone n_x is activated only when impulses are arriving from both S_1 and S_2.

In general terms, then, we may state that *when two stimuli act in combination, they activate not only the neurones that each acting alone would have activated but also certain other neurones.* It is the stimulation of these additional neurones that makes such "wholes" as the composite shape in Fig. 3 more than the sum of its parts. At other times the interaction may be due to the operation of direct inhibition (see p. 11) at synaptic zones, so that neurones that respond to one or other separate stimulus will not respond to the combination.

THE RELATION OF NEURAL EVENTS TO IMAGERY

There is still a surprisingly prevalent belief that whereas other animals may be "mere" mechanisms, man, although also made up largely of physical mechanisms, is "something more." This belief has its roots in the ancient idea that firmly bound to man's body until death is a soul endowed with free will, which, while standing aloof from the causal stream within the physical body, is nevertheless able to act upon the stream and influence its course. In psychology today the soul is rarely encountered. It has given place to another nonmaterial entity (mind). This has a "structure" of its own, obeys a set of laws within itself, and interacts with the physical body according to causal laws. The "mind" so understood plays a dominating part in the theorizing of psychoanalysts. (See, for example, Fenichel (1945, pp. 15–18), Jones (1948, pp. 171–72), Masserman (1946, pp. 26–29).

The standpoint will be taken here that every content of consciousness depends on specific, though no doubt complex, neural activity. Impressive support for this hypothesis is provided by experiments on the exposed human brain reported by Penfield and Rasmussen (1950) and Penfield (1954). They observed in many subjects that stimulation of points on the superior or lateral surfaces of the temporal lobe aroused imagery of past experiences. The phenomena were visual or auditory or both, and the same recollection could be repeated "as the result of successive stimuli at the same spot or by stimuli at a little distance from each other" (Penfield, 1954, p. 293).

Between a stimulus and the responses that follow it there must be an unbroken network of causally related events, potentially observable by an outside beholder, no matter whether or not some of the neural events have correlates in the consciousness of the subject. Any contents of the subject's consciousness would be *in parallel and not in series* with their neural correlates, and would in essence constitute the unique reaction of a specially placed observer (the subject) to these neural events. Thus, an image of which I am not conscious now will appear in my imagination if appropriate stimuli activate certain of my neurones. It can have no independent existence apart from the stimulation of these neurones. Within my nervous system, a *potentiality* which includes the evocation of this image may be said to exist, but *only in the same sense as it may be said that my nervous system harbors the potentiality of a knee jerk given the stimulus of a patellar tap*. If the relationship of images to the nervous system is so conceived, all talk of "mind structure" becomes nonsensical.

It is interesting to consider why people so readily believe that thoughts are in some way released from the brain and then "exist" somewhere outside, in detachment from the organism, as if they were "objects" in a shadowy realm. The origin of this illusion is easy to see. I may see a pencil, or I may imagine one. In either case, I have before me an image of a pencil. Since the image of the seen pencil has a localization which I recognize to be apart from me, I tend to localize the imagined pencil outside of me too. The truth appears to be that, just as the light rays from a pencil may initiate in my nervous system a series of changes leading to the specific neural events that are correlated with my *seeing* a pencil, so may other antecedents (such as the word "pencil") also have among their consequences these particular neural events, and I then have an *imagined* image of a pencil. Of course, there are also differences between what is seen and what is imagined, because the afferent neurones activated by a real pencil have other neural connections that are not shared by the neurones activated by the word "pencil."

2 | *The Making and Unmaking of Functional*

Neural Connections

The previous chapter espoused the thesis that the character of behavior depends upon the paths that neural excitation takes, paths determined by the disposition of functional connections between neurones. Some of these functional connections come into being during the course of the development of the organism, others as a result of the learning process. It is at present an academic question what physiological differences exist between the synapses that develop under these two different sets of circumstances. Certainly, connections established by the developmental process *appear* to be relatively unchanging in the absence of damage or disease, whereas connections formed through learning are notably modifiable. We shall give consideration to the behavior that stems from each, paying much the more detailed attention to learned behavior and to the laws of learning, just because, as will be shown, neurotic behavior is learned.

Maturation

Maturation (organismal growth and differentiation) determines the anatomical relations of neurones, and also establishes a large number of functional connections between them. That functional connections can be formed by maturation as such, and not as a by-product of activity, was demonstrated by Carmichael's classical experiments (1926, 1928), in which it was found that embryos of the frog (*Rana sylvatica*) and salamander (*Amblystoma punctatum*), developing in water containing a sufficient concentration of chloretone to prevent any body movements in response to external stimulation, were able, within 30 minutes of removal from the chloretone solution, to swim quite as well as those that had been allowed to move throughout development, and had been free swimmers for five days. In a later experiment (1928), Carmichael showed that the 30 minutes' delay could probably be attributed to the continuing action of the chloretone. Thus the organisms, solely as a result of maturation, had developed potentialities which would result in swimming, given the stimulations of an appropriate environment.

Simple responses that owe their occurrence to functional connections established by maturation are called reflexes. Examples are the knee jerk in response to a tap on the patella tendon, closure of the eyelid to a tactile stimulation of the cornea, and contraction of the pupil to a bright light falling on the retina. Frequently, chains of reflex responses are observed, in which each response provides at least some of the stimuli that set off the next response. Normal breathing movements are an example of this kind of succession. An example of more complex reflex responding which is less precise would be the violent generalized activity that may follow a noxious stimulus applied to a foot.

Some reflex responses have a homeostatic role. This adjective was introduced by Cannon (1929) to apply to those reactions by which disturbances within the organism due to changes in its environment are restricted in magnitude: "wide oscillations are prevented and the internal conditions are held fairly constant." Each relatively steady state of the organism, such as body temperature, blood sugar level, or the hydrogen ion concentration of the blood, is an instance of homeostasis. The reactions which maintain homeostasis are mediated by direct chemical action, by neural mechanisms, or by both. The neural mechanisms involve chiefly the autonomic nervous system; but, as Gellhorn (1943, pp. 266–67) points out, the somatic nervous system sometimes plays an important role. For instance, when the organism is exposed to cold, the activity of the striated muscles in shivering combines with the autonomically induced contraction of the blood vessels of the skin to effect the maintenance of body temperature.

When reflex behavior is of a considerable but ill-defined degree of complexity, it is customarily called *instinctive behavior*. A good example of complex behavior that obviously owes everything to maturation is provided by Hartman's account of the solitary wasp (1942):

The parents of last summer are dead and disintegrated. . . . With the warmth of summer the new generation will emerge, and, without parental instruction . . . build or dig a nest; find and capture appropriate prey, usually a given species to which the wasp species is "adapted"; sting the prey with a high degree of accuracy in the appropriate nerve centre or centres . . . ; with the prey as burden, find its way back to the nest, open this, store the prey, deposit an egg, close the nest, and leave the offspring to its fate.

Instinctive behavior is constituted of many reflex responses, both simultaneous and successive, to a given stimulus or series of stimuli. Modern researches have removed all justification for more mystical theories. For example, Rowan (1931), by subjecting snowbirds and crows artificially to daily *increases* in illumination during autumn, caused their gonads to increase in size and their general and migratory behavior to approximate that which they normally exhibit in springtime, in contrast to untreated controls. Thus, migratory behavior, for long attributed to the action of mysterious "spiritual" forces, is correlated with definite physiological changes, whose production is dependent on known stimuli. Similarly, Roule (1933) has presented evidence to show that the movement of young salmon downstream is related to alterations in their skin pigmentation causing inhibition of activity during the day, with the result that the fish, inert and passive, are carried downstream by the current; this is in contrast to the theory that the migration is caused by an "ancestral memory of the sea." More recent studies by Lorenz (1943) and Tinbergen (1951) among others have thrown light on the detailed mechanisms of many instances of instinctive behavior.

In general, the less complex the organization of an animal's nervous system the more completely does maturation determine the character of complex responses to stimuli (i.e., the more its behavior is a matter of instinct). For example, whereas male rats raised from birth in isolation from all other rats are able, at the first encounter with a receptive female, to copulate in a manner indistinguishable from that of experienced rats (Beach, 1942), young chimpanzees have to learn how to copulate success-fully (Bingham, 1928; Yerkes, 1939). Man himself has probably no ma-turationally established stimulus-response sequences that are complex enough to be called instinctive.

Learning and Unlearning*

Learning may be said to have occurred if a response has been evoked in temporal contiguity with a given sensory stimulus and it is subsequently found that the stimulus can evoke the response although it could not have done so before. If the stimulus could have evoked the response before but subsequently evokes it more strongly, then, too, learning may be said to have occurred (Wolpe, 1952a, p. 260).

It is presumed that the stimulus-response sequences set up by learning depend, just as maturationally established sequences do, upon the develop-ment of *functional* connections (synapses) between neurones appropriately in anatomical opposition. That specific neural connections are the basis of learning has been convincingly demonstrated by an experiment of Culler's (1938) that has not received the attention it deserves. This in-vestigator first of all conditioned some dogs to contract the right semi-tendinosus muscle in response to a tone. Then under complete anesthesia the left cerebral cortex was exposed for direct stimulation. It was found

---

* Parts of this section are reprinted from an article in the *Psychological Review* (Wolpe, 1950), by permission of the American Psychological Association.

that, so long as the semitendinosus muscle reacted to the tone, it reacted also to direct electric stimulation of a small spot not more than two square mm. in area on the anterior ectosylvian gyrus 20 to 25 mm. from the motor point for the semitendinosus muscle. When the tonal conditioned response was extinguished, so was the response to stimulation of the spot; and when the former response was reinstated, so was the latter. No other surface area with these properties was found. Dogs tested before conditioning showed no evidence of semitendinosus contraction on stimulation of the anterior ectosylvian area. Thus the reinforcing of the tone to the semitendinosus response was evidently correlated with certain neurones being linked to the neurones which subserve the semitendinosus response.

It is altogether reasonable to suppose that, where learning involves the formation of conscious associations, the process is basically similar although certainly more complex. Suppose, for instance, I learn that the word "window" means a window. Hearing the word spoken subsequently conjures up in me the image of a window. This implies that neurones responding to the word "window" have become so connected to the neurones subserving the visual image of a window that stimulation of the former results in stimulation of the latter.

FACTORS INFLUENCING LEARNING

The *process* of learning, of strengthening functional neural connections, is conveniently called reinforcement, and an individual event that has the effect of strengthening a functional neural connection is *a reinforcement*. It will be possible here to give only a brief account of some of the most central factors concerned.

Time Relations

The definition of learning given above refers to "temporal contiguity" between the stimulus and the response to which it is to be connected. This means relative closeness in time, but the exact details of the time relations greatly affect the degree of learning that occurs.

In an experiment in which a continuously sounding buzzer preceded an electric shock to the foreleg of a rat, Kappauf and Schlosberg (1937) found that the conditioning of the most constant response, a sharp inspiration, was at a maximum when the buzzer commenced at an interval of two-thirds of a second before a shock and then declined. Hull (1943, pp. 167–68) pointed out that this decline, having the form of a negative growth function, is strikingly similar to the decline found by Adrian (1928, p. 116) in the frequency of impulses in nerve during a continuous sensory stimulation. Much the same relationships were found by Wolfle (1932) for the case where the conditioned stimulus is momentary instead of continuous. However, the optimal interval is not invariable, for in experiments on conditioned avoidance reactions in dogs, Kamin (1954) and Brush, Brush, and Solomon (1955) have found it to be in the region of five seconds.

Several experiments have shown that the strength that accrues to the connection between a stimulus and a response also varies with the interval that separates the response from the reduction of a strong drive associated with a primary need. Perhaps the most satisfactory of these experiments, because of its relative freedom from complicating factors, has been that of Perin (1942). He trained rats to move a horizontal bar in a modified Skinner box by causing a pellet of food to be delivered when the bar was moved by an animal either to the right or to the left. When a preference had been established in the animal for movement in one direction, the setting of the apparatus was so changed that movement of the rod in the *preferred* direction now gave no food; while movement in the nonpreferred direction caused the rod to be instantly and silently withdrawn and a pellet of food to be delivered, at intervals varying from 0 seconds to 30 seconds. It was found that learning to move the bar in the nonpreferred direction was most rapid when the interval was 0 seconds, and that its rate decreased with increasing intervals to the food-need reduction with a negatively accelerated gradient. Other studies, reported by Anderson (1933), Hamilton (1929), and Wolfe (1934), point to the conclusion that the less the delay between a response and a major drive reduction, the stronger is the reinforcement of the response to a conditioned stimulus.

The Number and Distribution of Reinforcements

That the strength accruing to a connection is the greater the greater the number of reinforcements was recognized by Pavlov (1927, p. 40). A considerable number of subsequent investigators have endeavored to elucidate the precise quantitative relations involved. Hovland (1937), working on human subjects, used the tone produced by the vibrations of a beat frequency oscillator as a conditioned stimulus to the skin reaction evoked by a mild electric shock to the wrist. Four comparable groups, each comprising 32 subjects, were given 8, 16, 24, and 48 reinforcements respectively. The subjects who had received the larger numbers of reinforcements exhibited the more marked reactions. The increase in learning with increasing number of reinforcements was shown by Hull (1943, p. 103) to approximate to a simple positive growth function. Others who have found a similar relationship are Williams (1938), Perin (1940), and Shurrager and Culler (1940). Different relationships noted by workers using different material have been reviewed by McGeogh (1942). An investigation by Shurrager and Shurrager (1946) is of special interest.

In several spinal dogs they isolated a single all-or-none unit in the semi-tendinosus muscle which was conditioned to contract to a mild shock applied to the tail. Since the amount of conditioning in the isolated unit was found to be independent of the amount in neighboring units, the conditioning of the former was considered as representing a measure of the changes *at a single synapse*. It was observed that there was a *straight-line* correlation between the number of reinforcements and the percentage of responses to the stimulus being conditioned.

If reinforcements are closely crowded together, the amount of learning that accrues is less than if the temporal intervals between them are longer. For example, Calvin (1939) showed that conditioned eyelid responses in man, based on shock, were much more effectively learned if 3 conditioning trials were given per minute than if 9 or 18 were given. Similar results were obtained by Schlosberg (1934) in conditioning breathing reactions in rats, and Reynolds (1945), using trace-conditioned stimuli to the eyelid reaction in human subjects, found the same sort of relationship.

The Role of Drive Reduction

Building upon earlier work by Pavlov (1927) and Thorndike (1932), Hull (1943, pp. 68–83) was the first to regard the physiological concept of drive reduction as an essential component of the learning process. In many circumstances drive reduction plays a very obvious part in determining not only what is learned but also how much learning occurs at a given reinforcement. This is most clearly evident where the drive is a correlate of a primary need (see p. 6). For example, Gantt (1938) reported laboratory studies showing that an increase in the amount of food used during conditioning was correlated with increased strength of the conditioned response. Skinner (1938, pp. 360–61) found that rewarding thirsty rats with water immediately after lever-depressing activity resulted in augmenting the tendency for this activity to occur in the given situation. Grindley (1929) demonstrated that whereas the pecking responses of chicks to the sight of grains of rice were strengthened if they were allowed to eat the rice, the responses progressively weakened (after an initial improvement) if the eating was prevented by the interposition of a sheet of glass over the grains. An experiment by Wolfe and Kaplon (1941) showed that chickens receiving a large piece of food at each trial developed superior performance in speed of running down a straightaway track and in negotiating a T maze in comparison with chickens receiving a piece of food a quarter as large at each trial. Finally, as Hull (1943, p. 79) has pointed out, in situations in which a noxious stimulus is acting on an organism, out of the multitude of molar acts that may comprise the organism's responses, the one that is learned is the one that is followed by a removal of the noxious stimulus and a termination of the drive created by that stimulus.

Drive reductions that have antecedents other than primary need states are equally effective augmenters of learning. Mowrer (1940) was the first to show this in relation to the drive that is the antecedent of conditioned anxiety reactions. This finding was confirmed by May (1948), Miller (1948), and Farber (1948), and subsequently by numerous others. Berlyne (1950) has pointed out that novel stimuli arouse a drive state whose reduction reinforces exploratory activity. Other experimental examples of learning subserved by drive reduction not accompanied by the reduction of a physiological need are acquisition of a bar-pressing habit when bar-pressing is followed by a click that has previously been associated with feeding (Skinner 1938, p. 82) and the learning of a maze by male rats even when the only "reward" in the goal box has been the sight and smell of a receptive female (Kagan 1955). It may be presumed that the click produces an augmentation of hunger drive which is quickly succeeded by a decrement when no food follows. Similarly, sight of a receptive female leads to arousal of a sex drive which subsides upon removal of the sex object.

Mowrer (1947) not long ago put forward the view that while drive reduction is important in instrumental learning it plays no part in the acquisition of autonomic patterns of response such as anxiety. A number of experiments subsequently reported seemed to support his position. Barlow (1952) showed that more anxiety is conditioned to a stimulus present at the commencement of a shock lasting ten seconds than to a stimulus that appears during or after the shock. Mowrer and Aiken (1954) later demonstrated that there is a monotonic decrease in the amount of anxiety conditioned, the later the conditioned stimulus appears during the course of a ten-second-long shock; and Mowrer and Solomon (1954) showed that when the conditioned stimulus precedes shock of a given intensity the amount of fear conditioned is much the same whether the shock lasts five seconds or ten seconds, and whether the end of the shock is abrupt or gradual. These experiments constitute a formidable attack on the primacy of drive reduction in the conditioning of anxiety, and it is clear from the recent review by Solomon and Brush (1956) of the considerable controversy that has arisen that the attack has not been adequately met. A defense that may be suggested is that a longer shock produces a greater measure of drive—sufficient to compensate for the delay in reinforcement.

However, the argument of this book will not be affected if it should turn out that the onset of anxiety is all-important to its learning and its reduction of no moment at all. There are some apparently undeniable instances of learning reinforced by conditions of drive increment instead of drive reduction. One such instance is Sheffield and Roby's (1950) demonstration that saccharine ingestion has reinforcing effects on instrumental learning. Several workers have shown that *increases* in illumination can be reinforcing (Kish, 1955; Marx, Henderson, and Roberts, 1955; Hurwitz, 1956). In a similar way, it is evidently stimulation *increase* that reinforces approach behavior to a fragrant flower. In all these instances it seems that drive *increment* is the reinforcing agent. It is quite possible that some drive increments produce the same physiological change relevant to learning as is produced by drive reductions in other circumstances. The subcortical stimulation experiments of Olds and Milner (1954) seem to favor this supposition.

The innumerable instances of learning that occurs in the absence of reduction of any strong excitation, such as verbal learning and "sensory preconditioning" (e.g., Brogden, 1939), actually fit easily into drive reduction theory when drive is defined (as in Chapter 1) as excitation in the central nervous system. This makes no arbitrary distinction (ill-defined in any case) between strong excitations and weak ones, and implies that the excitations aroused by weak stimuli have *some* reinforcing power because even weak excitations are reduced when stimulation ceases. (Olds and Milner's work of course presents the possibility that the *induction* of at least some excitations may also have reinforcing effects.)

A neurophysiological hypothesis for learning based on drive reduction and applicable to both "classical conditioning" and instrumental learning has been presented elsewhere (Wolpe, 1952c; 1953b).

UNLEARNING*

Extinction: Conditioned Inhibition Associated with Fatigue (Reactive Inhibition)

The term extinction is applied to the more or less smoothly progressive weakening of the response to a conditioned stimulus when it occurs a number of times without reinforcement. A partial recovery of the strength of the response is noted if the stimulus is not applied for some time, and this is known as spontaneous recovery. The fact that spontaneous recovery is only partial indicates that in the inhibition of response associated with extinction two distinct elements are involved—an inhibitory state that dissipates with time (reactive inhibition), and an enduring diminution of response due to a negative conditioning having occurred. The recog-

---

* Much of this section was previously published in the *Psychological Review* (Wolpe, 1952b), and is reproduced by permission of the American Psychological Association.

nition of this dichotomy led to the first reasonably convincing explanation of the extinctive process, in the form of what Hull called the Mowrer-Miller hypothesis. The most thoroughgoing and elaborate exposition of this hypothesis is due to Hull himself (1943, pp. 277–302), although the basic propositions were originally put forward by Mowrer and Jones (1943) and by Miller and Dollard (1941).

The initial supposition of the Mowrer-Miller hypothesis is that each time an organism makes a response to a stimulus, whether the response is reinforced or not, a fatigue-associated state or substance is brought into being that has an inhibitory effect upon a closely following evocation of the same response. This fatigue-associated state is regarded as the basis of reactive inhibition, and in so far as fatigue implies a disturbance of the equilibrium of the organism, a state of drive is postulated as a direct function thereof. This drive will normally be reduced when the activity that produced it ceases. *Cessation* of the activity will be in closest contiguity with the drive reduction, and will consequently become conditioned to any afferent impulses or stimulus traces which chance to be present at the time. The stimuli conditioned to the response that caused the fatigue will be responsible for some such traces. These stimuli will therefore now in some measure be *conditioned to an inhibition* of the response to which previously they were positively joined. As a result, the strength of that response to the next presentation of these stimuli will be found to have decreased to some extent, even though an interval has been allowed to lapse long enough to permit the dissipation of all reactive inhibition. Of course, no decrement of response is, as a rule, noted when the response is a reinforced one; for in that case positive learning effects nullify the development of conditioned inhibition.

The mechanism of reactive inhibition. There is evidence that reactive inhibition is associated with fatigue of muscle. It has been found that reactive inhibition is cumulative in circumstances in which fatigue is cumulative. It is well known that fatigue mounts when responses are massed, and this is also the case with reactive inhibition. When reinforced responses are sufficiently massed, a *decreasing* strength of response may be noted. This phenomenon was first described by Pavlov (1927, p. 247). Like fatigue, the decremental influence disappears with time (Hilgard and Marquis, 1940, p. 148). In experiments in which extinction is commenced soon after massed learning trials, the presence of reactive inhibition seems to be revealed by an initial rise in the amplitude of the response (Hovland, 1936; Hudgins, 1933; Switzer, 1930). Accumulative reactive inhibition is also produced during extinction, as shown by the fact that the rate of extinction is increased if extinction trials are massed (Mikhailoff, 1933; Prosser and Hunter, 1936; Reyna, 1946; Rohrer, 1947). There is also evidence of a correlation between amount of fatigue per response evoked and degree of reactive inhibition. The greater the effort involved in a response, the sooner extinction is accomplished (Fitts, 1940; Mowrer and Jones, 1941; James, 1941; Solomon, 1948; Applezweig, 1951). (This last proposition has been challenged by Maatsch, Adelson, and Denny (1954), who have presented some contradictory data.)*

But however close the relationship between fatigue and reactive inhibition may be, they are not merely different labels for the same thing. Even though the fatigue-associated substance that underlies reactive inhibition is presumed to be produced in muscle, reactive inhibition *cannot be due to a local action of this substance*, because the same response that disappears after repeated nonreinforced presentations of a conditioned stimulus may at once reappear if another stimulus to which also it has been reinforced is presented. Pavlov (1927, p. 158) showed this in an experiment in which a dog was conditioned to make more or less equal salivary responses to tactile stimuli at any point on its skin. One minute after extinction of the response to stimulation of the left shoulder, stimulation of the left thigh evoked a practically undiminished response. This is in line with some observations of Sherrington on spinal reflexes (1947, p. 219). He found that when the scratch reflex elicited by stimulation of a point on the skin becomes weakened after many repetitions, it recurs with renewed vigor on stimulating a point two or more centimeters from the original one.

It seems, then, that *neural* mechanisms must play a part in the production of decrement due to repetition in both the spinal reflex and the conditioned response. If a substance produced by activity of muscle leads to the decrement, this substance presumably acts by stimulating nerves whose excitation creates an inhibitory effect at certain of the synapses transmitting impulses producing the muscular activity. A direct demonstration that this is indeed the mechanism of reactive inhibition is lacking, but there are facts that give important indirect support to the supposition. First, Gellhorn and Thompson (1944) have shown that muscular activity produces some substance that inhibits reflex responsiveness. They found, in ten subjects selected for their very active triceps reflexes, that making the arm ischemic did not diminish the reflex. But when, in addition, the muscle was repeatedly exercised until it became painful, the reflex could not be evoked in any of the subjects, even by strong stimulation. On restoring the circulation, the pain disappeared at once, and the reflex

---

. * It is quite possible that the situation is complicated by fatigue-like effects *in the central nervous system* such as suggested by Lion (1952) on the strength of experiments indicating that "ordinarily there is no such thing as fatigue of the extrinsic ocular muscles."

returned in one and a half to three minutes. Second, there is evidence that the afferent nerves of muscle carry fibers whose stimulation results in inhibition of that muscle's reflex responses. Sherrington (1924) found that if the central end of the cut afferent nerve to a muscle whose motor supply is intact is stimulated, not only is there no reflex contraction, "but the muscle, if reflexly contracting [to another stimulus] is thrown out of contraction." A possibly decisive experiment would be to determine the effect on extinction of depriving the chief muscles subserving a response of their afferent innervation.

A neurophysiological hypothesis. Meanwhile, going with the weight of evidence, and assuming the correctness of the above-mentioned view of the mechanism of reactive inhibition, it seems reasonable to attempt to show how conditioned inhibition *could* be subserved by synaptic processes. In the same way as positive learning seems to depend upon certain neural chains becoming increasingly conductive, it may be expected that conditioned inhibition implies decreased conductivity of these neural chains. We may see by reference to Fig. 5 how this may come about, always remembering that each neurone in the figure represents a very large number in the organism. The sequence of neurones n_1 to n_4 represents the linkage between an electrical stimulus applied to a foot (S_1), and the final common path (n_4) to a foot-lifting response (R_1). Owing to a functional connection having been established between n_9 and n_{11}, another stimulus energy, S_2, now evokes the response R_1 by means of impulses traversing the neural sequence n_5-n_6-n_9-n_{11}-n_4. The fatigue-associated substance (S_{IR}) which is produced in the muscles that carry out R_1 stimulates the endings of nerves whose central connections are inhibitory at certain synapses on all pathways to R_1. The inhibitory chain, in so far as it affects the n_9-n_{11} synaptic zone, is represented by n_{12}-n_{13}-n_{14}.

Inhibitory impulses, once set up, must be assumed to arrive indiscriminately at synapses on all pathways leading to the final common path to R_1(n_4). But since other pathways are evidently less affected when S_2 is extinguished than is the pathway subserving S_2 itself, it must be assumed that the inhibitory effect occurs most powerfully at synapses at which the recent transmission of impulses has produced certain sensitizing preconditions. Thus, in the figure, let S_3 be another stimulus energy also conditioned to the response R_1, and leading to R_1 by excitation of the sequence n_{15}-n_{16}-n_{17}-n_{18}-n_4. When S_2 has evoked R_1, inhibitory impulses arrive at the synapse $n_{17} \cdot n_{18}$ from the sequence n_{12}-n_{19}-n_{20}, but these impulses will not affect $n_{17} \cdot n_{18}$ if no impulses have recently been passing from n_{17} to n_{18}. Synapses whose activity has been instrumental in bringing about an effector response become, through this very activity, more sensitive to the inhibitory impulses that are consequent on the response.

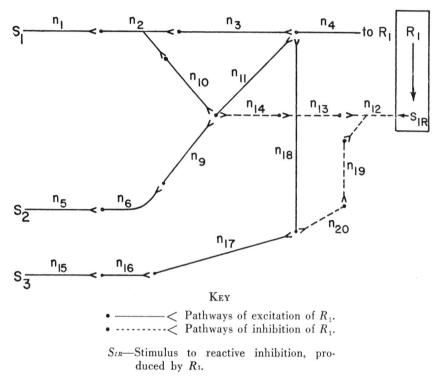

Fig. 5. Diagram illustrating the development of conditioned inhibition based on reactive inhibition.

With this in view, it is easy to see that *conditioned inhibition* can be understood in neurophysiological terms as a process that to a great extent parallels positive learning. It may easily be imagined that the *cessation* of impulses from the inhibitory neurone n_{14} is a drive reduction that acts on the synaptic zone $n_9 \cdot n_{11}$, sensitized by its previous activity, in such a way that conductivity between n_9 and n_{11} is diminished.

The above neurophysiological hypothesis has *an important immediate consequence*. It rescues the Mowrer-Miller hypothesis from the following devastating criticism. Suppose that a rat has learned to press a pedal as a result of previous food rewards. On any occasion when no food follows there will be, according to the Mowrer-Miller hypothesis, a weakening of this pedal-pressing habit, because cessation of the movement is closer in time than performance of the movement to the reduction of the fatigue-associated drive. But what happens when food does follow the pedal-pressing? Clearly, the ensuing hunger drive reduction is then also closer in time to the cessation of the pedal-pressing than to the performance thereof. Consistency would require one to expect that the hunger drive reduction would reinforce the cessation more than the act! As experience belies such an expectation, we must conclude that if drive reductions were altogether nonspecific the Mowrer-Miller hypothesis would be untenable. But there is not the slightest reason to assume such nonspecificity; and it is highly probable that special neural relations of the fatigue-associated drive make its reduction a reinforcer of conditioned inhibition only, by some such mechanism as suggested in the above neurophysiological hypothesis, while other drive reductions only reinforce *positively* the activities close to them in time.

It may be noted that our hypothesis dispenses with the Mowrer-Miller idea that in the conditioning of inhibition a *cessation* of an act is reinforced in the same sense as the act itself would be reinforced. Cessation of an act is relevant only in so far as it makes possible reduction of the fatigue-associated drive, for this is what determines *conditioned* inhibition—the "permanent" lessening of conductivity of the synapses subserving the evocation of the act in response to the particular stimulus constellation.

The Development of Conditioned Inhibition on the Basis of Reciprocal Inhibition

The term *reciprocal inhibition* was first introduced by Sherrington (1947, pp. 83–107) in relation to the inhibition of one spinal reflex by another, such as occurs when stimulation of an ipsilateral afferent nerve causes relaxation of a vastocrureus muscle contracting to a contralateral stimulus. Its use may be expanded to encompass all situations in which the elicitation of one response appears to bring about a decrement in the strength of evocation of a simultaneous response.

It has long been realized that habits are often eliminated by enabling new habits to develop in the same general situation (Hilgard and Marquis, 1940, pp. 108–14), but hypotheses as to the mechanisms by which this occurs have been notably vague. That reciprocal inhibition is concerned in the weakening of old responses by new ones was realized by Wendt (1936), but he did not suggest *how* a permanently weakened strength of reaction came to follow the temporary reciprocal inhibition of an activity. Like Guthrie (1935, pp. 64–84), Wendt was concerned with an explanation for extinction, and, like him, regarded competition between reactions as the basis for it; but, as Hilgard and Marquis (1940, p. 118) point out, this is contradicted by several facts, such as the increased rate of extinction with massing of trials.

If conditioned inhibition is built up during extinction because traces of the conditioned stimuli are contemporaneous with reactive inhibition of the conditioned response, it is reasonable to expect that if some other cause were to inhibit the conditioned response, conditioned inhibition could likewise be built up. When a response is inhibited by an incompatible response and if a major drive reduction follows, a significant amount of conditioned inhibition of the response will be developed. This process is illustrated by a striking experiment of Pavlov's (1927, pp. 29–31), where, however, the response to which conditioned inhibition was established was actually an "unconditioned" response. A weak electric current was made a conditioned stimulus for food in a dog. The current was in time gradually increased (with feeding) until it was extremely strong, but even then no defense reaction was manifested. In other words, the pathways normally connecting the electrical stimulus with the defense reaction had become inhibited. It would appear that at every stage of the experiment the performance of the feeding response involved a reciprocal inhibition of the mild defense reaction aroused by the electrical stimulus. Because of the drive reduction consequent on the feeding, this inhibition of response became progressively more strongly reinforced to the electrical stimulus. After many repetitions of the procedure, in the course of which the current was gradually stepped up, so great a degree of conditioned inhibition of the defense reaction to the current was established that even very strong electrical stimuli were unable to evoke that reaction, but evoked only the feeding response.

The experimental procedures described in Chapter 4 whereby neurotic anxiety reactions in cats were overcome through opposing them by feeding reactions appear to constitute further examples of learning based on reciprocal inhibition. In other experiments (p. 60) it was found that conditioned anxiety reactions, by inhibiting feeding reactions under special circumstances, produced conditioned inhibition of these reactions in relation to a particular environment. The therapeutic procedures described in Part II of this book also appear to have their lasting effects on a basis of reciprocal inhibition.

Another instance of unlearning through reciprocal inhibition is apparently provided by ordinary forgetting. This appears to be due to what is known as *retroactive inhibition*—the decrement in retention of learned materials resulting from activities interpolated between an earlier and a later test of retention. Osgood (1946, 1948) has suggested a hypothesis explaining retroactive inhibition in terms of increasing inhibitory habit tendencies based on reciprocal inhibition. In general agreement with him the following formulation is proposed. If, after the learning, another activity takes place which involves the same or similar cues but a dissimilar response, there will be at the time a reciprocal inhibition of the response originally learned. Because of the contiguous drive reduction—which is assumed to be present because every stimulation creates drive and therefore the potentiality of drive reduction (p. 24)—this reciprocal inhibition will leave in its wake a conditioned inhibition, a "permanent" weakening of the connection between the originally learned cue and its response. It would be expected, if this hypothesis is correct, that the amount of impairment of recall will be the greater the more closely the cue to an interpolated activity resembles the cue to the learned response; and given similar cues, the impairment will be the greater the more the responses differ.

There is considerable evidence in support of these expectations. McGeogh, McKinney, and Peters (1937) found that if an item A is the learned cue to a response B, and the association of $A-C$ is then learned, there is much poorer retention of the original association than if the association $D-E$ is interpolated. A decrement also occurs with the interpolation of $D-E$, but as McGeogh points out (1942, p. 492), there are aspects of D which are similar to A. Bunch and Winston (1936) showed that if, after $A-B$ has been learned, $C-B$ is interpolated, there is much less interference with the $A-B$ relationship than there is when $A-C$ is interpolated. It has been shown by McGeogh and McDonald (1931) and by Johnson (1933) that retroactive inhibition is the greater the more closely the learned and the interpolated *cues resemble* each other in meaning; and Osgood (1946, 1948) has found that if the learned and interpolated cues are identical, there is more interference the more the *responses differ* in meaning.

3 | *Definition of Neurotic Behavior*

A definition of neurotic behavior will be an inventory of as many constant characteristics of the behavior as are necessary to convey clearly to the reader how the writer conceives it to be distinct from other behavior. The raw material for such a definition is of course the behavior of patients who are clinically diagnosed as neurotic. Thus the definition will indicate what is thought to be common to the many varieties of behavior manifested by patients who are given such diagnoses as anxiety state, phobia, depression, hysteria, neurasthenia, and obsessional state. The following is the definition used in this book: *Neurotic behavior is any persistent habit of unadaptive behavior acquired by learning in a physiologically normal organism.* Anxiety is usually the central constituent of this behavior, being invariably present in the causal situations.

The following is a commentary on this definition and on its rider concerning anxiety.

Each of the distinguishable consequences of the behavior of an organism in a situation may be judged to be either *adaptive* or *unadaptive*. *Adaptive* consequences take the form of progress toward the satisfaction of a need (p. 6) or the avoidance of possible damage or deprivation. An *unadaptive* consequence would be the expenditure of energy or the occurrence of damage or deprivation. Many instances of behavior have a multiplicity of consequences both adaptive and unadaptive. The *adaptiveness of a given sample of behavior* may be said to be the resultant of all its adaptive consequences weighed against the unadaptive ones. It is adaptive if the latter are outweighed, and the more so the more they are outweighed. For example, despite the expenditure of energy, it is adaptive to pick blackberries, but less so if one is scratched by a thorn in the process. All this may be summarized by saying that behavior is adaptive to the extent that it is "worth while."

Since consequences vary, one performance of given behavior may be adaptive and another not. We shall then speak of the *adaptiveness of the habit* and this may be estimated in terms of the *probability* of favorable consequences.

Because their consequences are on balance unfavorable to the organism, neurotic habits are unadaptive. Their adverse effects take a variety of forms. The very feeling of fear when no real danger is present (for example, when going up in an elevator) is unpleasant and nonbeneficial. The fear may also lead to objectively wasteful expenditure of energy in the avoiding of feared situations (such as climbing stairs in the case of the elevator phobia). It may interfere with the efficiency of other activities, such as work or sex life. Finally, a variety of subsidiary patterns of response such as obsessional reactions may appear (see pp. 89–97). Some of these diminish the anxiety and others augment it, but in either event they themselves almost invariably have disadvantageous results for the individual. Occasionally, a patient obtains some concrete benefit from his neurosis—such as a pension for a paralyzed leg—but even here it is usually not true that he is *better* off than he would have been without the paralysis.* The unadaptiveness of neurotic reactions is usually overwhelmingly obvious.

If adaptiveness and its negative as defined above are considered in conjunction with the discussion of learning and unlearning given in the last chapter, it is obvious that when a response is adaptive the likelihood of its evocation in the particular stimulus situation tends to be reinforced. Each time a response is unadaptive, even if only in the sense that it produces nothing but fatigue, it tends to be extinguished. If the response is consistently unadaptive, its habit strength progressively weakens and eventually disappears. This is the usual course of events. Failure of unadaptive learned behavior to be extinguished—*its persistence*—is a feature of neurosis.

So remarkable is it that the normal extinction of an unadaptive response should fail to occur that most writers have assumed that some kind of pathology either organic or "functional" must be at the bottom of it. The Pavlovian theory of a pathology of nerve cells owes its existence to this assumption, and so to some extent does the Freudian theory of repressed complexes. It will be shown that the assumption is unnecessary; for the persistence of neurotic behavior is readily accounted for as a matter of learning under special conditions.

The *learned* character of neurotic behavior is of course not obvious from inspection of the behavior as such. It is indispensable to the definition because persistent unadaptive behavior often with prominent anxiety may be due to other causes, such as hyperthyroidism, epilepsy, or beri-beri. Chapter 4 describes how experimental neurotic behavior is learned

---

* Much has been made of the concept of "secondary gain," and it has led to the absurd idea that patients *want* their neuroses. The truth is that human beings are the unfortunate recipients of neurotic conditioning, just as animals may be; and I have never seen one who felt, when he was cured, that something valuable had been taken away from him.

and Chapter 6 describes some of the mechanisms of learning of human neuroses.

The significance, in the definition, of the words "in a physiologically normal organism" is that they exclude from its scope such persistent unadaptive habits as learning may establish in schizophrenia or any other condition whose primary basis is an abnormal organic state.

Anxiety and Its Derivatives

By anxiety is meant the autonomic response pattern or patterns that are characteristically part of the organism's response to noxious stimulation. A noxious stimulus is one that causes tissue disturbance of a kind that tends to lead to avoidance responses. When noxious stimulation itself evokes the anxiety responses, it is through nerve channels formed in the normal course of biological development of the organism. This is unconditioned (unlearned) anxiety. Unconditioned anxiety responses are also evoked by certain other stimulus conditions which are not obviously noxious—sudden strong auditory stimulation, falling, and ambivalent stimulus situations. Introspection suggests that the autonomic effects of these are much the same as those of noxious stimulation. In the case of ambivalent stimulus situations, striking experimental confirmation has been provided by Fonberg (1956) (see p. 65).

The word "anxiety" is used throughout this book synonymously with "fear." There is no reason to think that there is any physiological differ-. ence between the fear aroused by a stimulus that is associated with an objective threat, e.g., a rattlesnake, and fear that is unadaptive, aroused, let us say, by a kitten. Anxiety is the keystone of all neuroses, though it is not part of the symptom complex of some cases of hysteria.

A stimulus not previously capable of evoking anxiety responses may acquire the power to do so if it happens to be acting on the organism when anxiety is evoked by another stimulus. It then becomes a conditioned stimulus to anxiety, and the anxiety it evokes may, on subsequent occasions, be conditioned to yet other stimuli. An experimental illustration of this is given on page 60. The opportunities for the conditioning of anxiety are very numerous in human life, so that, even at an early age, there are far more anxiety responses to conditioned cues than to unconditioned ones.

The stimulus antecedents of neurotic anxiety responses have various sources. They may be well-defined situational stimuli such as thunderstorms, enclosed spaces, crowds, people in authority, being rejected, or being the center of attention. To be disturbing it is by no means always essential for these stimuli to be present in reality; their evocation in thought may be quite sufficient and in some cases plays the leading role in keeping the patient miserable. Anxiety responses are also evocable by more diffuse or pervasive aspects of the environment, being then more or less omnipresent, and giving the impression of being "free-floating." This is more correctly called *pervasive anxiety* (see pp. 83–85). Stimuli from the subject's own body may also be conditioned to produce anxiety responses. Besides the many patients who respond fearfully to symptoms such as headache or palpitations because of an association of these symptoms with the idea of a fatal disease, there are those who have anxiety as the direct response to a sensation without any mediating idea. For example, a man who had eaten a meal including a large amount of raw onion on an occasion of severe emotional stress felt distended and mildly anxious whenever he ate onions for years afterward.

The response elements that typically constitute an anxiety response are largely those associated with a widespread discharge of the autonomic nervous system, and predominantly of its sympathetic division. The usual manifestations are tachycardia, raised blood and pulse pressures, hyperpnea, pilo-erection, mydriasis, palmar hyperidrosis, and dryness of the mouth. The distribution of these effects varies with the individual and also, as Wolf and Wolff (1947) have shown, with variations in the details of the emotional state. Marked parasympathetic manifestations may also be observed. Extreme examples of the latter are evacuation of the bladder or bowels. Besides these somatic responses, the work of Hess (1947) suggests that there are other autonomic effects which may show themselves as increased irritability. It is possible that this is responsible for the diffuse rise in muscle tension that is characteristic of anxiety. Higher levels of muscle tension may be shown as restlessness or tremor.

The typical syndrome of anxiety is a very familiar one, and nobody who experiences it has any hesitation in labeling it appropriately. But there are many deviations from the typical—most of them probably due to variations in the balance of the elements. Some of the usual elements may become grossly dominant and swamp the others, or new elements may appear. The over-all distortion may be such that the subject will not now describe his state as one of "anxiety" or "fear," but may say he feels "a tense depression," or perhaps that he is having a horrible experience that he cannot describe and to which he can give no name. How these changes in the character of neurotic responses occur will be discussed at a later stage (pp. 100–101).

The severity of a neurosis will generally be judged in terms of amount of unadaptive anxiety. The amount varies in two dimensions—intensity and duration. A neurosis may be regarded as having a certain degree of severity *either* when particular stimuli that are relatively infrequently encountered evoke anxiety of high intensity *or* when more pervasive stimulation evokes almost continuous anxiety of relatively low intensity. A more severe neurosis will combine constancy of anxiety with high intensity.

Once anxiety is present, in whatever form, it may undermine the functioning of the organism in many ways. The generalized rise in muscle tension impairs coordination, which may matter a good deal where accuracy of movement is important. If the tension gives rise to tremor the patient may be embarrassed in certain social situations and may consequently avoid them. Localized tension may produce "fibrositis" or headaches (Jacobson, 1938, p. 88; Malmo et al., 1953; Sainsbury and Gibson, 1954). Mental concentration, ready flow of associations and recall may each be impaired by anxiety, and there may also be diminished registration of impressions (retrograde amnesia). There may be interference with sexual performance, shown in men by failure of erection, ejaculation without erection, ejaculation without pleasure, or premature ejaculation, and in women by frigidity.

The secondary reactions of the anxious subject to his anxiety complicate the clinical picture. The variations in the autonomic responses constituting anxiety that were referred to above may produce bizarre feelings such as "feelings of unreality," which may be greatly alarming either directly or because the patient concludes that he "must be losing his mind." Some of these strange feelings are produced by the hyperventilation that is frequently part of the primary anxiety reaction. Among other symptoms due to hyperventilation are paresthesias, tremors, myalgia, and precordial pain. Secondary conditioning of anxiety responses to any of these symptoms may then occur, so that a kind of vicious circle is created.

Special complications are apt to occur when the anxiety response is channeled to an unusual degree along particular (and perhaps unusual) pathways. Whether the neural dispositions that underlie such channeling are established by maturation or by learning is not known. But there are undoubtedly, as Wolff (1950) has put it, "stomach reactors, nose reactors, pulse reactors, and blood pressure reactors," and many others. Stomach reactors would presumably provide the bulk of the population in whom peptic ulcers develop, skin reactors would be prone to functional dermatoses, and respiratory reactors to asthma. Certainly the overcoming of anxious reactivity is frequently followed by the clearing up of such conditions.

Other consequences of anxiety that arise in special circumstances are considered in Chapter 6.

4 | *Experimental Neurosis: A Phenomenon*

*of Learning**

After the first experimental neuroses were reported from Pavlov's labora-
tories half a century ago, many other investigators produced them, employing a variety of methods. The conclusions drawn from this experimental
work were often exceedingly facile, and gave rise to much confusion. A
central belief common to most writers was that the neuroses were due to
some kind of *damage or disruption* in the nervous system due to conflict.
About ten years ago, I conducted a series of experiments at the University
of the Witwatersrand to test an alternative hypothesis—that neurotic behavior is the result not of damage but of *learning.* These experiments sus-
tained this hypothesis; and its corollary—that successful treatment of the
neuroses must also depend upon the learning process—was supported by
further experiments. The experiments are described later in this chapter.

A re-examination of the experiments of previous writers shows that the
neuroses they produced can also be explained in terms of the learning
process. It will be seen that their interpretations have often ignored important features of their experiments. If these features are consistently
taken into account, all the neuroses reported can be understood as being
the outcome of one or other (perhaps sometimes both) of two basic situations—the exposure of the organism to ambivalent stimuli or its exposure
to noxious stimuli, in either case under conditions of confinement. It will
be argued that these two kinds of situation have an effect in common upon
which the development of the neuroses depends—the induction of anxiety
at high intensity.

Analysis of Previous Experimental Findings

In the account that follows, the neuroses are grouped according to the
basic situation which seems to have determined their production, and it
will be seen repeatedly how experimental procedures may differ widely in
other respects and yet provide the same kind of basic situation.

* Extensive portions of this chapter are reprinted from my paper "Experimental
Neuroses as Learned Behaviour," *Brit. J. Psychol.*, **43**: 243–68, 1952.

An *ambivalent stimulus situation* is a situation to which opposing responses tend to be elicited simultaneously in more or less equal measure. The range of meaning is narrower than would be implied by "conflict situation," for not in every conflict are the opposing response tendencies equal. Examination of the literature reveals that three varieties of situations involving ambivalent stimulation have been effective in producing experimental neuroses. These will be considered under their headings below.

Neuroses Produced by Difficult Discriminations

Although the expression "difficult discrimination" carries an unwanted suggestion of conscious weighing-up, it is a conveniently brief term of reference for the ambivalent stimulus situation that occurs under the following circumstances: a positive and a negative response having respectively been conditioned to two stimuli at different points on a continuum, the animal is confronted with a stimulus at an intermediate point on the continuum such that the opposing responses are evoked in more or less equal strength.

Pavlov's experiment on neurosis production based on difficult discrimination was the first to be reported (1927, pp. 290–91). The projection of a luminous circle on a screen in front of a dog was repeatedly followed by feeding. When the alimentary response to the circle was well established, an ellipse with semiaxes in the ratio of 2:1 began to be projected among presentations of the circle, and was never accompanied by feeding.

A complete and constant differentiation was obtained comparatively quickly. The shape of the ellipse was now approximated by stages to that of the circle (ratios of semiaxes of 3:2, 4:3 and so on) and the development of differentiation continued . . . with some fluctuation, progressing at first more and more quickly, and then again slower, until an ellipse with ratio of semiaxes 9:8 was reached. In this case, although a considerable degree of discrimination did develop, it was far from being complete. After three weeks of work upon this differentiation not only did the discrimination fail to improve, but it became considerably worse, and finally disappeared altogether. At the same time the whole behavior of the animal underwent an abrupt change. The hitherto quiet dog began to squeal in its stand, kept wriggling about, tore off with its teeth the apparatus for mechanical stimulation of the skin, and bit through the tubes connecting the animal's room with the observer, a behavior which never happened before. On being taken into the experimental room the dog now barked violently.

Because of its close resemblance to the circle, the 9:8 ellipse presumably generated at least as great a positive alimentary response tendency due to primary stimulus generalization (Hull, 1943, p. 184) from the circle as negative alimentary response tendency due to generalization from previous ellipses. Since primary stimulus generalization depends on the common neurones activated by similar stimuli (Wolpe, 1952e), if the 9:8 ellipse activated a preponderating number of neurones in common with the circle, the negative response tendency to the ellipse could never become completely dominant, however often it were presented to the animal without reinforcement. Consequently, this ellipse would always evoke ambivalent response tendencies.

Other workers who have produced neuroses by difficult discriminations that are visual are Bajandurow (1932), who subjected doves to a circle-and-ellipse experiment similar to Pavlov's (although, it may be noted, he employed a conditioned avoidance response—which, as will be seen later, confuses the causal relations); and Jacobsen, Wolfe, and Jackson (1935), whose chimpanzee developed neurotic reactions in the following manner. The animal was allowed to observe the experimenter conceal a piece of food under one of two cups. An opaque screen was then lowered so as to hide the cups from her view. After an interval it was raised so that she could approach the cups and obtain the food if she lifted the correct one. In a first series of trials, the cups were separated by 30 inches, and the chimpanzee was able to go to the correct one even after the screen had been lowered for from three to five minutes. In a second series, the distance between the cups was 10 inches, and she then failed to recognize the cup covering the food. Normally highly emotional, she became profoundly upset whenever she made an error. Subsequently, she would watch the loading of the cup closely, and would often whimper as the cup was placed over the food. As the opaque screen was being lowered, she would fly into a temper tantrum, roll on the floor, micturate and defecate. After a few of these reactions she ceased to make responses to this test, though continuing to respond eagerly to other stimuli. Testing was continued daily for three weeks. By the end of this time she had to be taken by force to the experimental cage. It seems reasonable to suppose that there was so much intergeneralization of the responses to the approximated cups that the animal responded both positively and negatively more or less equally to each cup; and this is what would constitute an ambivalent stimulus situation.

Several investigators have produced neuroses by means of difficult discriminations of an auditory kind. Gantt (1944), using an apparatus very similar to that of Pavlov, made an ascending pair of tones a positive conditioned stimulus to eating, and the same pair in descending sequence a negative stimulus. Behavior disturbances were produced in dogs by narrowing the frequency difference between the two tones, so that, for example, one was eventually 21 cycles and the other 20. (It is worth remarking, however, that the famous dog Nick was probably hypersensitive to certain kinds of stimuli from the start, because the first time an artificial stimulus was presented to him [a tone of 1130 cycles for 10 seconds] he was disturbed enough to refuse food until the experimenter entered the camera; and the next day he was "terribly excited by the stimulus.") Dworkin, Raginsky, and Bourne (1937) used similar methods to bring about long-lasting neuroses in two dogs, except that discrimination depended on the difference in frequency between single tones, one positive and the other negative. Krasnogorski (1925) applied similar techniques to several children and obtained effects comparable to those observed in the animals. The findings in the above-mentioned experiments are so clearly parallel to those of Pavlov's circle-and-ellipse experiment that no separate comment is necessary.

Karn (1938) has described the production of a neurosis in a cat by a method that is of special interest in that a difficult discrimination of *intra-organismal cues* was involved. The animal was trained in a maze that was in effect a T maze, with the left turn followed by two further left turns, and the right by two further right turns, all segments being the same length as the stem of the T. The only place where food was ever given was at the end of the final segment. A door here opened to the starting point. The animal was required to learn at the choice point the double alternation—right, right, left, left. After 230 trials of the sequence it attained an average of 90 per cent correct in the last 30 trials. During the 232d trial, at its second arrival at the choice point the animal hesitated much longer than usual, and then raced to the right end point. During the remainder of the trial it moved slowly, whimpering. From this time onward the cat resisted being put into the maze, and mewed loudly and micturated at the choice point, especially at the second of the two occasions for a right turn. At later trials the signs of disturbance seemed to get worse, and accuracy of performance became progressively poorer. (In a later article, Karn [1940] states that he and E. R. Malamud have produced a neurosis in a dog by the above technique, and that Keller has done likewise with a rat.)

It is reasonable to interpret the results as follows. Each time the cat arrived at the choice point the external cues were the same, and these were equally conditioned to a turn in either direction. In the case of a first arrival at the choice point, traces of pre-maze stimuli and the distinctive cue of a completely empty stomach must have become strongly conditioned to right-turning. Difficulty would occur at the second arrival, for the internal cues conditioned to right-turning would be the proprioceptive cues from the right-turning movements of one run, plus cues consequent on having eaten once; while conditioned to left-turning would be the proprioceptive cues from the right-turning movements of two runs plus the internal cues consequent on having eaten twice. It is easy to believe that the difference between these two combinations of internal stimuli is minimal, so that at each second (and third) arrival at the choice point the right- and left-turning tendencies would be almost equal, constituting an ambivalent stimulus situation.

A special case of the production of neuroses by difficult discrimination seems to be provided by the use of *threshold stimuli* in experiments described by Dworkin (1939) and Dworkin, Baxt, and Dworkin (1942). Both dogs and cats were used. In conditions of constricted space, the animals were trained to raise the lid of a food box in response to pure tones of varying pitch. Over several months the loudness of the tones was gradually reduced. At first the behavior of the animals was normal. But in later experiments one or two loud tones would be used at the beginning of each session, and the loudness would then be progressively reduced to below threshold. The majority of animals of both species underwent changes in behavior, which in a few cases were very marked. The changes comprised increasing failure of response to conditioned stimuli, refusal to eat at all within the conditioning room, and, in the case of the cats, excessive general bodily movement. Three cats manifested severe symptoms that lasted for months. In these experiments the difficult discrimination seems to be discernible as follows. The experimental environment *with* the auditory stimulus stimulates approach responses to the food box. *Without* the auditory stimulus the environment has an inhibitory effect. A threshold stimulus provides intermediate conditions by which both responses tend to be evoked at once.

Neuroses Produced by Increasing the Delay Before
Reinforcement of a Delayed Conditioned Response

In Pavlov's laboratory (1927, pp. 293–94), a dog with a predominant tendency of excitation had become conditioned to make the alimentary response to any of six stimuli. Food was presented when a stimulus had been acting for five seconds. The duration of action of the conditioned stimulus before presentation of food was now prolonged by five seconds daily. All six stimuli were treated in this manner concurrently. When the delay reached two minutes, "the animal began to enter into a state of general excitation, and with a further prolongation of the delay to 3 minutes the animal became quite crazy, increasingly and violently moving all parts of its body, howling, barking and squealing intolerably. All this was accompanied by an unceasing flow of saliva . . ."

This neurosis is regarded as produced by ambivalent stimulation because of the following considerations. Pavlov (1927, p. 92) found that when a delayed conditioned reflex has been established, salivation is delayed until some time after the commencement of the conditioned stimulus. Presumably, then, certain durations of the conditioned stimulus have become conditioned to an inhibition of the alimentary response, and other, longer durations to an excitation of that response. If the delay until presentation of food is now increased in stages, at each stage a duration of the stimulus which had previously stimulated the response would begin to be conditioned to an inhibition thereof. Whenever the positive and negative tendencies were more or less equal, the stimulus would be an ambivalent one according to the definition given above. Experimentation with six stimuli for many days would add up to a very considerable exposure to ambivalent stimulation.

Neuroses Produced by Rapid Alternation of Stimuli Eliciting Opposing Responses

In the two types of ambivalent stimulus situation just described, the ambivalent effects are produced in the last resort by a single stimulus. The situation would be quite similar if the two opposing responses were elicited each by its own stimulus, provided that the stimuli followed each other rather closely. In one of Pavlov's dogs, among other positive and negative alimentary conditioned reflexes, conditioning was established positively to a tactile stimulation of 24 per minute and negatively to 12 per minute. One day the positive rate was made to follow the negative without any interval. For the first few days after this it was found that all positive conditioned reflexes had disappeared. This was followed by a period in which there were changing relations between the magnitudes of response to the various stimuli. The disturbances are said to have lasted five and a half weeks, but neither in Anrep's translation (1927, pp. 301–2) nor in Gantt's (1928, pp. 343–44) are any other changes in behavior described.

NEUROSES PRODUCED BY NOXIOUS STIMULI

A noxious stimulus is one that causes tissue disturbance of a kind that leads or tends to lead to withdrawal behavior. In man it is correlated with the experience of pain or discomfort.

In certain experiments in which noxious stimuli have been used to produce neuroses, a "clash" between excitation and inhibition has been involved in one way or another. In other experiments, feeding reactions have been interfered with by the presentation of the noxious stimulus. Because in both categories conflict is in some sense present, it has been regarded as the center point of the etiology in both. Nevertheless, these neuroses are grouped here among those due to noxious stimuli and not to ambivalent stimulation; the first category for reasons given below in the course of an examination of the experiments, the second for the following reasons. First, as shown above, to result in a neurosis, conflicting tendencies must be of approximately the same strength at the same time, whereas when the reaction to a noxious stimulus has interfered with feeding it has been overwhelmingly stronger than the feeding tendency. Second, in experiments to be described (p. 50), the writer has found that noxious stimuli alone, without the aid of any conflict, can be an entirely adequate cause of neurotic reactions. If anything, a more severe neurosis tends to be produced by shock alone than by shock associated with feeding.

In the following account of the various procedures that have been employed, more specific comments will be made. To unify the commentary the procedures are grouped according to what the experimenter has believed to be the crux of his method.

Noxious Stimuli in Experiments Involving "Clash"
Between Excitation and Inhibition

The Cornell experiments. The most extensive series of experiments coming under this heading has been reported from the Cornell Behavior Farm by Liddell and Bayne (1927), Anderson and Liddell (1935), Anderson and Parmenter (1941), and Liddell (1944). Sheep, goats, dogs, and pigs were used. It will be noticed that some of the experiments parallel those of Pavlov mentioned above, among the ambivalent stimulation neuroses, but the "unconditioned response" is a shock-avoidance reaction in place of the alimentary reaction. The basic procedure is described as follows by Anderson and Liddell (1935):

The sheep to be conditioned was led to the laboratory. It ascended a platform and stood on a table where it might eat from a basket of oats. Its freedom of movement was restricted by loops passing under the legs and attached to a beam overhead. With the incentive of food at the beginning and end of the experiment, the sheep within a few days would run on leash to the laboratory from the barn, mount the table and remain quietly for as long as two hours. A leather bracelet wrapped with brass wires was attached to the shaved skin of the upper part of the foreleg. . . . A brief tetanizing shock, not painful to the experimenter's touch . . . evoked a brisk flexion of the sheep's foreleg, after which the animal became quiet. . . . If the shock was regularly preceded by some neutral stimulus such as the ticking of a metronome, soon the ticking of the metronome would elicit movement of the leg in anticipation of the shock. . . . The signal that a shock was coming was invariably followed by the shock. The animal quieted down within a few seconds after the shock had been administered.

The variations of method used to produce neuroses in the animals are illustrated below by summarized case histories. The four headings indicate the *experimenters'* view of what is relevant.

1. *Subjecting the animal to a difficult discrimination.* "Sheep 3" in Anderson and Liddell's article learned to raise its foreleg to a metronome of 120 beats per minute when that rhythm was constantly followed by a shock. A metronome of 50 beats per minute was never accompanied by shock, and soon ceased to evoke the flexion response. Rates of 60, 72, 84, and 92 beats were then in turn successfully made negative signals, but 100 beats could not be differentiated from 120. A *neurosis did not follow on this failure of differentiation.* After this, the animal was subjected to a series of tests lasting two hours daily in which the whole range of rates was presented in turn, 120 beats being followed by shock, the others not. After a few weeks the defensive reactions to 120 beats were found to be greatly weakened; but after further presentations of 120 beats followed by shock, violent defense reactions developed to *all* the tempos. These reactions persisted for at least three years. Since they followed a single-stimulus phase of the experiment, they were certainly not due to the difficult discrimination providing an ambivalent stimulus situation.

2. *Rhythmic alternation of positive and negative conditioned stimuli.* A sheep (Anderson and Parmenter, 1941, p. 120) was subjected to the following schedule from the beginning of its training: pure tone of 435 cycles, shock, 7 minutes pause; pure tone of 900 cycles, no shock, 7 minutes pause. The whole cycle would be gone through twice at each session. At the seventh observational period, 26 days from the inception of the schedule, the animal resisted being brought to the laboratory, showed restlessness on the experimental table, and struggled vigorously when either tone was presented, a state of affairs which persisted for the rest of the animal's life. The only comment that need be made is that the 7 minutes' interval seems too long to make this an ambivalent stimulus situation.

3. *Increasing the daily number of reinforcements.* In the case of the sheep reported by Liddell and Bayne (1927), shock was administered to the foreleg at the sixth beat of a metronome at 60 beats per minute. Fifteen trials were given daily. After 98 trials a delayed conditioned flexion response was obtained. The number of trials was then increased to 20 per day. On the second day on which this was done, the animal for the first time resisted being led to the experimental room. Throughout the session the sheep was in almost constant movement. The delayed reflex was no longer obtained: instead, there was an exaggerated leg movement with each beat of the metronome. Continued experiment on the sheep led to increasing nervousness, even when tests were reduced to five per day.

4. *Giving a large number of unreinforced presentations of a general-*

ized stimulus. In Anderson and Liddell's "Sheep 2" a very stable conditioned response was formed after 120 combinations of a metronome at 120 beats a minute and shock. A metronome beating 50 times to the minute was now repeatedly presented without shock. The leg-raising response became weaker but did not disappear. At the end of a series of 42 presentations distributed over two days neurotic symptoms appeared. It does not seem reasonable to argue that the neurotic effects were due to a clash between excitation due to generalization and the developing inhibition that is the essence of the process of extinction (see p. 24). If this *were* the case, it would also occur during extinction of conditionings unrelated to shock; but disturbances do not seem to have been noted in Pavlov's numerous experiments on extinction, also on space-restricted animals.

A different factor is given causal prominence by the Cornell experimenters for each of the above-mentioned procedures. Yet there is *a common factor* whose character they persistently regard as a matter of indifference—the repeated evocation of the leg-flexion response, either by the noxious stimulus (shock) or by the conditioned stimulus or by a stimulus whose effects depend upon its similarity to the latter (generalization). Now, with the leg flexion, the noxious stimulus evokes a certain amount of emotional disturbance in the animals, as evidenced in particular by Anderson and Parmenter's detailed case histories. This disturbance, too, would be conditioned to the conditioned stimulus. How an anxiety reaction of great strength can be built up on the basis of this will be discussed at a later juncture. The point being made here is merely that the origin of the neuroses should be sought in what is common to all the procedures—noxious stimulation in conditions of confinement.

Strong support is given to this point of view by certain unpublished Cornell experiments quoted by Anderson and Parmenter. Goldman working with goats, Jensen working with sheep, and Daniel and Anderson working with dogs are stated to have produced experimental neuroses by *rhythmic stimulation with positive stimuli alone.* Anderson and Parmenter agree with Liddell (1944) in supposing *monotony* to be the operative traumatic factor here. But is monotony ever traumatic if no noxious stimulus is used? And would neurosis not result with positive stimuli alone even if they were not presented rhythmically? Liddell and Bayne's experiment described above shows that it would. It is evidently easier to produce neurosis when rhythmic stimulation is used, but this seems to be associated with the fact, observed by Anderson and Parmenter themselves, that the waiting time interval itself becomes an additional conditioned stimulus to anxiety responses.

Cook's experiments. Another series of neuroses alleged to be due to a clash between excitation and inhibition was produced by Cook (1939*a*) in movement-restricted rats. These were first trained to flex the right leg for a food reward in response to a bright light. If an animal raised its leg without a light appearing, it would be lightly shocked. The leg-flexion habit having been strengthened over several weeks, an "inhibitory stimulus," the shining of a dim light, was introduced. A flexion to this light brought a "punishing shock." If no flexion occurred the dim light would be extinguished after five seconds. After the differentiation had been strengthened over several periods, the final stage of the experiment was reached—gradually increasing the intensity of the dim light. There were two stages at which special stress seemed to be imposed on the rats, *and both occurred before the discrimination became difficult.* The first was when leg flexions unaccompanied by bright light were unrewarded and later punished, the second when leg flexions to the dim light were unrewarded and punished. Cook's explanation is that during these stages there was a clash between excitatory and inhibitory tendencies to leg flexion. Whether or not such a clash played any part could only be decided by control experiments separating the shock from the conditioned stimuli. But here it may be noted that in the circle-and-ellipse type of experiment of Pavlov no disturbance is mentioned concerning the stage when the first ellipse is being made a negative stimulus, even though here too there is a positive tendency due to generalization from the circle together with a negative tendency being built up by nonreinforcement of the ellipse. The difference may well be entirely attributable to the fact that Cook was using shocks at such a stage, while Pavlov was not. There is no doubt of the disturbing action of electric shocks; and no reason at present to suppose that a "clash" added in any way to the disturbance.

The Russian experiments. The neuroses produced by Pavlov (1927, pp. 289–90) and Petrova (1935) that come under the present heading are in somewhat different case. The animal was, as usual, held in position by a harness. Weak electrical stimulation of a spot on its skin was conditioned to the alimentary reaction by being repeatedly followed by food. The current was then gradually increased in strength from one experimental session to the next until it was "extremely powerful." The alimentary response continued to be evoked by this stimulus and remained stable for many months. There was never any sign of a defense reaction. Then the electric current began to be systematically applied to a different place daily. For some time the alimentary response continued to be evoked, but, on applying the current to yet another new place, "a most violent defense reaction" occurred. No trace of the alimentary reaction remained. In another dog, when the explosive reaction had not yet been brought about by application of the electrical stimulus to a thirteenth new place, it was produced by applying the stimulus to several of the places on the same day, and not, as before, to a single place only. Pavlov states that because of the special nature of the conditioned stimulus little attention was given to these results at first (presumably because they seemed to be what one would expect of a severe noxious stimulus). Later, when the similar outcome of the circle-and-ellipse experiment had been observed, it was concluded that in both types of case the disturbances were manifestations of a "pathological state" resulting from a clash between excitation and inhibition beyond a stage at which a balance could be maintained (1927, pp. 292–93).

However, the circle-and-ellipse and the shock experiment differ from each other fundamentally. In the former, the 9:8 ellipse repeatedly evoked simultaneous conflicting tendencies to make and not to make the alimentary response. In the latter, until the final phase, the shock evoked only the alimentary response, because conditioned inhibition of the defense reaction had been gradually built up on the basis of reciprocal inhibition (see p. 30); and in the final phase the defense reaction appeared, alone and unrestrained. The final phase only occurred when the shock was applied in a way that went beyond the scope of the conditioned inhibition. It is quite possible that the same or similar effects would have been produced if the animal had merely been given shocks of the final severity at his first visit to the experimental table. I have accomplished such results in cats (see below).

Noxious Stimuli Interrupting Conditioned Feeding Responses

Dimmick, Ludlow, and Whiteman (1939) were the first to produce animal neuroses by a method that falls under this heading, although they attributed their results to difficult discrimination—mistakenly, as will be shown. Using an experimental cage 36 x 28 x 16 inches, they trained cats to raise the lid of a food box in response to a lamp switched on simultaneously with the ringing of a bell. When 100 per cent correct responses had been acquired, the cat would be shocked through a grid on the floor of the cage if he opened the food box at any time except while the conditioned stimuli lasted or six seconds thereafter. (This shocking, of course, constituted an interruption of the feeding response conditioned, incidentally, to such stimuli as the sight of the food box.) A varying number of sessions after this was begun, it was found that at the conditioned stimuli the cat would stretch toward the food box but not touch it. When this happened the animal would be shocked at the end of the "correct" period for opening the food box. The effect of this was to produce progressively more negative behavior toward the experimental situation, and such symptoms as yowling, crouching, and clawing at the sides of the cage developed as responses to the conditioned signals. Also, the cats became less friendly in their living quarters.

Masserman (1943) has reported the production of numerous neuroses in cats by methods in many ways similar to the above. Using a cage 40 x 20 x 20 inches in size, he trained the animals to open the lid of a food box in response to a light-and-bell signal. When this was well established he produced neuroses as follows. At the feeding signal, or at the moment of food-taking, a blast of air would be applied across the food box, or the grid on the floor of the cage would be charged with two or three high-voltage, low-amperage pulsations. When the air blast was used, the characteristic reaction was a sudden rush to crouch at the far side of the cage. The usual reaction to a grid shock was "a startled jump as each impulse was felt, followed by a slow dignified stalking away from the food after the shocks ended." Sometimes the air blast and the shock were given together, and then the reaction usually resembled that to the shock alone. Whatever the noxious stimulation used (and the air blast seems to have been disturbing enough to deserve the adjective), neurotic behavior would afterward be observed in the experimental cage—agitation or immobility, vocalization, refusal of food, sensitivity to extraneous stimuli, and, on presentation of the feeding signal, crouching, trembling, mydriasis, and other signs of anxiety. Outside the experimental cage some animals became excessively timid, while others became aggressive toward their cage mates or toward humans.

The belief of Dimmick *et al.* (1939) that their animal neuroses were due to "difficult discrimination," and Masserman's that his were caused by "motivational conflict"—a clash between a feeding motive and an avoidance motive created by the air blast or shock—would probably never have been held if these experimenters had made control observations on the effects of shock on animals that had never been fed in the experimental cage; for I have shown (see below) that a cat shocked in this kind of apparatus develops much the same changes of behavior whether it has feeding motives at the time of the shock or not.

Noxious Stimuli Used Alone

The only previous report of neurosis production conforming to this heading appears to be that of Watson and Rayner (1920). They found that a usually phlegmatic 11-month-old infant called Albert would react fearfully to the sound of an iron bar loudly struck behind his head. They contrived to strike the bar just as the child's hand touched a white rat. This was done seven times and then repeated after a week. It was subsequently found that the child reacted with fear to the white rat, and also to a rabbit, a beaver fur, and a dog. A month later these fear reactions could still be elicited. After this the child was lost sight of.

MAIER'S "ABNORMAL BEHAVIOR FIXATIONS":
A DOUBTFUL CASE

Maier (1949) has reported a large number of experiments on rats, producing what he calls "abnormal behaviour fixations" which he regards as parallel to other experimental neuroses. He trained rats to jump to the cards on a Lashley jumping apparatus. During a "correct" jump, the card, being unlatched, would be knocked over, and the rat would land on a feeding platform to receive a food reward. The "incorrect" card was latched, so that an animal jumping to it would be bumped on the nose and fall onto a net below. If jumping to one of the two patterns or one of the two sides was consistently rewarded, the animal would learn to jump to the "correct" card. If, however, the cards were latched in no regular order, the animal would show a stage of variability in its choices and soon after refuse to jump. It would then be forced to jump by the administration of an electric shock at the jumping stand, prodding with a stick, or blowing a blast of air on it. Maier noted that the jumping so compelled occurred consistently to one side (position stereotype) or to one pattern (symbol stereotype), even if the animal had his nose bumped at each jump.

This unchanging habit is what Maier means by "abnormal behavior fixation." He regards it as abnormal because it is persistent although repeatedly punished by nose bumps, *and, he believes, unrewarded.* But he overlooks the fact that each time a jump is forced, e.g. by electric shock, *its occurrence ends the shock.* This means a reduction of the drive that impelled the jump; and a drive reduction brought about in this manner is undoubtedly an effective reinforcer of stimulus-response connections (see pp. 22–23). Jumping in the direction taken at the first forced jump is thus reinforced, and is consolidated at each repetition. The firm establishment of this manner of jumping as the response to the electric shock stimulus is therefore nothing but ordinary adaptive learning, and not "an abnormal fixation." Being adaptive, it is not neurotic behavior in terms of our definition.

Unadaptiveness could, of course, be claimed for the seizures displayed by some of Maier's animals in other experiments, but these are evidently due to an innate hypersensitivity to strong stimuli (Finger, 1945). Maier (1949, pp. 135–39) denies this on the ground that such seizures occur more easily in confined space (Maier and Glaser, 1942) or when an animal is forced to jump to a card toward which it has an avoidance attitude (Maier and Longhurst, 1947); but this argument is untenable, since reactions dependent upon innate organization are also influenced by contingent circumstances. Unadaptive behavior that is innate falls outside the scope of our definition of neurosis.

Author's Experiments in Neurosis Production

I performed these experiments between June 1947 and July 1948 in the Department of Pharmacology of the University of the Witwatersrand.

SUBJECTS AND APPARATUS

The subjects were domestic cats ranging in age from about six months to three years. They were housed in airy cages eight feet long, five feet wide, and nine feet high, built into a brick cage house on the roof of the Medical School. When experimentation began, an animal would have been in these quarters for at least four weeks. Experiments were always done between 11:00 A.M. and 1:00 P.M., when the animals had not eaten for 19–21 hours, except occasionally, when prolonged observations were necessary.

The experimental center was a laboratory on the floor below the cage house. Animals were carried to and from the laboratory in "carrier cages" of which the dimensions were 9 x 9 inches and 16 inches high.

The experimental cage (40 x 20 x 20 inches high) was practically identical with that of Masserman, except that the long sides and roof were made of stout three-quarter-inch wire netting in place of glass. A metal funnel delivered pellets of minced beef into the food box as required. The conditioned signals used were auditory—a buzzer and a whirring sound made by the armature of an automobile hooter (somewhat inaccurately referred to as a "hoot"). The grid on the floor of the cage could be charged by depressing a telegraph key in the secondary circuit of an induction coil continuously vibrating 25 feet away. The current delivered, being of high voltage but low amperage, was very uncomfortable to the human hand but not productive of tissue damage.

In the course of the experiments it became evident that the experimental laboratory, and, indeed, the experimenter himself, could well be regarded as part of the apparatus. For convenience the experimental laboratory was called Room A. Experiments were also conducted in three other rooms which were labeled B, C, and D. These rooms, in the order stated, seemed, to the human eye and ear, to have decreasing degrees of resemblance to Room A. Rooms A and B were both situated about 30 feet above ground level overlooking eastward a fairly busy street, but Room A was the brighter of the two, as it also had windows on its north side. Both rooms contained very dark laboratory furniture, the greater quantity being in Room A. Room C faced south, was about half the size of A or B, and contained laboratory furniture lighter in color and less in quantity than that in B. It was out of earshot of the street. Room D was situated on the roof of the Medical School, and was extremely bright with whitewashed walls and large windows north and west. Besides a concrete trough and odd packages it contained only a light-colored kitchen sink in one corner.

PROCEDURE

Experimentation commenced only after an animal's original reactions had been recorded to the experimental cage, to the auditory signals and various other sounds, and to one or more of Rooms B, C, and D. In all cases these reactions were found to be inconsequential.

Six experimental animals were subjected to the main experimental procedure (Schedule I) and six to a control procedure (Schedule II). In brief, it may be said that Schedule II corresponds to the method for producing neuroses described by Masserman (1943), and Schedule I differs from it in omitting what Masserman would regard as an essential step—the conditioning of a feeding response.

Schedule I. Not more than two days after the control observations detailed above, the cat was reintroduced into the experimental cage and given five to ten grid shocks, each immediately preceded by a "hoot" lasting 2 to 3 seconds. The grid shocks were separated by irregular intervals ranging from 15 seconds to 2 minutes. With the exception of Cat 8 who received five shocks in all, these animals were subjected to a second series of shocks one to three days later.

Schedule II. The first part of this schedule consisted of conditioning animals to perform food-approach responses to the buzzer. There were two variations differing from each other in a minor respect. Four of the six animals were trained to raise the lid of the food box to the stimulus, the other two to orientate themselves to the *open* food box. When either response had been strongly reinforced over eight to sixteen experimental sessions each consisting of about twenty reinforcements, each animal would be subjected to shocks from the floor of the cage, as follows. The buzzer had just sounded, the cat had made its learned response, the pellet had fallen into the food box, and now the animal was moving forward to seize it. Before the pellet could be reached, a grid shock was passed into the cat, which immediately recoiled, howling. Shocking under these conditions was repeated until the cat ceased to make its previous conditioned response to the buzzer. Four was the mean number of shocks required to accomplish this. One cat required nine shocks distributed over three separate sessions.

IMMEDIATE EFFECTS OF THE SHOCK

The immediate responses to shock followed the same pattern in all cats, whether they had previously acquired a feeding response in the experimental situation or not. This pattern was made up of various combinations of the following symptoms—rushing hither and thither, getting up on the hind legs, clawing at the floor, roof, and sides of the experimental cage, crouching, trembling, howling, spitting; mydriasis, rapid respiration, pilo-erection, and, in some cases, urination or defecation.

LASTING EFFECTS OF THE SHOCK

Effects Noted in the Experimental Cage

When tested at subsequent sessions, *all* animals, irrespective of the schedule employed, displayed neurotic symptoms in the sense of the definition given in Chapter 3. The effects of the two schedules were broadly the same, with a few differences that will be mentioned below. Three manifestations were constant and common to all animals: (1) resistance to being put into the experimental cage; (2) signs of anxiety when inside the cage (muscular tension and mydriasis were invariable); (3) *refusal to eat meat pellets anywhere in the cage even after 1, 2, or 3 days' starvation.*

Quantitative change in general activity was almost invariable. An increase or decrease was usually constant for an individual animal. Increased activity took the forms of restless roving, clawing at the wire netting, butting the roof with the head, and ceaseless vocalizing. Decreased activity varied between tense infrequent movements in the standing posture and very intense immobile crouching.

Symptoms that were observed intermittently in all animals were hypersensitivity to "indifferent" stimuli, pilo-erection, howling, crouching, and rapid respiration.

Certain cats displayed special symptoms in addition to those that were common to all. The respiratory rate of Cat 9 always rose from about 30 to about 60 as soon as he was put into the cage. Cat 15, who had micturated while being shocked, invariably micturated a few seconds after being placed in the cage. Cat 6 manifested almost continuous trembling. Cat 8 developed a symptom that it seems permissible to call hysterical. He jerked his shoulders strongly every few seconds in the experimental cage, and also in his living cage *if I entered it.* This jerking suggested an abortive jumping movement, and may well have had its origin in the fact that on the first occasion on which this animal was shocked he jumped through a hatch in the roof of the cage that had been left open inadvertently. All but the first-mentioned of these four cats had been through Schedule I.

Whatever symptoms an animal showed in the experimental cage were invariably *intensified by presentation of the auditory stimulus* that had been contiguous with the occurrence of the shock.

Generalization of Neurotic Responses Outside Experimental Cage

All cats showed some symptoms outside the experimental cage of the same kind as inside it. In two Schedule I animals and four Schedule II animals these effects were limited to slight tenseness and fluctuating mydriasis in the experimental room, together with inhibition of feeding responses anywhere in the room at the sound of the buzzer or "hooter" as the case might be. However, in the remaining six cats (four of Schedule I, and two of Schedule II) such symptoms were very marked, and were observed also outside the confines of the experimental laboratory. That is to say, they were observed in one or more of the Rooms B, C, and D. One animal also refused meat pellets in the passage in front of the living cages. Any animal that showed symptoms of tension in Room D showed them more strongly in Room C, and still more in Room B. A cat free of symptoms in Room B would also be free in Rooms C and D. Thus it would appear that the anxiety-producing effect of these various rooms was a function of their resemblance to Room A as judged in a rough way by the human eye and ear. More exactly, the magnitude of the anxiety response in Room C, for instance, seems to have depended upon the number of stimuli common to Rooms A and C. As will be seen below, the successful use of these rooms to build up a conditioned inhibition of the anxiety responses provides strong support for this supposition.

An interesting instance of apparent failure of generalization was noted in Schedule II cats. These learned during their food-approach training in the experimental cage to jump spontaneously into the open carrier cage placed upon the floor of the living cage. *Even after they had been made neurotic they continued to jump into the carrier cage,* and only began to manifest anxiety while being carried downstairs to the experimental room. Apparently, this is an example of the steeper gradient of generalization of avoidance responses than of approach responses pointed out by Miller (1944).

Neurotic Responses to the Experimenter

Three Schedule I animals developed phobic reactions toward the experimenter which were manifested even in the living cages. The jerking shoulders of Cat 8 when I entered his cage have already been mentioned. Two others would crouch with pupils widely dilated as soon as they saw even my entry into the cage house. Such effects were never noted in Schedule II animals.

Some Differences Between the Effects of the Two Schedules

The general similarity between the effects of the two schedules has been mentioned. However, it is only to be expected that the preliminary conditioning of feeding reactions in Schedule II animals would result in some differences. The fact that only Schedule I animals became phobic toward the experimenter was noted in the last paragraph. The explanation seems to be that for Schedule II cats "approach" attitudes toward the experimenter had at first been built up as a result of his previous association with feeding responses; and at the time of shocking, the experimenter was relatively remote as a stimulus since the animal was oriented toward the food box. Schedule II animals were alone found to show phobic responses to meat pellets dropped in front of them wherever they might be—starting with pupils widely dilated. This is easily understood, as these animals were responding strongly to the sight and smell of these pellets when they were shocked.

A DEMONSTRATION OF ADAPTIVE LEARNING IN THE TRAUMATIC SITUATION UNDER SPECIAL CONDITIONS

Cat 14 was trained to orientate himself to the open food box at the sound of the buzzer during nine sessions by rewarding this response on 160 occasions by a pellet of food in the food box. The response having been thus firmly established, a pellet was dropped into the food box *without* being preceded by the buzzer. Upon moving toward it, the cat was given a grid shock. He ran howling to the rear compartment. After a time, in response to repeated presentations of the buzzer he crept cautiously back to the food box and ate the pellets that had accumulated in it.

In subsequent sessions pellets preceded by the buzzer were irregularly interspersed with pellets not so preceded. If the animal tried to eat a pellet of the latter kind he was shocked. However, after a period which varied from 2 to 15 minutes from the dropping of the pellet, the buzzer would be sounded; after which the animal would be allowed to eat the pellet. Sometimes the buzzer was sounded several times at half-minute intervals before he did so. In the course of 21 sessions of this sort he received 215 reinforcements of the feeding response to the buzzer and 12 grid shocks. In the earlier sessions there was a strong tendency not to respond to the buzzer after having been shocked, but this tendency gradually lessened until eventually this animal manifested anxiety only when a pellet fell into the food box without prior presentation of the buzzer. He would recoil sharply, with pupils dilated and hair on end, and then very slowly withdraw, staring at the food box. This could not be called a neurotic reaction (see definition), for had he advanced instead of withdrawing, he would surely have been shocked. He did not develop any kind of avoidance reaction to the experimental situation as a whole, as shown by the fact that at the beginning of every session he jumped spontaneously, usually within a few seconds, from the open carrier cage into the experimental cage. The explanation for this is as follows. While the drive reduction following each shock reinforced an avoidance response to stimuli from the experimental environment, each feeding reinforced a conditioned inhibition of this avoidance response based upon reciprocal inhibition. Since feedings were far more numerous than shocks, the effective response to the experimental situation remained an approach response. Only to pellets unaccompanied by the buzzer (which alone were consistently followed by shock) did an avoidance response become reinforced.

Curative Measures Involving Reciprocal Inhibition

The fact that the neurotic reactions of the cats were associated with inhibition of feeding suggested that under different conditions feeding might inhibit the neurotic reactions: in other words, that the two reactions might be reciprocally inhibitory.

In order actively to inhibit the anxiety reactions the feeding would have to occur in the presence of anxiety-producing stimuli. Either, then, some factor that would favor feeding had to be added to the stimulus situation in the experimental cage, or else feeding had to be attempted somewhere *outside* the experimental cage where anxiety-producing stimuli would be less numerous and less potent. Both principles were used, as described below.

THE ADDITION TO THE EXPERIMENTAL ENVIRONMENT OF
A FACTOR FAVORING FEEDING

The Human Hand as a Stimulus to Feeding

Since in their living cages the cats were accustomed to have food cast to them by the human hand, it was expected that the hand had become a conditioned stimulus evoking approach responses to food. Consequently, the experiment was tried of placing an animal in the experimental cage and moving toward its snout pellets of meat on the flat end of a four-inch rod held in the experimenter's hand, in the hope that the presence of the hand would overcome the inhibition to eating. This procedure was applied to nine animals (six Schedule I, and three Schedule II), and after some persistence four of them (three Schedule I, and one Schedule II) were induced to eat. These animals at first approached a pellet hesitantly, sometimes refusing it. But after several had been eaten, they ate fairly freely from the rod, and soon after would also now and then eat a pellet on the floor of the cage or in the food box. In the case of Cat 3, the only one of these four cats that had been through Schedule II (in which shock interrupted a movement toward the food box), eating out of the food box did not occur until he had eaten more than fifty pellets on the floor of the cage in the course of several sessions. As the number of pellets eaten in the situation increased, each of these animals ate more freely, moved about the cage with greater freedom, and showed decreasing anxiety symptoms. By the time Cat 10 had eaten about fifty pellets and Cat 11 about eighty they were jumping spontaneously out of the carrier cage into the experimental cage; and inside the cage were showing no sign of anxiety whatever. Cat 8, which, it will be remembered, had the "hysterical" jerking movement of the shoulders, lost all trace of his symptoms only after he had eaten 216 pellets in the experimental cage in the course of eleven sessions.

Masserman's "Forced Solution"

The three Schedule II cats on which the human hand technique was not tried were each subjected to procedures based on the "forced solution" described by Masserman (1943, p. 75), with like results. The essence of this method is that a hungry neurotic cat in the experimental cage is gradually pushed by means of a movable barrier toward the open food box which contains appetizing food. This accentuates the manifestations of anxiety, but after a while the animal snatches at the food in one or more hurried gulps. Repeating the procedure over several days has the effect of diminishing and then eliminating the neurotic reactions.

FEEDING IN THE PRESENCE OF RELATIVELY WEAK ANXIETY RESPONSES

It has already been stated that the inhibition of eating, together with the rest of the neurotic picture, occurred not only in the experimental cage but also anywhere in the experimental room and in other rooms resembling this room in various ways—an effect presumably due to primary stimulus generalization (see pp. 11–13). The slighter the resemblance of a given room to the experimental room, the less marked were the anxiety reactions. In the case of the five cats that had remained unaffected by the delivery of food in the experimental cage by the human hand, it was decided to try to obtain feeding responses in the rooms where the anxiety reactions were less marked. It was thought that somewhere in this "hierarchy" of rooms there would be found for each animal a place where the anxiety responses were mild enough to permit eating, at least at times. Starting in the experimental room (Room A), each cat was patiently plied with meat pellets on the floor. If it did not eat after about 30 minutes, the experiment was repeated on the following day in the next room lower in the "hierarchy." One cat ate initially in Room A, one in Room B, one in Room C, and one in Room D. The fifth animal could not be persuaded to eat even in Room D, but did so eventually in the passage that separated Room D from the living cages. Once an animal had eaten in a given place it was given about twenty pellets there, always responding to their presentation with increasing rapidity, and with decreasing signs of anxiety. The next day it was tested in the room next in order of resemblance to Room A. (From time to time control tests of response in the experimental cage were also made.) By this method of gradual ascent all the animals were eventually enabled to eat in Room A. Then, within the room, gradual approach was made to the experimental cage in similar fashion, the animal being fed on the floor increasingly close to the experimental table, then on the table next to the cage, on the roof of the cage, and at last inside the cage. It was found that when feeding became possible in the cage, anxiety reactions were much more rapidly eliminated there when the pellets were tossed at widely distributed points than if they were confined to the food box. Apparently, scattered placing of the pellets resulted in reciprocal inhibition of the anxiety responses to stimuli from all parts of the experimental situation, and this made possible the development of conditioned inhibition of the responses to all parts, so that after 50–100 pellets had been eaten in the cage, manifestations of anxiety ceased to be observed.

THE ELIMINATION OF NEUROTIC RESPONSES TO THE
CONDITIONED AUDITORY STIMULI

The fact that an animal, after subjection to the procedures just described, would behave without anxiety in the experimental cage can be attributed to the elimination of the neurotic responses that had previously been conditioned to the various visual (and olfactory) cues in the vicinity of the cage. But if the *auditory* stimulus that had preceded the shocks was now presented, the animals again manifested a high degree of anxiety. The effect was such that the animal could be inhibited by the auditory stimulus from completing any movement toward a pellet of meat in the experimental cage, and in most cases, at various points in the experimental room as well. The problem was to present the auditory stimulus in such a way that the anxiety reactions would be weak and there would be no inhibition of eating. There were two possible solutions to this: (1) diminishing the strength of the stimulus either by reducing its physical intensity or by increasing the distance between the animal and the stimulus; or (2) making use of the stimulus trace and the fact that the effects of a brief sensory stimulus on the nervous system gradually decline in intensity with passage of time (Adrian, 1928). The first solution was applied to two animals and the second to seven.

Feeding in Conjunction with the Auditory Stimulus at Reduced Strength

Both cats upon whom this procedure was used had been through Schedule I. The minimum distance at which Cat 11 would eat with the conditioned auditory stimulus ("hooter") sounded continuously was found by trial and error to be 40 feet. Here, though continuously tense and mydriatic, the animal ate eight pellets, but would not eat at a point 10 feet nearer. The next day, after two pellets at 40 feet, he ate ten at 30 feet, at first only when dropped a few inches away from him, but afterward even at distances of 3 or 4 feet. Pellets were then dropped increasingly near the hooter, and by the time eight more had been given he had eaten two only 17 feet away. After eating each pellet he would run back to the 30-foot point, or even beyond it. Day by day, the distance at which the animal would eat was reduced. When he had had a total of 160 pellets at progressively decreasing distances, he was at last able to eat inside the experimental cage during the sounding of the hooter, although manifesting considerable anxiety. At the end of his fourth session spent in eating in the cage, by which time he had eaten a total of 87 pellets there, the note was made, "There is now absolutely no sign of avoidance reaction or anxiety to the auditory stimulus."

Cat 8, whose anxiety responses to the auditory stimulus were much milder than those of Cat 11 at the commencement of this procedure, ate as little as 20 feet away from the "hooter" in the beginning, and required only 33 pellets at decreasing distances to enable him to eat in the presence of the sound in the experimental cage. He lost all tenseness there after 45 pellets given over four sessions.

Feeding in the Presence of the Trace of the Conditioned Auditory Stimulus

Four of the cats treated in this way had been through Schedule I and the other three through Schedule II. The animal was placed inside the experimental cage and, though showing no sign of disturbance, was given one or two meat pellets on the floor of the cage. Then, after an interval of about a minute, the auditory stimulus was sounded for about one-fifth of a second, and *immediately afterward* a pellet was dropped in front of the animal, who had in the meantime become tense and hunched-up, with pilo-erection and mydriasis. After a variable interval, usually about 30 seconds, the animal would have lost most of its tenseness and would move forward cautiously to the pellet and eat it. Not less than one minute later, the auditory stimulus would again be presented and be followed by a meat pellet, but this time the animal would eat after a shorter interval. This procedure was repeated 10 to 20 times during a session, and the interval before the eating of the pellet would gradually diminish until the animal ate without delay. In illustration of the above, the intervals recorded (in seconds) for one cat during the first session of this kind were: 40, 15, 20, 7, 5, 6, 6, 6, 4, 8, 8, 11, 4, 6, 4, 4, 5, 3, and 4. At the next session the intervals were 3, 3, 2, 3, 2, and 2 seconds for the first six presentations of stimulus and thereafter she consistently responded practically at once.

The next step was to *increase the duration of the auditory stimulus.* First, every fourth or fifth stimulus was given a duration of about a second; and then, gradually, depending on the responses of the animal, the duration was increased. Eventually, the animal would show no vestige of anxiety even to a stimulus of 30 seconds' duration, and would make alert food-seeking movements as soon as he heard the auditory stimulus.

Demonstration That the Neurotic Reactions Were Not Merely Overshadowed

Whichever of the above two procedures had been employed, the question remained whether the neurotic reactions had really been eliminated or had merely been overshadowed by a stronger reaction of feeding beneath which they lay dormant. The decisive experiment was *to extinguish the food-seeking response to the auditory stimulus* and then observe whether or not the neurotic reactions were reinstated. Each of the animals was given 30 irregularly massed extinction trials on each of three successive days. Long before the end of the third day's session they all showed almost complete indifference to the auditory stimulus. Immediately after the conclusion of the third extinction session the following test was made. A pellet was dropped on the floor of the experimental cage about two feet away from the animal, and as he began to approach it the auditory signal was sounded continuously, to see if extinction had reinstated the inhibitory effect on eating that had originally been noted. *In no instance was there observed any semblance of the restoration of an anxiety response or any suggestion of an inhibition of eating.* Moreover, observation for many weeks afterward never revealed recurrence of anxiety responses in any animal.

THERAPY IN REVERSE: THE SPREAD OF NEUROTIC REACTIONS TO NEW STIMULI

A special experiment was performed on two Schedule I cats (11 and 8) before the anxiety-evoking effects of the auditory stimulus were removed as described above. The procedures were not identical but complemented each other in demonstrating that by changing the relations in an experiment in which a stimulus to feeding and an anxiety-evoking stimulus are brought together, not only does therapy fail to occur but there is *a spread of anxiety-evoking potential to new stimuli*. This provides incidentally a further demonstration of the reciprocal relationship between feeding behavior and anxious behavior.

After the anxiety responses of Cat 11 to the visual (and olfactory) stimuli of the experimental cage had been thoroughly eliminated, he was one day placed in the experimental cage and a minute or two later a pellet of meat was audibly dropped into the food box. As he moved forward to seize it, the hooter was hounded. He withdrew his head sharply, his pupils dilated momentarily, and he then sat still, crouching close to the food box. At intervals of about two minutes, two other pellets were dropped into the food box, and the hooter was again sounded each time when he approached. During the next 15 minutes' observation he maintained his crouched, "negativistic" attitude continuously. He started at every sharp sound. His pupils gradually became fully dilated, and his respiratory rate went up to 80, but after about 10 minutes both of these symptoms began to diminish. In subsequent sessions, the hooter was again sounded on the occasions when he was about to eat a pellet out of the food box; and then it was seen that he was ceasing to try for pellets in the food box, and that his previous free movements had taken on a kind of slow, squirming character. However, he still readily ate pellets dropped on the floor of the cage. The hooter was now employed to inhibit his eating there as well. When eating on the floor had been inhibited several times, he not only refused pellets *unaccompanied* by the hooter on the floor of the cage, but resisted violently being put into the experimental cage which he had once eagerly entered. On the experimental table outside the cage he still ate pellets voraciously. But by sounding the hooter during approaches to pellets, eating on the table became inhibited, and eventually, by the same means, so did eating anywhere in the room unless the pellet fell within a few inches of the animal. Moreover, this normally exceptionally active cat, when once in the laboratory, sat tense and immobile next to a wall. Thus, an ever-widening range of stimuli had been made to evoke anxiety reactions. This is understandable on the basis that with cessation of the hooter commenced a reduction of the drive state that the hooter itself had brought into being. The reinforcing state of affairs provided by this drive reduction would reinforce the withdrawal reaction and its autonomic concomitants to any stimuli that happened to be contiguous in time.

In the case of Cat 8, the arousal of anxiety responses by the hooter was similarly used to condition anxiety to two places in the experimental room (Room A).

Interpretations of the Phenomena of Experimental Neurosis

The interpretations that follow have reference primarily to my own experiments described above. In these, as in the experiments of others who employed severe electric shocks (see above), the neurotic behavior is so dramatically produced that the pertinent factors are relatively easy to identify. We shall first see what can be learned from these experiments and then consider how much similarity can be found in the production of neuroses by other methods.

CONFORMITY OF THE BEHAVIOR CHANGES
TO DEFINITION OF NEUROSIS

The central point at issue here is whether experimental neurosis and clinical neurosis are, at bottom, the same. It is worth remarking that the *impression* of similarity between neurotic animals and neurotic humans (taking into account the greater complexity of the human nervous system) is very striking; so that even a psychoanalytically oriented experimenter like Masserman has had no doubts of it. But it is necessary to approach the matter more rigorously and to ask whether the animal neuroses conform to the definition abstracted from human neuroses that is given in Chapter 3. To do so they must satisfy the criteria of *anxiety, unadaptiveness, persistence,* and *acquisition through learning.*

The constant presence of *anxiety* is obvious from the account of the experiments and requires no emphasis. *Unadaptiveness* is evident in two ways—the inhibition of feeding responses in a hungry animal in a situation in which feeding would not again be followed by shock (and in the case of Schedule I animals had never been followed by shock); and the mere fact that the anxious responses were causing fatigue without in any way favoring the organism's life processes (i.e., were without reward).

The criterion of *persistence* is satisfied by (1) maintenance of tenseness and other manifestations at an undiminishing level throughout a long session; (2) recurrence of manifestations at unabated strength session after session; and (3) re-evocation of manifestations after long periods free from experimentation—for example, in all of three cats rested for six months. The following extract from the protocols of a Schedule I cat illustrates the unremittingness of the neurotic tension and shows how complete the inhibition of feeding can be.

On September 1, 1947, seven days after she had been shocked, Cat 7, unfed for 22 hours, was taken to the experimental laboratory. She resisted being put into the experimental cage. Inside the cage, she crouched with pupils widely dilated. She was kept there for 2 hours, during which her pupils remained dilated, although their size fluctuated a good deal, reaching a maximum at any sharp sound or sudden movement. At times she became very restless, mewed plaintively, and clawed at the sides of the cage. She showed no response at all to meat pellets put in front of her nose on an ebony rod, and left untouched a pellet which lay on the floor of the cage during the whole of her two hours' confinement. A few minutes later, in the living cage, she ate her daily ration with extreme voracity.

In order to decide whether or not the neurotic behavior was *learned*, it is necessary to recall that in the definition given in Chapter 2 it was stated that learning may be said to have occurred if a response has been evoked in temporal contiguity with a given sensory stimulus, and it is subsequently found that the stimulus can evoke the response although it could not have done so before. In the case of our experimental cats there was no qualitative difference between the immediate responses to the shock and the later responses to the experimental environment. In other words, the responses produced by the shock in the originally "neutral" experimental environment were subsequently found to be producible by the experimental environment itself. This clearly implies the occurrence of learning as defined. It was particularly well shown in the development of the "special" symptoms noted earlier. For example, the cat that displayed the jerking shoulders was the one that had once jumped out of the cage when shocked, and the one that regularly micturated in the experimental cage had micturated when shocked.

THE LEARNING PROCESS IN NEUROSES
PRODUCED BY SEVERE SHOCK

As stated above, what the animals learned in acquiring their neuroses was to make, in the absence of the electric shock, whatever responses the electric shock had produced in them. These responses had become conditioned to the stimuli that were acting on the animal at the time of the shock or just before it—stimuli from the cage, the experimenter, the experimental laboratory, and the buzzer or hooter.

It has seemed incredible to some that so great a measure of learning can occur in so few trials. But (as stated in Chapter 2) amount of learning at a single trial depends upon amount of drive reduction, and since a severe shock produces an enormous amount of central neural excitation, the drive reduction consequent on its cessation will be very great indeed. Unusually rapid learning is thus possible; and as the responses evoked by the shock are very strong ones, it is not surprising that very striking learning occurs in very few trials.

After the first shock, and increasingly as further shocks are added, stimuli from the experimental environment are able to elicit anxiety responses on their own. These, of course, have anxiety drive as an antecedent. This implies that a second source of reinforcement of anxiety responses is now present; each time the animal is removed from the experimental environment the anxiety drive due to this environment is reduced, and this further reinforces the anxiety responses to the stimuli of this environment. The role of anxiety drive reduction as a reinforcing agent has been discussed (pp. 22–23). An informative experiment that needs to be done would show whether animals frequently introduced into and removed from the experimental cage would eventually have more severe neurotic reactions than animals who spent an equal length of time in the cage during a few long visits. The former would clearly have had more anxiety drive reductions.

THE LEARNING PROCESS IN NEUROSES
PRODUCED BY MILD SHOCK

It will be recalled (p. 43) that mild shocks were employed for the production of experimental neuroses by the Cornell investigators. Nevertheless it is clear from their accounts that there was always some evidence of general disturbance, even if the animal took only "a few seconds" to quiet down. This is consonant with the human experience that an electric shock which, though weak, is strong enough to evoke a motor response will also probably cause some emotional disturbance. As might have been expected, the mild shocks had to be administered many times more than severe ones to produce a similar measure of "permanent" change of response involving emotional disturbance.

It is necessary to explain how a severe anxiety reaction could arise from what is apparently nothing more than the repeated conditioning of a mildly disturbing emotional reaction. After the first conditioning trial the stimulus (e.g., buzzer) evokes a small amount of anxiety. Let us call this 2 units and let it be one-sixth the amount evoked by the shock (12 units). At the second trial, when the shock follows shortly on the conditioned stimulus the anxiety from the two sources will add together, giving a total of 14 units. The amount of conditioning of anxiety to the buzzer at this trial will now be one-sixth of 14 (2.3). This adds to the 2 units previously established to make up a total of 4.3 units to be evoked by the next presentation of the buzzer. Table I shows how repetition creates a cycle in which each increase in the amount of anxiety evoked by the conditioned and the unconditioned stimulus in combination increases the amount of anxiety conditioned to the buzzer, and this increases at an accelerating rate the total anxiety evoked by the combination. After five repetitions of the sequence the buzzer evokes more anxiety than the shock. It is obvious that after a large number of repetitions a very high degree of anxiety will be evocable. The gradual building up of anxiety is clearly evident in Anderson and Parmenter's detailed case histories (1935).

TABLE I

Conditioning trial	1st	2d	3d	4th	5th	6th
Amount of anxiety due to buzzer...	0	2.0	4.3	7.0	10.2	13.9
Amount of anxiety due to shock...	12.0	12.0	12.0	12.0	12.0	12.0
Total amount of anxiety..........	12.0	14.0	16.3	19.0	22.2	25.9
Amount of anxiety newly conditioned to buzzer.........	2.0	2.3	2.7	3.2	3.7	4.3

This hypothetical statement has obvious deficiencies. It leaves out of account the usual decrement in amount of learning with each successive reinforcement (p. 21). The choice, for the sake of clarity of exposition, of one-sixth as the ratio of newly conditioned anxiety to evoked anxiety is quite arbitrary. The real proportion may well be much less. Another possible variable that is ignored is the amount of anxiety evoked by the shock itself. It is possible that with repetition this either rises or falls. Our hypothesis merely shows in a schematic way how it is *possible* for high intensities of anxiety to be conditioned by the use of mild shock.

It should be noted, regarding the Cornell experiments, that it was not only to the special auditory stimuli that anxiety responses were being conditioned, but to the whole experimental environment. In the "rigid time schedule" experiments, conditioning occurred also to the internal changes associated with a particular time interval, as Anderson and Parmenter point out, and this may have accounted for the easier production of neurosis in these cases. It seems gratuitous to postulate "monotony" as a self-sufficient factor in the way Liddell (1944) has done. (See discussion p. 45.)

THE LEARNING PROCESS IN NEUROSES
PRODUCED BY AMBIVALENT STIMULATION

If neuroses produced by ambivalent stimulation are the same as neuroses produced by noxious stimuli, the same essential processes must presumably bring them into being. Certainly, in terms of symptoms the end result is much the same. The question is, is there any evidence of similar antecedents? Noxious stimulation produces neurosis as a result of the anxiety it evokes. There are two sources of evidence that ambivalent stimulation also evokes anxiety. First, it is a matter of everyday human experience that ambivalent stimuli arouse feelings of tension. Second, Fonberg (1956) has shown in a cleverly devised experiment that the emotional responses in an experimental neurosis produced by ambivalent stimulation are similar to the emotional responses due to noxious stimulation. In several dogs she conditioned defensive motor responses to a noxious stimulus. Subsequently she produced experimental neurosis in the animals by means of ambivalent auditory stimuli. Simultaneously with the appearance of emotional disturbances the previously elaborated motor reactions reappeared. Since nothing resembling a noxious stimulus was present in the external situation, it is reasonable to suppose that the motor response was mediated by an internal state of affairs that is also present with noxious stimulation—namely, anxiety.

At an early stage of an experiment to produce neurosis through ambivalent stimulation, the anxiety drive that is a by-product of the conflicting tendencies is likely to be slight. Even then the drive reduction constituted by its cessation results in the anxiety responses becoming reinforced to whatever stimuli are contiguous with them, and among these is the ambivalent stimulation itself. In the same way as suggested above for the case of mild noxious stimuli, the strength of the anxiety responses is conceived to be gradually stepped up at each presentation of the ambivalent stimulus situation while the drive reduction potential correspondingly grows. Eventually very powerful anxiety responses are evoked, and strong avoidance behavior entirely replaces the approach responses to the experimental situation which were previously established by repeated feeding.

THE FACTOR OF CONFINEMENT

Anderson and Liddell (1935) pointed out long ago that all animal neuroses have been produced *in conditions of confined space.* Cook's experiments (1939b), using different degrees of space constriction with other factors constant, indicate that it is a potent factor in neurosis production. There are at least three ways in which confinement could exert its influence. First, the prevention of an effective escape response allows the cumulative action on the animal of stimuli that have become conditioned to anxiety, so that there is a rising magnitude of potentially reducible anxiety drive. Second, the drive reductions occur in the presence of a limited number of stimuli, and the anxiety responses can be conditioned to these in greater strength than would be the case if the environment were a changing one. Third, it seems likely that autonomic responses are stronger when freed from the reciprocally inhibiting effects of the well-defined musculoskeletal response that would occur if escape were possible. This supposition is supported by the experiments of Freeman and Pathman (1940), Haggard and Freeman (1941), and Mowrer and Viek (1948). (See p. 89.)

THE REASON FOR PERSISTENCE OF NEUROTIC HABITS
(RESISTANCE TO EXTINCTION)

As stated in Chapter 2, learned responses that are unrewarded (and so unadaptive) ordinarily undergo extinction by a mechanism that is associated with fatigue. Since fatigue occurs whether there is reward or not, there is *always* a fatigue-associated drive state that tends toward a weakening of the connection between the response and the stimulus that led to it. But it is only when there is no significant reward that the connection is *actually* weakened (see pp. 25–26). When reward counteracts this tendency toward weakening it does so through reducing the central drive state due to, say, hunger.

Now, the neurotic responses are unrewarded (unadaptive). Yet they necessarily have a central state of drive as an antecedent. This drive is automatically reduced by the retreat of the organism from the anxiety-producing stimulus, or by any other means that removes the organism from the action of this stimulus. Any responses that may be occurring at such a time will be reinforced, and their fatigue-associated tendency to be extinguished will be counteracted. Farber (1948) has presented a clear demonstration in rats of the manner in which anxiety drive reduction interferes with extinction.

Each time a neurotic cat was passively removed from the experimental cage, anxiety drive was reduced, and this reinforced the neurotic responses, counteracting whatever fatigue-associated extinctive tendencies the evocation of the responses had produced. It is quite possible that a similar, though doubtless weaker, counteracting effect could occur *within* the cage, if the animal was oriented toward a part of the cage that was strongly anxiety-evoking and then turned toward a spot evoking relatively weak anxiety. Unless there were marked perseveration of the effects of the stronger stimulus, some drive reduction would take place that would reinforce the anxiety responses. This implies that an environment unevenly conditioned to anxiety responses would maintain them better than one evenly conditioned. Experiment will decide whether this is so or not.

Frequently repeated or continuous consequents of the anxiety drive (e.g., the autonomic responses) are much more likely to coincide in time with drive reductions than are responses that occur only occasionally. That is why, in our experiments, the autonomic responses, whose evocation was continuous, were always persistent, whereas such intermittent responses as clawing the sides of the cage were often soon extinguished.

Another factor that probably contributes greatly to the persistence of neurotic anxiety response habits is the low level of reactive inhibition presumably generated by autonomic responses, whose energy expenditure is small by contrast with that of musculoskeletal responses.

THE MECHANISM OF CURE OF EXPERIMENTAL NEUROSES

The effectiveness of the procedures that overcame the neurotic responses can be accounted for as follows: in every instance feeding was made possible in the presence of stimuli conditioned to anxiety responses which, under other circumstances, inhibited feeding. When stimuli to incompatible responses are present simultaneously, the occurrence of the response that is dominant in the circumstances involves the reciprocal inhibition of the other. As the number of feedings increased, the anxiety responses gradually became weaker, so that to stimuli to which there was initially a response of the anxiety pattern there was finally a feeding response with inhibition of anxiety. This "permanent" change implies a new positive conditioning *pari passu* with a conditioning of inhibition of anxiety, and this could have been subserved by at least two drive reductions—hunger drive reduction, and reduction by the reciprocal inhibition itself of the drive antecedent to the anxiety responses. That the conditioned inhibition was due to a *neural change* and was not merely a correlate of the occurrence of the alternative response seems a clear inference from the fact that eventual extinction of the alternative response did not result in reinstatement of the original one. The mechanism has been more fully discussed in Chapter 2.

In the case of the so-called "forced solution" first described by Masserman (1943) in which the maximally hungry cat is physically forced toward very attractive food and at a certain proximity eats, the process is essentially similar. This is another way of raising the strength of the food-approach tendency against the anxiety that opposes it. An act of feeding inhibits the anxiety and leaves its habit strength slightly weakened, so that feeding will occur more readily on the next occasion; and so on.

A Critique of Other Theories of Experimental Neurosis

The theories considered below differ widely in their details, but each one presumes that damage or disruption of some kind underlies the neurosis, and not "mere" learning.

PAVLOVIAN THEORY AND ITS MODIFICATIONS

Pavlov's theory of the causation of neurosis follows from his general proposition that normal cortical function requires a balance between excitatory and inhibitory processes. The theory is essentially this (1927, pp. 292–93): if, at a given locus of the cortex, excitation and inhibition come into conflict at high intensity, the neural elements concerned may be unable to bear the strain, and may consequently be thrown into a pathological state.

The purport of this hypothesis depends entirely upon the meaning to be ascribed to the word "pathological." Pavlov does not mean merely that the clashing of excitation and inhibition are the necessary preconditions for establishing the neural connections that subserve the neurotic behavior, which would then be regarded as "pathological" just because it is unadaptive. On the contrary, he implies that certain nerve cells are changed physically in some way that makes their functioning different from that of normal cells.

There is an extremely cogent reason for rejecting the idea of a physical pathology—the very fact that it is possible to eliminate neurotic responses by providing conditions which enable other responses to become reinforced to the anxiety-connected stimuli. If the neurotic responses can be unlearned they must presumably have been established in the first place by learning. A *lesion* in the nervous system could scarcely be expected to heal just because some specific new learning has occurred.

An interesting modification of Pavlov's theory was proposed by Anderson and Liddell (1935). Realizing the importance of restraint in the production of experimental neuroses, they proposed the hypothesis that suppression of the animal's "spontaneous activity" results in an accumulation of nervous tension that may be too great for the nervous system to withstand. Their views, however, resemble those of Pavlov in that they too believe that the undesirable effects of the tension are due to "actual damage to the nervous system." Essentially the same views have been expressed more recently by Anderson and Parmenter (1941) and by Liddell (1944).

Most other writers who have dealt with experimental neuroses—for example, Dworkin and his associates (1941), Cook (1939), Babkin (1938), and Ischlondsky (1944)—have accepted the interpretations of Pavlov and of the Cornell workers, and have not offered any significant elaborations of the theory. The conception of "physiological disruption" put forward by Hebb (1947) is basically similar, although expressed in somewhat different terms.

FENICHEL'S PSYCHOANALYTIC THEORY

Fenichel (1945), taking the view that the experimental neuroses correspond to those human neuroses that are due to conflict, has tried to explain the experimental neuroses in terms of psychoanalytic principles. He says that in the neurosis-producing situation the animal feels contradictory impulses "between an instinct striving for discharge and the defensive forces of the ego"; but the conflict makes it impossible for him to discharge the impulses in the usual way. As a result, tension accumulates, and the organism is subjected to an amount of excitation greater than it can master. The neurotic symptoms are regarded as "distorted discharges as a consequence of the state of damming up."

Now, even if it were to be accepted that an organism may be overwhelmed at a given time by powerful excitations with results as envisaged by Fenichel, the "permanence" of the neurotic reactions remains to be explained. The explanation suggested by Fenichel is that the excessive excitation has left some kind of nervous damage behind. This, oddly enough, is the same as Pavlov's theory which was criticized above.

MASSERMAN's "BIODYNAMIC" THEORY

This theory of experimental neurosis is also basically psychoanalytic in character. However, for Masserman the conflict is not between the animal's id and ego, but between two or more motivations. He states (1943, p. 103): "When in a given milieu two or more motivations come into conflict in the sense that their accustomed consummatory patterns become incompatible, kinetic tension (anxiety) mounts and behavior becomes hesitant, vacillating, erratic, and poorly adaptive (neurotic) or excessively substitutive, symbolic and regressive (psychotic)." Thus, when conflict produces neurosis it is because "behavior is disrupted." Masserman does not suggest by what mechanism the disrupting conflict leaves lasting effects on the behavior of the animal. If a group of cells were physically disrupted their subsequent behavior might be expected to change. But "disruption of behavior" by conflict merely implies the interrupting and distorting effects of an activity that intrudes upon the ordinary course of another. The mere occurrence of such interference is not in itself an explanation of subsequent *lasting* changes in behavior. Criticisms of other aspects of Masserman's position have been made elsewhere (Wolpe, 1956).

SOLOMON AND WYNNE's THEORY
OF PARTIAL IRREVERSIBILITY*

Solomon and Wynne (1954) believe that to explain the peculiarities of neurotic reactions (intense pain-fear reactions), it is necessary to postulate that their acquisition involves certain distinctive processes. To begin with, they accept Mowrer's view (1947) that the learning of emotional reactions in general occurs through a mechanism different from that by which instrumental acts are learned. Then, because neurotic reactions are very resistant to ordinary extinction procedures, they postulate that

---

* This and the following section are derived from a commentary previously published (Wolpe, 1956).

strongly terrifying experiences in particular produce some change that is permanent and irreversible, such as "a decreased threshold phenomenon or a sensitization phenomenon." This change is distinguished from learning, and thus some kind of lesion is implied.

It has been shown with reference to a neurophysiological model (pp. 19–30) that a single all-embracing learning process such as Hull envisaged (1943) subsumes facts like those for which Solomon and Wynne find it necessary to seek special mechanisms. The difficulty of extinction of high-intensity autonomic fear responses falls into line when, as stated above (p. 66), it is realized that each time an animal is removed from exposure to an anxiety-evoking stimulus, the process by which the anxiety responses would be removed is nullified. This seems to be well demonstrated by the experiment (p. 60) in which, when an auditory stimulus to which intense anxiety has been conditioned in a cat is repeatedly presented in a given "neutral" visual environment, the latter acquires the power to evoke anxiety in the animal. The only apparent drive reduction is that which occurs when the ending of the auditory stimulus removes the source of anxiety. If this drive reduction can condition anxiety to *new* stimuli, then *a fortiori* it can maintain an already existing anxiety conditioning, in this case of the auditory stimulus, against the extinctive tendency.

SCHAFFER'S THEORY OF RELATIVE FUNCTIONAL DECORTICATION

Basing his case largely on the fact that in certain ways neurotic reactions resemble those of decorticate preparations, Schaffer (1954) has proposed that neurotic behavior is due to a "shift in dominance from cortical to sub-cortical centres" (p. 327). He believes this shift to be due to a "pathological state resulting from stress." He rejects the possibility that neurotic behavior can be due to "ordinary" learning, mainly on the strength of objections raised by Maier and his school. (These objections are criticized elsewhere: Wolpe, 1953a.)

Because the cortex loses its dominance, the responses acquired "are the result of subcortical learning" (pp. 330–31). Thus, although learning of a kind is postulated, it has its special features only because of a pathological state resulting from stress. Now, there is indeed probably a subcortical dominance in neurotic behavior, but its occurrence is entirely explicable in terms of "ordinary" learning. The reaction patterns produced by noxious stimulation or conflict are apparently subserved predominantly by subcortical pathways, and when these patterns are evoked in a suitable temporal relationship to a given "neutral" stimulus, that stimulus becomes itself capable of evoking those reaction patterns.

5 | *Reciprocal Inhibition*

as a Therapeutic Principle

Chapter 4 described how neurotic cats were treated by getting them to eat in the presence of small and then gradually increasing "doses" of anxiety-evoking stimuli. The treatment was uniformly successful and I gave reasons for concluding that this was so because the anxiety responses were inhibited by the eating, which resulted on each occasion in setting up a measure of conditioned (learned) inhibition of the anxiety responses to whatever stimuli had evoked them. With repetition more and more conditioned inhibition was built up, so that the anxiety-evoking potential of the stimuli progressively diminished—eventually to zero.

The observations led to the framing of the following general principle:

If a response antagonistic to anxiety can be made to occur in the presence of anxiety-evoking stimuli so that it is accompanied by a complete or partial suppression of the anxiety responses, the bond between these stimuli and the anxiety responses will be weakened.

This hypothesis does not deny the possibility that these bonds may be weakened by other means too; but the only other known process by which habits are broken down—experimental extinction (see p. 24)—is singularly ineffective when it is anxiety that has to be extinguished. Certainly neurotic anxiety responses are not often extinguished by repeated evocation. Even with mild degrees of anxiety the ineffectiveness of the extinctive mechanism is striking. Miller (1950) for example found that a fear-accompanied motor habit required hundreds of trials to be extinguished. If there had been only a conditioning of fear, and no motor habit, the process would probably have taken even longer, since the motor activity itself would tend to inhibit anxiety (see below). The poor extinction of anxiety responses is apparently due to (a) the small amount of reactive inhibition generated by autonomic responses, and (b) the reinforcement of the anxiety responses by anxiety drive reduction when the organism is passively removed from anxiety-evoking stimuli (see Chapter 4).*

---

* Nevertheless reactive inhibition can have a therapeutic role, typified by Dunlap's (1932) "negative practice." A very well worked out case has recently been reported by Yates (1957).

When the reciprocal inhibition principle was first formulated about ten years ago on the basis of the experiments on cats, the possibility of its clinical use hinged on the answers to two closely interrelated questions: (a) Were there other responses besides eating by which anxiety responses could be inhibited and could have their habit strength weakened? (b) Would it be possible to apply the findings to the treatment of human neurotic states? An attempt was made to answer both questions simultaneously by experiments on neurotic human subjects, employing responses other than feeding in the presence of anxiety-evoking stimuli. It was hoped that some of these responses would prove to be antagonistic to the anxiety responses, would inhibit the latter and thereby decrease their habit strength.

In selecting responses to oppose the anxiety responses I was guided by the presumption that responses that largely implicate the parasympathetic division of the autonomic nervous system would be especially likely to be incompatible with the predominantly sympathetic responses of anxiety. Although there is evidence (Gellhorn, 1943; Babkin, 1946) strongly suggesting that sympathetic and parasympathetic responses are usually synergic, in many circumstances they are by and large opposed and one or other clearly dominant.

In the first three classes of responses that I came to use in clinical therapy—(a) assertive responses, (b) sexual responses, and (c) relaxation responses—there are, as far as the autonomic system is concerned, persuasive indications of parasympathetic ascendancy. A good deal of the evidence in favor of this with regard to assertive (angry) responses has been summarized by Arnold (1945). Ax (1953) has questioned Arnold's position, but his own observations reveal a tendency for the pulse and respiratory rates to be raised in fear and lowered in anger. In the realm of sexual responses, erection is subserved by the *nervus erigens* which emanates from the sacral parasympathetic plexus (Langley and Anderson, 1895). This plexus also supplies part of the innervation of the female sex organs. Parasympathetic responsiveness during sexual excitement is not confined to the sex organs, being manifested, for example, in increased gastric secretion (Dumas, 1928). Sympathetic responses, such as raised pulse rate, are also present, but in the genital organs they become prominent only in relation to ejaculation (Langley and Anderson, 1893). The parasympathetic effects of muscle relaxation are easily observed in anxious subjects trained in relaxation. In the course of a few minutes I have known the pulse rate to drop 30 beats or more, breathing to become slower, and sweating palms to become dry or nearly dry. Decrease in blood pressure as well as pulse rate has been shown by Jacobson (1939, 1940) to accompany relaxation.

Parasympathetic dominance also seems to characterize the emotional responses (evoked during an individual's ordinary day-to-day commerce with the world) that have been held to account for the beneficial fluctuations in neurotic reactivity referred to in Chapter 6. However diverse their details may be, the responses concerned appeared to have a pleasantness of tone in common. The correspondence of feelings of pleasantness with parasympathetic effects on the circulation is evident from Leschke's review (1914) of the work of numerous investigators. The rate of the pulse drops and its amplitude usually rises, in contrast with a constant increase in rate and decrease in amplitude accompanying unpleasantness, pain, or fear. To the same effect is Gellhorn's statement (1953, p. 336) that pleasurable emotions induced by gustatory and olfactory stimuli cause parasympathetic excitation. Similarly, while exciting or disturbing music raises both blood pressure and pulse rate, calm or heroic music has the opposite effect (Washco, 1933). But it would be a mistake to assume that unless an emotional response constellation manifests parasympathetic dominance it is incapable of inhibiting anxiety. Just as, in the motor sphere, to walk and to jump are mutually antagonistic, although they may utilize many muscle elements in common, an emotional response that utilizes many elements in common with anxiety may be antagonistic to the total anxiety response. The central nervous system is the fountainhead of emotional excitation, and the distribution of responding elements depends upon previously organized complex units of neural organization. Thus it is essentially a *pattern* of emotional responses that is excited or else inhibited.

About four years ago I made an effort to procure a response that was theoretically the diametric opposite of anxiety, in the hope that this would be a particularly effective therapeutic instrument. The method used was to present a word stimulus at the moment of cessation of an uncomfortable electric shock in order to condition to this word the bodily changes that ensued upon its cessation. These, presumably, would be the negative of such anxiety responses as the shock had evoked. In a few cases the expected conditioning was successfully accomplished (see pp. 180–81).

It seemed reasonable to look in other directions too. There was no a priori reason for assuming that inhibition of anxiety could be accomplished only by responses that were themselves physiologically opposite to anxiety. Evidence is available that there are arrangements in the nervous system which make it possible for motor responses also to produce inhibition of anxiety. Freeman and Pathman (1940) found that the galvanic skin response (GSR) to disturbing stimuli reverted to its initial level most rapidly in subjects responding with overt muscular action, even if this took such apparently unadaptive forms as squirming and giggling. Haggard and Freeman (1941) subsequently found that motor activity directed to a relevant problem leads to subsidence of the GSR to its pre-existing level more rapidly than activity consisting of nondirected restless movements. It is doubtless in consequence of this ability to inhibit anxiety responses that motor responses can diminish the habit strength of anxiety responses. This has been illustrated in the clearest way by an experiment by Mowrer and Viek (1948) which led directly to the use of a new therapeutic method (see pp. 173–80).

Probably just such a mechanism accounts for the fact that in the learning of a fear-connected activity (e.g., the learning by a young child to cross a street) the fear that is present during early performances disappears after repeated practice. It is also quite possible that in some instances of the therapeutic use of assertive behavior the motor responses play as important a part as the aggressive emotional responses in inhibiting anxiety responses.

Intense respiratory responses such as produced by single deep inhalations of 50–70 per cent carbon dioxide (p. 166) have also turned out to be anxiety-inhibiting, although in themselves these responses seem in no way to be physiologically opposite to anxiety.

As will be shown in detail below, success has attended the therapeutic use of each one of the above-mentioned classes of responses (although in the vast majority of cases two or more are used, and relaxation is nearly always one of them). The results are presented in detail in Chapter 14. The three classes mentioned as the earliest to be tried—assertive responses, relaxation responses, and sexual responses—have had by far the widest application, and I refer to them with good reason as my "bread and butter" responses.

In addition to the responses whose evocation is deliberately planned, and undoubtedly of foremost importance in some cases, are the interview-induced emotional responses. These arise in some patients in response to the very presence of a situation in which they entrust their happiness to the special knowledge and skill of another human being. There is reason to believe that these responses, in so far as they are anxiety-inhibiting, are the cause of the remarkably uniform proportion of satisfactory results (about 50 per cent apparently cured or much improved) that are yielded by a variety of older methods of therapy ranging from reassurance to psychoanalysis.

Of course the use of techniques based on the reciprocal inhibition principle does not preclude the evocation of these nonspecific interview-induced emotional responses. They presumably occur as frequently as in any other kind of therapy; with effects as desirable. But in order to meet any suggestion that the reciprocal inhibition techniques themselves also have as little real effect as the special methods that other therapists use and regard (mainly erroneously) as having special virtues — in other words, that the therapeutic success that follows the use of reciprocal inhibition techniques is also entirely or mainly due to nonspecific emotional responses—the following facts must immediately be stated:

1. Out of a total of 210 patients who have had these techniques applied to them, nearly 90 per cent have been either apparently cured or much improved, in contrast with a percentage not exceeding 60 in almost all other reported series.

2. The average number of interviews per patient is low (mean = 31).

3. Patients frequently improve rapidly in a small number of interviews after having had prolonged psychoanalytic or other therapy with little or no success.

4. There is almost always an obvious direct relationship between the amount of application of a given procedure and the amount of improvement. This is especially clear with the desensitization technique based on the use of relaxation (Chapter 9).

6 | *The Etiology of Human Neuroses*

This chapter deals with the etiology of human neuroses in terms of modern learning theory. An origin in learning is clearly evident for many common manifestations of neurosis, and in the case of others testable hypotheses* embodying an origin in learning are suggested. It will be seen that the causation of clinical neuroses is essentially similar to that of experimental neuroses. The richer symptomatology of the former is explained by the far greater complexity of the human nervous system enabling the use of language, intricate serial learning, and an enormous variety of discriminations. The account that follows will be brief; a full exposition of the etiology of human neuroses is projected for a separate volume.

The causal relations of some of the commonest phenomena of human neurotic behavior are summarized in Figure 6.

Predisposing Conditions

A predisposing condition is any factor that facilitates the acquisition of neurotic behavior in a subject exposed to characteristic precipitating conditions. It is likely that individuals differ in general emotional reactivity because of maturationally established physiological differences. Observations in infants (e.g., Shirley, 1933) uniformly indicate the presence of such differences. A highly reactive individual exposed to given anxiety-evoking conditions would obviously have a greater intensity of conditionable anxiety evoked in him than an individual whose reactivity was low.

Sensitivity may be increased by learning too. If anxiety reactions have been previously conditioned to particular stimuli, the involvement of these stimuli in a neurosis-producing situation will result in a higher level of anxiety than would otherwise have been the case. It is because of this that, on the whole, a severe neurosis is more likely to develop in a person

---

* Professor Karl Popper (1956) has pointed out that a hypothesis is confirmed (strengthened) only if it has survived an experiment that has set it at risk; i.e., an experiment such that if the observations had gone the other way the hypothesis would have been negated. Because Freudian and similar theorists rarely frame their hypotheses in a testable way and, even when they do, do not often test them in Popper's sense, their hypotheses tend to survive indefinitely—until someone else undertakes to do the testing! (See Chapter 12, p. 186 n.; Chapter 14, p. 216.)

Special predisposing preconditions (not essential)

↓

Subject exposed either to stimuli directly evoking anxiety or to ambivalent stimulation so that anxiety of high intensity is evoked. (Many variables are involved, e.g., degree of constriction of psychological space [limitations of response possibilities], strength of anxiety at each exposure, number of exposures, degree of stimulus constancy at different exposures.)

↓

Conditioning is established
of

high-intensity anxiety responses and/or other responses, e.g., hysterical responses

to

specific stimuli and/or pervasive stimuli ("free-floating" anxiety)

Secondary anxiety-relieving behavior may ensue:

a) Physical avoidance of stimuli conditioned to anxiety

and/or

b) Displacement of attention

and/or

c) Drug-taking

and/or

d) Anxiety-relieving obsessions

Modifications in the constitution of neurotic responses following their evocation in contiguity with certain other responses

Figure 6

who already has many unadaptive anxieties conditioned in him than in a relatively "nonneurotic" person. High anxious reactors constitute the *dysthymic* group of Eysenck's recent studies (1955a, 1957).

It is possible that certain transient factors are also capable of influencing the acquisition of neurotic conditionings—fatigue, chemical agents such as drugs or hormones, and special conditions of consciousness such as hypnagogic states. Properly designed studies of these factors have yet to be made.

The Basic Precipitating Conditions

All human neuroses are produced, as animal neuroses are, by situations which evoke high intensities of anxiety. In animals anxiety of the requisite intensity can be built up as a response to previously neutral stimuli in one of three ways. The animal can be (1) subjected to difficult discriminations on the Pavlovian model, or (2) exposed to a relatively small number of severe noxious stimuli, or (3) exposed to a relatively large number of small noxious stimuli, as in the Cornell experiments. Where noxious stimulation is used, the anxiety is directly evoked by one stimulus, whereas in the conflict type of neurosis, the anxiety is indirect, that is, it requires a special combined effect of two stimuli. It will be contended here that the production of human neuroses is analogous to that of animal neuroses.

DIRECT EVOCATION OF ANXIETY

No doubt a human being exposed to the same sort of experimental conditions as the cat which is shocked in a cage could be conditioned to have neurotic reaction. But, except in such exceptional cases as concentration camp experiences, very few human neuroses are produced in this way. However, there are a number of stimulus conditions which innate organization apparently makes capable of arousing a good deal of anxiety in the human subject, anxiety to which other "neutral" stimuli could become conditioned. These are painful stimuli, very intense stimuli, and falling. In addition, pathological states such as coronary thrombosis or the toxic actions of certain drugs sometimes produce symptoms that, presumably on an innate basis, are grossly disturbing. The accidental injection of procaine into the vein of a young woman about to undergo a minor dental operation led to severe muscle spasms, tachycardia, nausea, intermittent partial blackouts, and alternating feelings of heat and cold. She reacted to those symptoms with severe anxiety and, when they subsided, was flaccid and exhausted. The next morning she felt completely normal, but in the afternoon, on sitting down in a hairdresser's chair, instantly had an anxiety reaction—a conditioned response explicable by the tactile similarity between the dentist's chair and the hairdresser's, clearly based on the anxiety that had been aroused by the effects of the procaine.

In human subjects, however, the direct evocation of anxiety of the kind that leads to neuroses is much more commonly produced by conditioned stimuli to anxiety. For example, neuroses produced in war often have as their basis the arousal of intense fear in a situation that is really dangerous. The apprehension of danger depends on previous learning, and the fear reaction aroused is conditionable to any stimuli which happen to be present at the time, such stimuli as the sound of machine-gun fire, the smell of gunpowder, the broad blue sky, open spaces, or desert sand.

Severe anxiety can equally well be evoked in circumstances where there is no *objective* threat. For example, a girl of 11 brought up in a strictly Calvinist home in which hell-fire played a prominent part, reacted with great anxiety when she first felt pleasurable genital sensations. Thus, anxiety was strongly conditioned to sexual sensations, and this persisted even after her marriage ten years later, even though she at this time no longer retained the fears of hell-fire. A similar case is that of a person who experiences unusual emotional feelings and concludes that this means he is going insane. Because of previous conditioning involving the idea of insanity, this evokes a tremendous fear reaction to which contiguous stimuli may become conditioned. The neurotic anxiety so produced often persists even though the person becomes assured that in fact he is not threatened with insanity. Neurosis production in the examples given above is analogous to the experiments in animals involving *strong* noxious stimulation. A clinical parallel to the weak noxious stimulus situation of the Cornell experiments is the case of a schoolboy who developed violent emotional reactions to classroom situations on the basis of multiple pinpricks by a teacher who viciously disliked him.

CONFLICT

Although Krasnogorski (1925) produced minor neurotic disturbances in young children by subjecting them to difficult discriminations on the Pavlovian model, it is doubtful whether human neuroses ever occur spontaneously in this way. The usual way in which conflict enters into the production of neuroses in human subjects is patterned on the following. A woman finds herself engaged to a man whom she actually dislikes. She would like to get out of the engagement but does not because, for example, she fears the criticism of her friends. She is continuously tense, and more so when she is in the company of her fiancé. The tension gradually mounts, reaching a tremendous pitch as the wedding day draws near. Whether she breaks the engagement or not, she is likely to have a variety of stimuli, previously neutral, conditioned to anxiety. It seems quite likely that the mechanism that leads to this very high tension is not dissimilar to the mechanism that produces neurosis when there is discriminatory ambivalence. Apparently, simultaneous, strong, conflicting action tendencies somehow generate high degrees of anxiety within the nervous system. The similarity between the anxiety produced by noxious stimulation and that produced by conflict has been convincingly demonstrated by Fonberg (1956) (see p. 65).

An interesting question that arises is: if the girl finds this engagement and the prospect of the marriage that is threatened so unpleasant, should this not arouse more anxiety in her than the possibility of upsetting her friends, and why does the stronger anxiety not drive her out of the engagement? Apparently, the prospect of taking the action that would lead out of the situation simply adds new anxiety to that which already exists and this is what inhibits the action. In other words, in the approach to a transition between being inside the situation and being out of it, fiancé-induced anxiety actually *summates* with disproval-of-friends-induced anxiety! The relations are represented graphically in Figure 7.

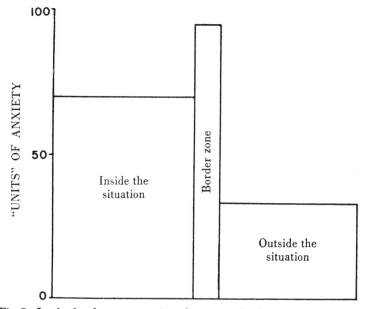

Fig 7. In the border zone, anxiety from outside the situation summates with that from inside.

This means that though the conflict involved here belongs to Miller's avoidance-avoidance type (1944), there is a very important point of difference. Because Miller's animals stand in *spatial* relation to the stimuli leading to the opposing activities, the effect of each stimulus is a function of its distance from the animal, so that the progression to the point of maximum conflict is a gradual one. By contrast, the two stimulus constellations that affect our engaged girl act on her more or less on an all-or-none basis. While she is within the situation she can either "accept" it or be orientated toward escape. During moments of "acceptance" the tension evocable by her fiancé and his implications are maximal. When she thinks of getting out, this decreases a little, and then soon has added to it the full weight of tension associated with the implications of getting out. One patient reported that while she was desperately seeking a way out of such a situation her tension became so great that she felt her "head was bursting."

THE CONFINEMENT FACTOR

It will be recalled that experimental animals can be made neurotic only when the noxious stimulation or the ambivalent stimulation occurs under conditions of spatial restriction. It was shown how in this way a very high level of anxiety evocation is procured in the animals. While physical confinement is certainly not implicated in the production of the vast majority of human neurosis, a human being may be confined within a situation by virtue of his conditionings. So confined, as the instance of our engaged girl illustrates, he is subject to the same heights of tension as are the spatially restricted animals.

Both physical and psychological confinement restrict the range of stimuli acting on the animal, but in the human case stimuli are as likely to become relevant because of their dominating presence in thought as because of their prominence in the outside world. It is to these stimuli that neurotic responses are especially likely to become conditioned.

OTHER FACTORS IN THE CONDITIONING OF NEUROTIC ANXIETY

In neurosis formation, as in other learning, all that can be learned is present in that which is evoked. Even the intensity of the response learned is determined by the strength of its evocation in the conditioning situation. This was clearly demonstrated by Dykman and Gantt (1956). In a number of dogs they conditioned a different auditory stimulus to the responses to each of three intensities of electric shock applied to the left forepaw. They found that the heart rate and the amplitude of the leg-withdrawal response subsequently evocable by the respective auditory stimuli were directly proportional to the intensity of electric shock that had been used.

Since typical anxiety responses are the most common to be evoked by the stimulus situations associated with the production of neuroses, these are the responses which will characterize most neuroses. But the picture may be complicated or distorted, sometimes very grossly. Sometimes the learned responses contain features that do not ordinarily belong to anxiety, apparently as a consequence of the intensity of the anxiety itself. For example, in a case with markedly fluctuating pervasive ("free-floating") anxiety (see below), it was regularly observed that beyond a certain level of anxiety there gradually appeared paraesthesia of the hands, forearms,

and knees whose extent and intensity were directly correlated with increases in the intensity of anxiety beyond this "threshold" level. A possible
explanation for this would be that when excitation of neurones subserving
anxiety reaches a certain high intensity, there is an overflow of impulses
into related neurones normally refractory (probably due to spatial and
temporal summation—see pp. 10–11).

In other cases, there appears to be a mutual inhibitory action between
anxiety and some other simultaneously aroused emotion, usually sexual.
What emerges from this is described by the patient as a feeling of emotional
"deadness" or "unreality." To this there are usually added fragments of
the original emotions which combine oddly to produce bizarre feelings for
which no words exist. Any stimuli that at the time happen to be acting on
the patient become conditioned to the "deadness" and the positive bizarre
responses. Quite commonly, the patient is greatly disturbed by these feelings which he may regard as indicative of disease, insanity, or emotional
disintegration. This secondary disturbance may take the form of a super-
added "normal" anxiety, of an intensification of the bizarre response, or
various syntheses of the two. Very often the bizarre feelings are continuously present during all the patient's waking hours, constituting a distorted
variant of pervasive ("free-floating") anxiety.

It is particularly then (but not only then) that he is likely to observe
a diminution or absence of expected emotional responses to situations
that have nothing to do directly with either sex or anxiety. He no longer
feels the subtle pleasures that he previously derived from the normal experiences of a day—the glory of a bright morning, the pleasant familiarity
of a street scene, the many-toned moods that music can arouse, or the ro-
mantic suggestiveness of perfume. There is a peculiar wretchedness for
which the lines of Henry Cust are singularly appropriate.

> Not unto us, O Lord, the rapture of the day
> The peace of night or Love's divine surprise . . .
> To us thou givest the scorn, the scourge, the scar,
> The ache of life, the loneliness of death,
> The insufferable sufficiency of breath . . .

More than one patient has described the state as embodying all the root-
lessness and futility of Kafka's *The Castle*. Less pleasant normal feelings
like sadness and pity may also fail to be evoked in the situations associated with them. But usually it is only in more trivial situations that no
emotional response whatever is discerned. In "stronger" ones various
unpleasant feelings appear, nearly always indescribable. One patient
stated that sad scenes in films produced nothing but "inadequate cold
shivers" down his spine.

The Causal Relations of Pervasive ("Free-Floating") Anxiety

Under certain circumstances it is not only to well-defined stimulus configurations that anxiety responses are conditioned, but also to more or less omnipresent properties of the environment, of which extreme examples would be light, light and shade contrasts, amorphous noise, spatiality, and the passage of time. Since each of these enters into most, if not all, possible experience, it is to be expected that if any of them becomes connected to anxiety responses the patient will be persistently, and apparently causelessly anxious. He will be suffering from what is erroneously called "free-floating" anxiety, and for which a more suitable label would be *pervasive anxiety*.

It must be unequivocally stated, in case it is not quite self-evident, that there is no sharp dividing line between specific anxiety-evoking stimuli and stimuli to pervasive anxiety. The pervasiveness of the latter is a function of the pervasiveness of the stimulus element conditioned; and there are degrees of pervasiveness ranging from the absolute omnipresence of time itself through very common elements like room walls to rarely encountered configurations like hunchbacks.

What reason is there for believing that pervasive anxiety has definable stimulus sources?

Questioning of patients with pervasive anxiety usually reveals that definable aspects of the environment are especially related to this anxiety. For example, one patient reported increased anxiety in the presence of any very large object; another an uncomfortable intrusiveness of all sharp contrasts in his visual field—even the printed words on a page, and particularly contrasts in the periphery of the field. A third felt overwhelmed by physical space. Frequently, patients with pervasive anxiety observe that noise causes a rise in the level of their anxiety. In some cases the noise need not be loud, and in some even music is disturbing.

Although pervasive anxiety is usually felt less when the patient lies down and closes his eyes, it does not disappear. To some extent this may be explained on the basis of perseveration due to prolonged reverberation of the effects of the stimulus in the nervous system. But this does not account for the fact that usually *some* anxiety is already felt at the moment of waking. An obvious explanation is that anxiety evocable by stimuli that enter into the very structure of experience is likely to be produced by the first contents of the awakening subject's imagination. Anxiety increases when the outside world makes its impact; and it is consonant with this that, very commonly, the level of pervasive anxiety gradually rises as the day goes on.

This diurnal rise in level is less likely to occur when the general level of pervasive anxiety is low; for then there is a greater likelihood of the arousal, during a normal day's experience, of other emotions which may be physiologically antagonistic to anxiety, so that the anxiety will be inhibited and its habit strength each time slightly diminished. On the other hand, invariably (in my experience) the patient with pervasive anxiety also has unadaptive anxiety reactions to specific stimuli, and if he should encounter and react to any one of the latter during that day, the level of pervasive anxiety will promptly rise. In the normal course of events it is to be expected that level of pervasive anxiety will fluctuate because of "chance" occurrences which strengthen or weaken its habit strength.

Sometimes, when a patient is fortunate enough not to meet with any specific disturbing stimuli over an extended period, his pervasive anxiety may practically cease, but subsequent response to a relevant specific anxiety-evoking stimulus will condition it lastingly again. This reconditioning was beautifully demonstrated in one of my patients, who, in addition to pervasive anxiety, had a number of severe phobias on the general theme of illness. The pervasive anxiety responded extremely well to La Verne's carbon dioxide–oxygen inhalation therapy (see Chapter 10). The patient stopped coming for treatment until several months later when the pervasive anxiety was reinduced after he had witnessed an epileptic fit in the street. The pervasive anxiety was again speedily removed by carbon dioxide–oxygen and the patient again stopped treatment after a few more interviews. The essence of this sequence was repeated about ten times before the patient finally allowed desensitization to the phobic stimuli to be completed.

The question naturally arises: What factors determine whether or not pervasive anxiety will be part of a patient's neurosis? At the moment two possible factors may be suggested on the basis of clinical impressions. One seems to be the intensity of anxiety evocation at the time of the induction of the neurosis. It is hypothesized that the more intense the anxiety the more stimulus aspects are likely to acquire *some* measure of anxiety conditioning. Indirect support for this hypothesis comes from the observation that, on the whole, it is the patient who reacts more severely to specific stimuli who is also likely to suffer from pervasive anxiety.

The second possible factor is a lack of clearly defined environmental stimuli at the time of neurosis induction. For example, one patient's pervasive anxiety began after a night in a hotel during which he had attempted intercourse with a woman to whom he felt both sexual attraction and strong revulsion. He had felt a powerful and strange, predominantly nonsexual excitation, and ejaculation had occurred very prematurely without pleasure. The light had been switched off, and *only the dark outlines of objects could be seen.* After this, so great was his feeling of revulsion to the woman that he spent the remainder of the night on the carpet. This experience left him, as he subsequently found, with an anxiety toward a wide range of sexual objects, along with much pervasive anxiety, characterized by a special intrusiveness of all heavy dark objects.

The Causal Process in Hysteria

Hysterical reactions are clearly distinguishable from the rather diffuse discharges of the autonomic nervous system that characterize anxiety reactions (whether typical or modified; see pp. 35–36). In most instances hysterical reactions do not find expression in the autonomic nervous system at all, but in the sensory system, the motor system, or groups of functional units involved in the production of imagery or of consciousness in general. Thus, they may take the form of anesthesias, paresthesias, hyperesthesias, or disturbances of vision or hearing; of paralyses, pareses, tics, tremors, disturbances of balance, contractures or fits; of amnesias, fugues, or "multiple personality" phenomena. Occasionally, hysterical reactions do appear to involve functions within the domain of the autonomic nervous system— in the form of vomiting (or nausea) or enuresis, but it is noteworthy that each of the two functions involved is to some extent within voluntary control.

Anxiety frequently accompanies hysterical reactions and then they occur side by side as two distinct forms of *primary* neurotic response. This state of affairs must be sharply distinguished from that in which sensory or motor phenomena are secondary effects of the normal components of anxiety, and as such do not qualify as hysterical. For example, a headache due to tension of the temporal muscles, backache due to tension of the longitudinal spinal muscles, or paresthesia due to hyperventilation are not to be regarded as hysterical.

It is necessary also to differentiate hysterical from obsessional reactions (p. 89). Hysterical reactions are at a relatively low level of organization, affecting well-defined sensory areas and specific motor units, and causing changes in the general character of consciousness or the exclusion from consciousness of "blocks" of experience limited in terms of a time span or some other broad category. The details of the reactions tend to be fixed and unchanging. Obsessional reactions consist by contrast of highly organized movements or of elaborate and complex thinking, in either of which there is a great variety in the individual instances of expression of a specific constant theme.

Like other neurotic reactions, hysterical reactions are acquired by learning. It is intriguing to note that Freud's very early observations on hysterical subjects could easily have led him to this conclusion had he not been sidetracked by a spurious deduction from observations on therapeutic effects. In a paper published in 1893, speaking of the relation of the symptoms of hysteria to the patients' reactions at the time of the precipitating stress, he states:

The connection is often so clear that it is quite evident how the exciting event has happened to produce just this and no other manifestation; the phenomenon is determined in a perfectly clear manner by the cause; to take the most ordinary example, a painful effect, which was originally excited while eating, but was suppressed, produces nausea and vomiting, and this continues for months, as hysterical vomiting. A child who is very ill at last falls asleep, and its mother tries her utmost to keep quiet and not to wake it; but just in consequence of this resolution (hysterical counterwill) she makes a clucking noise with her tongue. On another occasion when she wishes to keep absolutely quiet this happens again, and so a tic in the form of tongue-clicking develops which for a number of years accompanies every excitement. . . . A highly intelligent man assists while his brother's ankylosed hip is straightened under an anesthetic. At the instant when the joint gives way with a crack, he feels a violent pain in his own hip joint which lasts almost a year. . . . [pp. 25–26]

The attack then arises spontaneously as memories commonly do; but they may also be provoked, just as any memory may be aroused according to the laws of association. Provocation of an attack occurs either by stimulation of a hysterogenic zone or by a new experience resembling the pathogenic experience. We hope to be able to show that no essential difference exists between the two conditions, apparently so distinct; and in both cases a hyperaesthetic memory has been stirred. [p. 40]

Apart from the reference to the possibility of attacks arising "spontaneously" (which Freud later explicitly repudiated) we have here an account of the formation by learning of stimulus-response connections. That Freud did not *see* this was mainly because, having observed patients cured when they recalled and narrated the story of the precipitating experience, he concluded that the symptoms were due to the imprisonment of emotionally disturbing memories. He states ". . . we are of opinion that the psychical trauma, or the memory of it acts as a kind of foreign body constituting an effective agent in the present, even long after it has penetrated. . . ." There can be little doubt that this statement would not have been made, and the mind-structure theory that is psychoanalytic theory would not have been born, if Freud could have known that memories do not exist in the form of thoughts or images in some kind of repository within us, but depend on the establishment, through the learning process, of specific neural interconnections that give *a potentiality* of evocation of particular thoughts and images when and only when certain stimulus conditions, external or internal, are present.

When a clear history of the onset of hysterical symptoms is obtained, it is usually found, as illustrated in Freud's cases quoted above, that the hysterical reaction displays a repetition of features that were present in response to the initiating disturbing experience. The stimulus to the reaction varies. Sometimes it is a fairly specific sensory stimulation. For example, a 33-year-old woman had as a hysterical reaction an intolerable sensation of "gooseflesh" in her calves in response to any rectal sensation such as a desire to defecate, ever since, three years previously, a surgeon had unceremoniously performed a rectal examination upon her, while, drowsy from premedication with morphia, she was awaiting the administration of an anesthetic for an abdominal operation.

In other cases it appears that the hysterical reaction is aroused by ubiquitous stimuli, being then the hysterical equivalent of pervasive ("free-floating") anxiety. An example of this is wryneck that is present throughout the working day and relaxes the moment the patient falls asleep. In yet others anxiety appears to *mediate* the hysterical reaction. The hysteria of one of my patients had both a pervasive component and an anxiety-mediated component. This was a 58-year-old woman who 18 months earlier had encountered a deadly snake in a copse. She had been terrified and momentarily paralyzed; her ears were filled with the sound of waves and she had been unable to speak for two hours. The sound of waves had never left her, and any considerable anxiety such as might arise from tension in her home would intensify this sound and then lead to vertigo, loss of balance, and a feeling of great weakness in all her limbs, so that she sometimes fell.

The central feature of hysterical reactions is the conditioning, in situations of stress, of neurotic reactions other than anxiety, although anxiety is often also conditioned as well. It is necessary to ask what determines this. There are two possible answers. One is that these reactions are conditioned when they happen to be evoked in addition to anxiety. The other is that although such reactions may be evoked by stress in all subjects, they become the neurotic responses conditioned only in those in whom some special factor is present that gives preference to nonanxiety conditioning. Since, in fact, the immediate response to neurotigenic stimulation always seems to implicate all response systems, the latter possibility is the more likely to be relevant. And there is evidence that it is people with distinct personality features who usually develop hysterical reactions.

Jung (1923) long ago observed that hysterics tend to exhibit extravert character traits while other neurotic subjects tend to be introverted. In this partition of personalities he was followed by other writers who, while differing in many ways, agreed, as Eysenck (1947, p. 58) concluded from a survey, in the following particulars: (*a*) the introvert has a more subjective, the extravert a more objective outlook; (*b*) the introvert shows a

higher degree of cerebral activity, the extravert a higher degree of behavioral activity; (c) the introvert shows a tendency to self-control (inhibition), the extravert a tendency to lack of such control. Eysenck
(1955b) has pointed out on the basis of experiments performed by Franks
(1956) and himself (1955a) that extraverted subjects besides learning
more poorly also generate reactive inhibition more readily than introverts
do. He postulates (1955b, p. 35) that subjects in whom reactive inhibition is generated quickly and dissipated slowly "are predisposed thereby
to develop extraverted patterns of behaviour and to develop hysterico-
psychopathic disorders in cases of neurotic breakdown." Clearly what his
facts actually demonstrate is that the hysterical type of breakdown is particularly likely in subjects in whom reactive inhibition has the feature
stated. The *causal* role of reactive inhibition is not shown, nor is a possible
mechanism suggested.

A possibility is this: that in addition to their easily generated and persistent reactive inhibition (and perhaps in some indirect way bound up
with it) extraverted people have one or both of the following characteristics: (a) when exposed to anxiety-arousing stimuli they respond with
relatively low degrees of anxiety so that other responses are unusually
prominent; (b) when anxiety and other responses are simultaneously
evoked in them, contiguous stimuli become conditioned to the other responses rather than to the anxiety—by contrast with introverts.

This hypothesis lends itself readily to direct experimentation. In the
meantime a survey from my records of the 22 patients with hysterical symptoms has yielded some suggestive evidence. Nine of them (41 per cent)
had initial Willoughby scores below 30. This is in striking contrast to 273
nonhysterical neurotic patients, in only 50 (18 per cent) of whom were the
initial scores below this level. The Kolmogorov-Smirnov test shows the
difference to be significant at the .05 level. It is interesting to note that
insofar as this supports our hypothesis it accords with the time-worn conception of the hysterical patient with little or no anxiety—*la belle indif-
férence.* It is relevant to the same point that the hysterical patients with
low Willoughby scores all benefited by procedures that varied greatly but
did not obviously affect anxious sensitivity. By contrast, in the 13 patients
whose hysterical reactions were accompanied by much anxiety there was a
direct correlation between diminution of anxious sensitivity and decreased
strength of hysterical reactions except in two cases where this consisted
purely of amnesia, which was unaffected. (In one of these the events of
the forgotten period were later retrieved under hypnosis, in the other they
remained forgotten. It seemed to make no difference either way to the
patient's recovery.)

Summarizing the above facts, it may be said that hysterical reactions may either accompany anxiety or occur on their own. In the former case their treatment is the treatment of anxiety, in the latter it is different in a way that will be discussed in the chapter on treatment. It is supposed that anxiety is a feature when hysteria occurs in subjects relatively far from the extraverted extreme of Eysenck's introversion-extraversion dimension, just because the hypothetical preferential conditioning of responses other than anxiety to neurotigenic stimuli is less marked in these people. This supposition needs to be tested.

Meanwhile it may be noted that there is experimental evidence of a competitive relationship in certain contexts between autonomic and motor responses. Mowrer and Viek (1948), using two groups of rats, placed each animal after a period of starvation on the electrifiable floor of a rectangular cage and offered him food on a stick for ten seconds. Whether the animal ate or not, shock was applied ten seconds later. In the case of one group of ten rats, jumping into the air resulted in the experimenter switching off the shock (shock-controllable group). Each animal in this group had an experimental "twin" to which the shock was applied for the same length of time as it had taken its counterpart to jump into the air (shock-uncontrollable group). One trial a day was given to each animal. The animals in each group whose eating responses during the ten seconds were inhibited (by conditioned anxiety responses resulting from the shocks) were charted each day, and it was found that in the shock-controllable group the number of eating inhibitions was never high and declined to zero, whereas in the shock-uncontrollable group the number rose to a high level and remained there. Apparently, the constant evocation of jumping in the former group resulted in a gradual development of conditioned inhibition of anxiety. By contrast with this, in the typical Cornell technique for producing experimental neuroses (p. 43) a very localized musculoskeletal conditioned response comes to be increasingly dominated by autonomic anxiety responses. This whole matter has been discussed in more detail elsewhere (Wolpe, 1953a).

Obsessional Behavior

Sometimes, besides the autonomic discharges characteristic of anxiety, ideational, motor, and sensory responses are prominent in a neurosis. If simple and invariate in character, they are labeled *hysterical* (see p. 85). The term *obsessional* is applied to behavior that is more complex and variable in detail, consisting of well-defined and often elaborate thought sequences or relatively intricate acts which, though they may differ in outward form from one occasion to the next, lead or tend to lead to the same kind of result. The term is applicable even to those cases characterized by an obstinate impulse to behavior that rarely or never becomes manifest.

Examples of obsessions predominantly of thought are a woman's insistent idea that she might throw her child from the balcony of her apartment, or a man's need to have one of a restricted class of "pleasant" thoughts in his mind before he can make any well-defined movement such as entering a doorway or sitting down. Exhibitionism and compulsive handwashing are characteristic examples of predominantly motor obsessional behavior.

Sometimes the word *compulsive* has been preferred to obsessional for those cases in which motor activity predominates. However, as most cases display both elements, there is little practical value in the distinction. Furthermore, the term compulsive is open to the objection that *all* behavior is compulsive in a sense, for causal determinism implies that the response that occurs is always the only one that could have occurred in the circumstances. The feature of any example of obsessional behavior is not its inevitability but its *intrusiveness*. Its elicitation or the impulse toward it is an encumbrance and an embarrassment to the patient.

If hysterical and obsessional reactions involve similar elements, we may expect that borderline cases will be found. An example of this is a 47-year-old male nurse employed in an industrial first-aid room who for 17 years had an uncontrollable impulse to mimic any rhythmic movements performed before him, e.g., waving of arms or dancing, and to obey any command no matter from whom. In this was combined the basic simplicity of hysteria and the situationally determined variability of obsessional behavior. (See p. 188 for an account of this patient's treatment.)

It may be stated almost as dogma that the strength and frequency of evocation of obsessional behavior is directly related to the amount of anxiety being evoked in the patient. Pollitt (1957) in a study of 150 obsessional cases noted that obsessional symptoms became more severe and prominent "when anxiety and tension increased for whatever causes." However, it is not always that the source of the anxiety is irrelevant. Sometimes the obsessional behavior is evident only when anxiety arises from specific, usually neurotic sources. For example, an exhibitionist experienced impulses to expose himself when he felt inadequate and inferior among his friends but not when he was anxious about the results of a law examination.

ANXIETY-ELEVATING OBSESSIONS

Two types of obsessional behavior are clearly distinguishable in clinical practice. One type appears to be part and parcel of the immediate response to anxiety-evoking stimulation and has secondary effects entirely in the direction of increasing anxiety. When a motor mechanic of 45 had neurotic anxiety exceeding a certain fairly low level, he would have a terrifying though always controllable impulse to strike people. From the first moment of awareness of the impulse he would feel increased anxiety, and if at the time he was with an associate or even among strangers—for example, in a bus—he would thrust his hands firmly into his pockets "to keep them out of trouble." In the history of such patients one finds that behavior similar to that constituting the obsession was present during an earlier situation in which conditioning of anxiety took place. In 1942 this motor mechanic, on military service, had been sentenced to 30 days' imprisonment in circumstances which he had with some justice felt to be grossly unfair. Then, as he had resisted the military police rather violently in protest, he was taken to a psychiatrist who said there was nothing wrong with him and that the sentence should be carried out. At this his feeling of helpless rage had further increased and he was taken out by force. Then for the first time he had had "this queer feeling" in his abdomen and had struck a military policeman who tried to compel him to work. Horror at the implications of this act intensified his disturbed state. The obsession to strike people made its first appearance in 1953, eleven years later. He had been imprisoned overnight (for the first time since 1942) because, arriving home one night to find his house crowded with his wife's relatives, he had shouted and been violent until his wife had called the police. After emerging from jail, burning with a sense of injustice much like that experienced during his imprisonment in the army, he had felt the impulse to strike a stranger who was giving him a lift in an automobile, and then again, much more strongly, a few days later toward his wife at their first meeting since his night in jail. This time he had gone into a state of panic, and since then, for a period of five months, the obsession had recurred very frequently and in an increasing range of conditions, e.g., at work he would often have a fear-laden desire to hit fellow workmen with any tool he happened to be holding. (There was subsequently a secondary conditioning of anxiety to the *sight* of tools, including knives and forks.)

ANXIETY-REDUCING OBSESSIONS

The second type of obsessional behavior occurs as a *reaction* to anxiety, and its performance *diminishes* anxiety to some extent, for at least a short time. It occurs in many forms—tidying, handwashing, eating, buying—activities which are of course "normal" when prompted by usual motivations and not by anxiety; rituals like touching poles, perversions like exhibitionism, and various thinking activities. In some of these cases secondary heightening of anxiety occurs as a response to some aspect of the obsessional behavior. For example, in a case of obsessional eating, the anxiety was at first reduced by the eating, and then its level would rise in response to the idea of getting fat.

Obsessional behavior of this kind owes its existence to the previous conditioning of anxiety-relieving responses. This has been strikingly demonstrated in a recent experiment by Fonberg (1956). This writer conditioned each of several dogs to perform a definite movement in response to several auditory and visual stimuli using food reinforcement. When these instrumental conditioned responses had been firmly established, she proceeded to elaborate defensive instrumental conditioned responses, employing stimuli and responses distinct from those of the alimentary training. The noxious stimulus used was either an electric shock to the right foreleg or a strong air puff to the ear. As a result of this conditioning, upon presentation of the conditioned stimulus an animal would be able to avert the noxious stimulus—for example, by lifting a particular foreleg. The dogs were then made neurotic by conditioning an excitatory alimentary response to a strong tone of 50 cycles and an inhibitory response to a very weak tone of the same frequency, and then bringing the two differentiated tones nearer and nearer to each other from session to session either by progressive strengthening of the inhibitory tone or by both strengthening the inhibitory and weakening the excitatory. In all animals, as soon as neurotic behavior appeared it was accompanied by the previously elaborated defensive motor reaction. Besides this deliberately conditioned reaction, "shaking off" movements were observed in those dogs in whom the noxious stimulation had originally been air puffed into the ear. The more intense the general disturbance the more intense and frequent were the defensive movements. The alimentary conditioned reflexes disappeared completely. With the disappearance of general disturbed symptoms, the defensive movements subsided, reappearing with any new outburst of behavioral disturbance.

It appears clear from these observations that in elaborating the conditioned defensive reaction to the auditory stimulus, anxiety-response-produced stimuli were also conditioned to evoke the defensive reaction, and this reaction was consequently evocable *whenever* the animal had anxiety responses, no matter what the origin of these may have been.

Similarly, in the history of patients displaying this kind of obsessional behavior, it is found that at an earlier period, some important real threat was consistently removed by a single well-defined type of behavior, and this behavior later appears as a response to *any* similar anxiety. The behavior must owe its strength to its association with exceptionally strong reinforcement-favoring conditions—either very massive or very numerous anxiety-drive reductions or both. Its development is also, no doubt, greatly favored when from the outset no other significant anxiety-relieving activity has occurred to compete with it. Its maintenance depends upon the reduction of anxiety it is able to effect at each performance.

One patient was the youngest daughter of a man who despised females and would not forgive his wife for failing to bear him a son. She was very clever at school, and found that intellectual achievement, and that alone, could for brief periods abate her father's blatant hostility and therefore her own anxiety. Consequently, "thinking things out" became her automatic response to *any* anxiety. Since there are many objective fears for which careful thought is useful, there were no serious consequences for years. But when a series of experiences in early adult life led to a severe anxiety state in her, she automatically resorted to her characteristic "problem-solving" behavior. Because the anxiety responses now arose from such sources as imaginary social disapproval, and could not be removed by the solution of a well-defined problem, she began to set herself complex problems in which she usually had to decide whether given behavior was morally "good" or "bad." Partial and brief alleviation of anxiety followed both the formulation of a "suitable" problem and the solution thereof, while prolonged failure to solve a problem increased anxiety sometimes to terror. Although the anxiety soon returned in full force, its temporary decrements at the most appropriate times for reinforcement maintained the problem-finding and problem-solving obsessions, and could well have continued to do so indefinitely.

In other cases obsessional behavior is less episodically determined because everyday circumstances contain aspects of the special situation in which the obsessional mode of behavior alone brought relief from severe anxiety. A history of more than 100 undetected thefts of money by a 17-year-old university student began at the age of 5 when his mother joined the army and left him in the care of an elder sister who beat him severely or tied him to a tree for a few hours if he was slightly dirty or did anything "wrong." He feared and hated her and retaliated by stealing money from her. He was never caught and the possession of the stolen gains gave him a feeling of "munificence and security." The kleptomania continued all through the early home life and school life and was clearly connected with the chronic presence of punishment-empowered authority in the shape of parents or teachers.

It is not surprising, if obsessional behavior is so consistently followed by reduction of anxiety drive, that it is apt to become conditioned to other stimuli too, especially any that happen to be present on repeated occasions. Thus, after therapy had rendered the young woman with the problem-solving obsession mentioned above practically free from neurotic anxieties, mild problem-solving activity was still occasionally aroused by a trifling question, such as "Is it cloudy enough to rain?" The conditioned stimulus was apparently the mere awareness of doubt. Similarly an exhibitionist whose exhibiting had almost entirely disappeared with the overcoming of his anxious sensitivities, still had some measure of the impulse when he saw a girl dressed in a school ("gym") uniform, because he had in the past exhibited to schoolgirls particularly frequently and with special relish. Of course, in this instance sex-drive reduction may have played as important a role in the reinforcement as anxiety-drive reduction.

Amnesia and "Repression"

The amnesias that are usually encountered in the course of neurotic states can be conveniently divided into two classes, according to the emotional importance of the incidents forgotten. Patients who are in a chronic state of emotional disturbance frequently fail to register many trifling events that go on around them. For example, a patient may go into a room and conduct a brief conversation with his wife and an hour later have no recollection whatever that he went into that room at all. Here we seem to have a simple case of deficient registration of impressions (retrograde amnesia). Apparently, the patient's attention is so much taken up by his unpleasant anxious feelings that very little is left to be devoted to what goes on around him.

The forgetting of the contents of highly emotionally charged experiences has been given foremost importance by Freud and his followers as the cause of neurosis. It seems, however, that forgetting of this character is rather unusual, and when it does occur it appears to be merely one more of the conditionable occurrences in the neurotigenic situation. It does not appear that the repression as such plays any part in the maintenance of neurosis. It is quite possible for the patient to recover emotionally although the forgotten incidents remain entirely forgotten. The following case illustrates this.

A 37-year-old miner was seen in a state of intense anxiety. He had had a very marked tremor and total amnesia for the previous four days. He gave a story that his wife, on whom he was greatly dependent, had cunningly got him to agree to "temporary divorce" six months before and was now going to marry a friend of his. No attempt was made at this juncture to recall the lost memories. The patient was made to realize how ineffectual his previous attitudes had been and how he had been deceived. As a result, he angrily "had it out" with his wife (and a few others, incidentally); anxiety rapidly decreased, and he soon felt strongly motivated to organize his whole life differently. At his fifth interview (ten days after treatment began) he said that he felt "a hundred per cent"—and looked it—and he was full of plans for the future. Yet he had still recalled nothing whatever of the forgotten four days.

Since the possible effects of restoring the memories at this stage were obviously a matter of great interest, the patient was then deeply hypnotized and told to recount the story of the four days. He narrated in detail how he had traveled 300 miles to his rival, meaning to strangle him; how he had been fobbed off, and how, on returning and at last hearing from his wife's own lips that she was in love with the rival, he had staggered out of the house, had made his way to his sister's house, and there collapsed. He told all this quietly, with little emotion, except where he described meeting his rival. Then he moved his hands as if about to throttle someone. He was given the posthypnotic suggestion that he would remember the whole story on waking. When he woke, he told it again briefly, expressing slight amusement at it and surprise at having remembered. There were no important consequences. A few months later he married another woman and was apparently very well adjusted generally. After four years there was no evidence of relapse.

Secondary Neurotic Responses

Many patients suffer more or less passively the discomforts due to their neurotic responses. Others have recourse to activities that diminish anxiety in a variety of ways.

PHYSICAL AVOIDANCE OF ANXIETY-EVOKING STIMULI

Retreat from anxiety-arousing stimulus situations and avoidance of them when they can be anticipated may be expected to be the rule. This is not because the patient sits down and works it out as a good plan but because the reduction of anxiety drive following an activity that removes him from the anxiety-arousing stimulation increases the tendency for that activity to occur as an automatic response to that situation. Thus, the amount of anxiety to be endured is cut down by, for example, not entering elevators, staying out of the way of superiors, passing over obituary notices, keeping quiet in company—avoiding whatever may be fearful. When anxiety is more or less continuous, as in the case of pervasive ("free-floating") anxiety (p. 83), clear-cut avoidance behavior is of course less likely to develop. But even in patients who do have avoidance patterns, removal from a tensing situation frequently is inhibited by other motivations, usually of a social character. For example, a patient who has a conditioned anxiety reaction to physical illness in others visits a friend and finds him in bed with a heart attack. It will usually be difficult for him to obey his impulse to depart at once.

It is not uncommon to encounter patients who repeatedly get into situations that they know to be disturbing. The reason is that a prospect that seems entrancing from afar may contain aspects highly disturbing at close quarters. This conforms to Miller's experimental paradigm (1944) in which the approach behavior gradient is shown to have a gentler slope than the avoidance gradient. It is also in keeping with the observation (p. 53) that cats who are made neurotic after having had feeding conditioning in the experimental cage continue to jump spontaneously into the carrier cage that will take them down to the now fearful experimental room.

DISPLACEMENT OF ATTENTION

In many respects similar to physical avoidance are those activities that diminish neurotic anxiety by distracting attention from anxiety-evoking stimuli through a focusing upon stimulus configurations that do not arouse anxiety. There is a very wide range of activities which may have this effect, and while one patient may confine himself to only one of them, another may resort to many. Some patients become engrossed in work and feel miserable as soon as they stop working. Others "lose themselves" in social activities and cannot bear to be alone. There are those who obtain relief in participation in sports, in playing cards and other games, or even in solitary activities like solving crossword puzzles. Another important group find solace in sexual activities, which may be of many kinds—reading lewd stories, looking at pictures of voluptuous women, speaking to attractive women, making love, working toward "conquests," and forming lasting sexual relationships. Finally we may mention those who "escape into danger," which seems paradoxical until, going into details, it is seen that these people either do not react fearfully to the "dangers" that they tempt, or experience a pleasant thrill stronger than the fear that is also present, or find the fear evoked by a real danger more tolerable than the bizarre horror that characterizes the particular neurosis.

Obviously, none of the activities listed above, except perhaps certain cases of danger-seeking, is in itself "abnormal." But any of them will constitute a secondary neurotic reaction insofar as it has its instigation in the existence of neurotic anxiety—because, perhaps by chance, the patient has previously found it to be anxiety-reducing. It is not necessary for him to *remember* that it was anxiety-reducing. In terms of the principles enunciated in Chapter 2, it is clear that reduction of anxiety drive following the activity leads to the formation of a neural connection that makes this activity an automatic response to the bodily sensations characteristic of anxiety. On each subsequent occasion when the behavior again reduces the anxiety, its tendency to be performed is augmented.

The learning that underlies this automatic response may have occurred either after the onset of the neurosis or at any previous time, and may have had many reinforcements, large or small, during the years of the patient's life. A man's anxiety-relieving devotion to his work may as easily have its origin in the fact that, at the beginning of his anxiety state, work happened to reduce his anxiety, as in the fact that during his childhood he could allay his father's wrath by a display of scholastic diligence.

All, or nearly all, of the attention-displacing types of activity arouse emotional states that have the *potentiality* of inhibiting anxiety. If the arousal occurs in an appropriate time relation to anxiety-evoking stimulation and is strong enough, some measure of "spontaneous" therapy will of course ensue. But when no enduring benefit is observed, it is evidently just because there is a complete removal from the action of neurotic stimulation during involvement in the activity.

TAKING DRUGS

If a person's neurotic symptoms have been ameliorated following the taking of a drug, it is to be expected that he will make further use of it when his symptoms are troublesome. Their efficacy in this direction accounts in part for the widespread use of alcohol and narcotic alkaloids, as also for the use of the barbiturates and the so-called tranquilizers such as chlorpromazine (Largactil), meprobamate (Miltown, Equanil), or methylpentynol (Oblivon). Unless a chemical addiction is produced (which seems to happen among these only with alcohol, narcotics, and, less often, the barbiturates), the tendency to take the drug disappears when the neurosis is overcome. This is hardly surprising when one considers that the unpleasant sensations produced by the neurotic responses are the stimulus to the taking of each dose of the drug. If the stimulus does not appear, neither can the responses. This is in conformity with the observations of Masserman and Yum on neuroses in cats (1946). Neurotic animals spontaneously choose food containing a low percentage of alcohol in preference to food free from alcohol. But, confronted with the same choice after cure of the neurosis, they revert to the nonalcoholic food.

The Determinants of Change in Neurotic Symptomatology

The presence of neurotic responses implies that certain objectively nonthreatening stimulus conditions have become capable of evoking anxiety responses. The character of the responses, though varying with transient physiological states such as fatigue, usually has an approximate stability. There are three "dimensions" in which variation can occur: (1) the range of stimulus conditions capable of eliciting the anxiety response may increase or decrease; (2) the strength of the response to a particular stimulus situation may increase or decrease; and (3) the anxiety response may change in character through losing or gaining components, or through alteration in the relative strength of components.

THE SPREAD OF ANXIETY-EVOKING POTENTIAL TO NEW STIMULI

Since every exposure to anxiety-producing stimuli involves the evocation of anxiety drive and subsequent drive reduction, every such stimulation carries the potentiality of new stimuli becoming conditioned to anxiety responses in a way analogous to that described above (p. 60), in the experiment in which the repeated presentation of an anxiety-evoking buzzer whenever an animal approached a particular corner of a room gave that corner the power to evoke anxiety independently. Figuratively, there occurred a "spread" of anxiety from one stimulus to another.

In the human subject there are two methods of spread which are roughly separable but often simultaneous. The first of these may be called involvement through continuity, because the progression is among stimuli that share some feature with an original conditioned stimulus. For example, a woman developed a fear of anesthetic masks as the result of experiencing a terrifying sensation of suffocation during the administration of an anesthetic. This fear spread to other stimuli in many steps along a central thread of "suffocation feeling." For example, her feeling of heat and stuffiness in a crowded elevator aroused anxiety which became a secondarily conditioned response even to being in an uncrowded elevator. From this it was very easy for the anxiety to spread by steps to all situations where she could not easily leave at will—for instance, playing cards. One day, an exceptionally severe hailstorm evoked in her a feeling of suffocation, of not being able to get away, and this experience conditioned her to be anxious even during quite light rain.

The other method of spread may be called involvement by contiguity. Here anxiety-evoking power is acquired by a new stimulus merely because it happens to be in the environment of the subject in a context favorable to conditioning. For example, a man who already had a conditioned anxiety reaction to the sensation of rapid beating of his heart experienced the onset of an attack of paroxysmal tachycardia just after he had walked to the telephone in his office, while the western sun shone in upon him strongly through the window. After this, he felt tense in sunlight and avoided the sunny side of the street.

In addition to the above, there is frequently an apparent spread of anxiety to new stimuli based upon "symbolism." For example, a woman of 30 came for the treatment of claustrophobia of two years' standing. The onset of this turned out to be related to a marriage in which she felt "caught like a rat in a trap." Many years earlier she had had a fearful experience in a confined space, and this had led to slight uneasiness in such places as elevators. Her marital situation now generated a chronic undertone of "shut-in" feeling, with which the physical enclosement of elevators now summated to produce a substantial fear reaction.

INCREASE IN STRENGTH OF ANXIETY RESPONSES

Anxiety responses to a stimulus can increase in strength either through contiguity of that stimulus with other stimuli that can evoke stronger anxiety responses, or through repeated evocation of anxiety by the stimulus itself. The former process was discussed in considering precipitating conditions. The following is an example of the latter process. A young man, after a series of severe experiences with women, had become conditioned to react anxiously to physical contact with any woman whom he could not completely accept. Every physical contact with such a woman increased his anxious sensitivity to her, with generalization, as would be expected, to other women in the same category.

DECREASE IN STRENGTH OF ANXIETY RESPONSES

In the discussion on experimental neuroses, it was shown that mere repetition of anxiety responses does not result in their weakening, for two reasons—removal of the animal from the anxiety-arousing stimulus leads to anxiety drive reduction and also, apparently, anxiety responses generate relatively little reactive inhibition. The therapeutic experiments showed that the anxiety responses can be overcome by opposing other incompatible responses to them. The arousal of such incompatible responses takes place to a variably effective extent in the normal course of human life. The effectiveness will obviously be greater when the level of anxiety is low and when the intensity of the opposing emotional response is high. It is because of this that the anxiety conditioning produced by many frightening experiences is easily overcome in a short time during the ordinary course of life. Here are some examples of the operation of spontaneously occurring responses antagonistic to anxiety. (1) The anxiety of a man with mild claustrophobia sitting in a theater is inhibited by an exciting film. (2) Sexual anxiety is inhibited by the strong positive emotion aroused by an encouraging approach from an attractive person of the opposite sex. (3) A shy man has pleasant emotions aroused by an interesting conversation. (4) A medical student has the anxiety, aroused in him by the sight of a dead body being cut open, inhibited by a feeling of interest in what he sees at the post-mortem. In these situations and thousands of others, there can obviously be inhibition of the anxiety only if the opposing response does not involve a complete distraction from or removal of the anxiety-producing stimulation. Weakening of the anxiety reaction can occur only if some fraction of the response to the anxiety-evoking stimulus is present. This is the process that accounts not only for the spontaneous cure of neuroses, and particularly the overcoming of very numerous minor neurotic reactions, but also for the fluctuations in strength of evocation of anxiety even in relatively severe neuroses.

The emotional effects of aesthetic experiences of various kinds are not infrequently important in this connection. Some patients report decreased levels of pervasive anxiety after holidays and excursions into beautiful surroundings, or after looking at paintings, listening to music, or reading poetry. An interesting example of the effectiveness of the last was recently noted by Farrar (1957) in the biography of John Stuart Mill (1924). At the age of 22 Mill became emotionally disturbed and took to reading poetry by Wordsworth. This unexpectedly brought him relief. He states:

> What made Wordsworth's poems a medicine for my state of mind was that they expressed not mere outward beauty, but states of feeling, and of thought coloured by feeling, under the excitement of beauty. They seemed to be the very culture of the feelings which I was in quest of . . . And I felt myself at once better and happier as I came under their influence.

THE OCCURRENCE OF CHANGE IN THE CONSTITUTION
OF NEUROTIC RESPONSES

If a neurotic animal is brought back to the cage where the neurotic conditioning was obtained, he will, of course, manifest the responses previously conditioned. If the neurotigenic stimulus, e.g., electric shock, is now again administered, the responses it elicits may not entirely coincide with the ongoing conditioned responses. To take a gross example, if the animal is clawing at the side of the cage, the shock may now inhibit this movement and produce a tense crouching. This response is thus added to the responses previously conditioned, interacting with them, modifying them, and being modified by them upon subsequent exposure to relevant stimuli. Thus, at the animal's next return to the cage his initial response will not be quite the same as before. Each additional presentation of the shock, insofar as it produces responses differing from and interfering with the ongoing ones, will produce further modification of the immediate responses to the cage. A great deal of indirect experimental support for this proposition is available. For example, in attempting to condition a stimulus to an animal's response to an electric shock on the leg, when the shock is administered without respect to what the animal is doing (so that in fact it is doing something different on each occasion), variable responses are conditioned (e.g., Brogden *et al.*, 1938). Complex alterations in the character of response to the "unconditioned" stimulation have been demonstrated by Kawamura and Yoshii (1951), who found that when rats suspended by a jacket enclosing their trunks were given 10–15 shocks to their hind legs on repeated occasions, the responses of the animals changed from time to time, some animals manifesting as many as five different patterns of behavior. An exact parallel to this is difficult to find in human subjects, since they are not often twice exposed to precisely the same neurotigenic conditions, and since, in any case, unconditioned noxious stimulation is but infrequently the crucial precipitating factor. Some kind of similarity is afforded by the case of a bomber pilot who developed a severe anxiety reaction toward flying when his plane had been hit by flak on two successive flights. After a third flight a depressive element was added to his anxiety when the plane was again hit and everybody else within it was killed.

Change in response constituents also occurs as a result of the evocation of *conditioned* anxiety responses. The change is then determined by the simultaneous occurrence of response elements evoked by other stimuli incidentally present, when such response elements are found to participate in the next evocation of the neurotic response. Gantt (1944, 1949) has provided experimental demonstrations of this. He has shown, for example, that a neurotic animal may in time have sexual responses incorporated among anxiety reactions which at the outset had nothing at all to do with sexual behavior. Whatever the precise origin of the first evocation of sexual responses may have been, once they appeared they were constantly present in given conditions evoking neurotic responses. A clinical example of this is the case of a young woman with certain social fears who one day had these fears strongly evoked in a situation that also produced marked blushing. Thereafter, blushing accompanied the evocation of fear under all circumstances.

PART II: PSYCHOTHERAPY

7 | The Approach to the Patient:

Interview Procedure

It is desirable to give a full account of the way in which interviews are conducted, not only for the sake of those who may desire to repeat the procedures to be described but also to give the critical reader some opportunity to judge whether or not factors whose relevance I have not noticed have been influencing the course of events.

The Initial Interviews

Typically, the first interview lasts an hour, later ones about 45 minutes. At all of them the patient faces the therapist across a desk. He is asked to give his name, address, age, and telephone number. These particulars are written down on a card on which notes are openly inscribed at every interview. If the patient displays any discomfiture at the note-taking, he is assured that the record is confidential and will be read by nobody but me. But occasionally I am constrained to use a pseudonym on the record card in place of the real name.

The first step in the sequence of therapeutic operations is to obtain from the patient a detailed history of his difficulties and symptoms. A special effort is made to identify precipitating events and also any factors that have appeared either to aggravate or ameliorate the symptoms. Many patients are able to connect the onset of various reactions with specific occurrences or chronic states of affairs. Others can establish within reasonably narrow limits the time of onset of symptoms without being able to identify any relevant circumstances. A third group of patients can recall nothing of the onset of their neurotic reactions. I coax these to think back more carefully in the hope of arousing some recall; but if significant facts are not brought forth within a few minutes, I cease to press the point, telling the patient that I have no intention of devoting a great deal of time to raking up past history, because although it would be interesting and perhaps helpful it is not necessary: *for to overcome his neurotic reactions it is of greater relevance to determine what stimuli do or can evoke them at the present time.* However, the history of particular sequences of events is often sought later when the case presents new aspects. Also some patients spontaneously proffer relevant data from time to time.

Next, attention is directed to the patient's life history, starting with the circumstances in which he grew up. He is asked about his relationships with and attitudes toward parents, siblings, and other people, how his parents got on with each other, whether they punished him and in what ways, his religious training, his fears and difficulties, and any outstanding incidents that come to his mind. He then gives an account of his experiences in educational institutions, his attitudes to them, his academic and athletic accomplishments, and any emotionally important reactions to teachers or fellow students. This leads on to his occupational history in both its technical and its interpersonal aspects. He is then questioned about his sex life, his first awareness of sexual impulses, masturbation and his attitudes to it, and early heterosexual (and/or homosexual) reactions. This is followed by a history of his sexual relationships, with particular emphasis on those with high degrees of emotional involvement—whether pleasant or unpleasant, and his marital history in all its social and sexual aspects. Finally, he is asked to recount any fearful or distressing experiences not previously mentioned. The order of the above topics is varied if the natural flow of the story demands it.

All that the patient says is accepted without question or criticism. He is given the feeling that the therapist is unreservedly on his side. This happens not because the therapist is expressly trying to appear sympathetic, but as the natural outcome of a completely nonmoralizing objective approach to the behavior of human organisms. For example, when the patient shamefully recounts an extramarital love affair, it is sincerely pointed out that this is no reason for shame, because factors in the circumstances made it a natural thing to happen—as indeed they must have.

In so far as this kind of expression of an attitude by the therapist can free the patient from some unadaptive anxieties, it must be regarded as psychotherapeutic. It amounts essentially to an authoritative correcting for the patient of the connotation of certain stimulus configurations: the patient has reacted unpleasantly to x because he has wrongly believed it to imply y, and now the therapist convinces him that x does not imply y (see Chapter 13). This is different from the central therapeutic aim stated above—the removal from various stimulus configurations of the power to evoke useless unadaptive fears. In other words, here it is y that is feared, *wrongly*, and the problem is to "disconnect" the fear responses from y. It is worth noting that therapeutic effects of the latter variety also begin early in some of those patients in whom nonspecific emotional responses to the interview situation are strong enough to inhibit the anxieties evoked by verbal stimuli that arise during the interviews (see Chapter 13).

Formal history-taking may consist of between one and a dozen interviews. At the end of the last anamnestic interview the patient is given Bernreuter's (1933) self-sufficiency questionnaire to do as homework. Despite the ambiguity of some of its 60 items the questionnaire is of some value as a guide to the probable duration of therapy. A score lower than about 20 (33 per cent) suggests that the patient will have difficulty in carrying out the active psychotherapeutic tasks that will later be assigned to him. This is in agreement with the experience of Salter (1950).

The Willoughby Schedule

The next interview commences with the answering of Willoughby's (1932, 1934) questionnaire, which is reproduced below. This is a test for neuroticism, i.e., persistent unadaptive anxiety reactions; and the neuroticism revealed by the questionnaire relates mainly to common types of social situations. Each question is answered on a five-point scale in which 0 is negative and 1 to 4 are positive in increasing degrees. Examination of the individual questions shows that positive answers to numbers 1, 3, 5, 7, 11, 13, 15, 16, 18, 19, 20, 22, and 23 give direct indications of unadaptive anxiety reactions (by definition, pp. 32–33). For example, when one is fearful at the prospect of displaying before an audience an activity one can otherwise do well, the fear arises *in relation to no objective threat*. Positive answers to the remaining questions, numbers 2, 4, 6, 8, 9, 10, 12, 14, 17, 21, 24, and 25 give indications of emotional sensitivity in a variety of different ways, but not explicitly in terms of anxiety. However, the anxious basis of such sensitivities is shown by falling scores on these questions in patients who are improving under therapy.

It is important for each question to be put to the patient in such a way that the anxiety or other emotional sensitivity is clearly brought out by the answer. This is ensured by the therapist going through the questionnaire with him, and carefully explaining the meaning and intention of each question as he comes to it. For example, for question 3, "Are you afraid of falling when you are on a high place?" I explain that a positive answer will indicate being afraid in situations where there is *no actual danger of falling*. Again, regarding question 22, "Are you self-conscious about your appearance?" the patient is told that this refers to being self-conscious about his appearance even though his mirror has revealed him to be clean, well-groomed, and suitably dressed for the given occasion.

WILLOUGHBY PERSONALITY SCHEDULE

Instructions:

The questions in this schedule are intended to indicate various emotional personality traits. It is not a test in any sense because there are no right and wrong answers to any of the questions in this schedule.

After each question you will find a row of numbers whose meaning is given below. All you have to do is to draw a ring around the number that describes you best.

0 means "no", "never", "not at all", etc.
1 means "somewhat", "sometimes", "a little", etc.
2 means "about as often as not", "an average amount", etc.
3 means "usually", "a good deal", "rather often", etc.
4 means "practically always", "entirely", etc.

1. Do you get stage fright?—0 1 2 3 4
2. Do you worry over humiliating experiences?—0 1 2 3 4
3. Are you afraid of falling when you are on a high place?—0 1 2 3 4
4. Are your feelings easily hurt?—0 1 2 3 4
5. Do you keep in the background on social occasions?—0 1 2 3 4
6. Are you happy and sad by turns without knowing why?—0 1 2 3 4
7. Are you shy?—0 1 2 3 4
8. Do you day-dream frequently?—0 1 2 3 4
9. Do you get discouraged easily?—0 1 2 3 4
10. Do you say things on the spur of the moment and then regret them?— 0 1 2 3 4
11. Do you like to be alone?—0 1 2 3 4
12. Do you cry easily?—0 1 2 3 4
13. Does it bother you to have people watch you work even when you do it well?—0 1 2 3 4
14. Does criticism hurt you badly?—0 1 2 3 4
15. Do you cross the street to avoid meeting someone?—0 1 2 3 4
16. At a reception or tea do you avoid meeting the important person present?— 0 1 2 3 4
17. Do you often feel just miserable?—0 1 2 3 4
18. Do you hesitate to volunteer in a class discussion or debate?—0 1 2 3 4
19. Are you often lonely?—0 1 2 3 4
20. Are you self-conscious before superiors?—0 1 2 3 4
21. Do you lack self-confidence?—0 1 2 3 4
22. Are you self-conscious about your appearance?—0 1 2 3 4
23. If you see an accident does something keep you from giving help?— 0 1 2 3 4
24. Do you feel inferior?—0 1 2 3 4
25. Is it hard to make up your mind until the time for action is past?— 0 1 2 3 4

Your name...................... Date............

As the highest score for any question is 4, the highest total possible on the questionnaire is 100. The distribution of scores for 295 unselected patients at first answering is shown in Fig. 8. On the Kolmogorov-Smirnov test (Miller, 1956; Siegel, 1956) the distribution for the 160 males does not differ significantly from that of the 135 females. It will be observed that 236 patients (80 per cent) gave scores of 30 or over and 277 (94 per cent) of 20 or over.

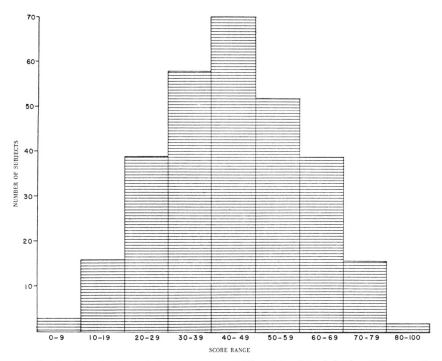

Fig. 8. Distribution of first scores on Willoughby Schedule for 295 neurotic patients.

In view of the fact stated above, that positive answers to questions on the Willoughby schedule to a great extent indicate neurotic anxiety as defined in this book, comparison of the above distribution with scores that would be found in a "normal" group of subjects would constitute an important check of correspondence of the definition with the clinical realities. Unfortunately, no study that is strictly comparable is available since nobody has gone through the schedule with a "normal" group of subjects in a similar way question by question. But some indication is obtainable from one of Willoughby's own studies (1934) in which out of 262 university students, about 50 per cent of the scores exceeded 30 and 75 per cent exceeded 20. This corresponds closely with the distribution found by Harvey (1932) using the Thurstone schedule upon which the Willoughby is based. Figure 9 compares the sample cumulative distribution function of Willoughby's subjects with that of our patients. The maximum difference is 21, at the 30–39 level of scores. On the two-sided Kolmogorov-Smirnov test this is significant at the .001 level. This means that what the Willoughby measures is far more prevalent among people who come for treatment of a condition that is diagnosed as neurotic than among a group from the "normal" population.

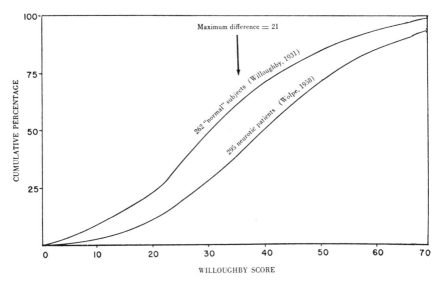

Fig. 9. Sample cumulative distribution functions comparing the Willoughby scores of normal and neurotic groups. The maximum difference (21) is significant at the .001 level.

The information that the Willoughby gives about neurotic reactivity is confined to a limited number of areas in which such reactivity is very common. It is to be expected that, whereas in some patients it will very adequately convey the extent of neuroticism, in others it will reveal only a part, or none at all if the neurotic responses are all to stimuli in areas that the questionnaire does not encompass. For example, a man whose neurotic reactions were for all practical purposes confined to sexual situations had an initial score of 17; a business executive who had been very well and happy until 18 months previously, when certain alarming experiences had conditioned fear of heart disease, gave a score of 15. Another group of patients in whom the schedule gives low scores is the nonanxious hysterics discussed in Chapter 6.

Taking the above into account, it seems reasonable to state that while high scores to the Willoughby schedule denote that neurotic reactivity is high, low scores do not prove that it is low. The question naturally arises: where is the dividing line between a high score and a low one? One answer would be that any score above zero is high because it means that there is *some* neuroticism, and to aim to remove all of it would be quite defensible. But for practical purposes the question to be asked is: at what level do neurotic reactions begin to intrude in a patient's life sufficiently to affect his happiness? Of course there can be no absolute level that applies to everybody; but my experience has generally been that when the level drops to 20 or 15, neurotic reactions are ceasing to bother the patient in a way that makes him want to do anything at all about them. However, it is not only the total score that matters but also how that score is made up. A score of 10 made up of two 4's and two 1's clearly indicates more important neurotic sensitivity than a score of 20 made up of 1's.

Introductory Statement to the Patient

After disposing of the Willoughby schedule I make a statement to the patient along the following lines:

"I want to give you some idea of the nature of your disturbances and of the means we shall adopt to overcome them. Your trouble is basically that you react with fear too often or too strongly. You may say that the word 'fear' is not a correct label for some or any of your disturbed feelings. You may feel that 'anxiety' or 'tension' or 'disturbance' or 'distress' is a better word, or the feelings may be so unusual that no words can describe them. Even so, fear is the root emotion, but various factors may modify the physiological responses that produce the fearful feeling. Not all fear is undesirable. In some circumstances it is an entirely reasonable and even useful response. You would not come for treatment if your fears were only of such things as poisonous snakes or an actual threat of losing all your money on the stock exchange. But if you are afraid of going in a lift or of walking in a street or of entering a room full of people, then you are afraid in situations in which there is no actual danger. Such fears are useless fears. Nevertheless they do not exist for nothing. Always, definite circumstances have brought these useless fears into being. These circumstances vary greatly in detail but they have a common central core which I shall illustrate by means of a simple example.

"A young child goes into his mother's kitchen, puts his hand on the big, black stove and burns himself. At that moment he experiences pain and fear and makes a movement of withdrawal. A lasting after-effect of this experience is that on subsequent occasions when the child enters the kitchen and sees the stove, he reacts with fear and with an impulse to keep away from it. In other words, he has now learned a reaction of fear and avoidance of a dangerous object. This, of course, is desirable.

"But another, seemingly odd reaction may also be observed. Suppose that in the bedroom of the child's mother there is a large black chest of drawers. It may now be noticed that the child is also afraid of this chest of drawers, just because, in common with the stove, it has the characteristics of largeness and blackness. The resemblance has thus made the child uselessly afraid of a harmless object. Even in this limited example the disadvantages of such a useless fear may readily be seen. First, merely to experience unnecessarily the unpleasant emotion of fear is undesirable. Then, if the chest of drawers should happen to be in the child's path, he has to make a detour. Finally, if his mother keeps candy in one of the drawers this is no longer accessible to him.

"This example is a model of the learning of all useless or neurotic fears. Whenever a person is subjected to an intensely fearful experience or to a fearful chronic situation, he is liable to become conditioned to react with fear whenever subsequently, in actually benign circumstances, he encounters things or stimuli similar to any that were closely associated with the situation of fear. Here is an example: A young woman came to see me, primarily because she was inexplicably terrified of her employer. It turned out that she had had an extraordinarily cruel father of whom she had been rightly afraid. By the principle of resemblance I have described, she had become afraid of practically all other people too, and her special fear of her boss was due to the fact that he had certain mannerisms strongly reminiscent of her father."

On the basis of the patient's history, I attempt to show him how experiences in his own past have led to his present sensitivities. If no satisfactory tie-ups can be established, he is told that it is not essential to establish them; and that our time can be used in other and more fruitful ways than delving into the past; for although it is interesting to know what led to his neurosis, the mere possession of this knowledge will not in itself make his unadaptive anxieties disappear. I tell him that measures have to be taken to break down the anxious habits; that some of these are applied in the life situation, others in the consulting room, but the essence of all measures is opposing to the anxiety other emotional states incompatible with it.

The stage is now set for the introduction of deliberate methods of psychotherapy—the formal use of particular responses that, through inhibiting anxiety (or, in some instances, other neurotic responses), weaken neurotic habits. As mentioned earlier in this chapter, some weakening of these habits may already have been taking place spontaneously because in certain patients the interview situation itself evokes responses antagonistic to anxiety (see Chapter 13). The responses at the disposal of the therapist by which therapeutic change may be *deliberately* brought about are listed below. The list certainly does not exhaust the possibilities and may be expected to acquire additions as time goes on.

1. Assertive responses
2. Sexual responses
3. Relaxation responses
4. Respiratory responses
5. "Anxiety-relief" responses
6. Competitively conditioned motor responses
7. "Pleasant" responses in the life situation (with drug enhancement)
8. *a*) Interview-induced emotional responses
   b) Abreaction

Abreaction and "pleasant" responses in the life situation may occur spontaneously, but their occurrence may be favored by suitable manipulations on the part of the therapist. The utility of each of the other responses listed (1–6) depends upon action by the therapist who must see to it that they are evoked in such circumstances that they will effectively inhibit anxiety. The responses and their use in therapy will be discussed below under their headings.

The first problem is always, of course, to decide which of the responses can most appropriately be used to obtain reciprocal inhibition of a patient's neurotic anxiety responses. This will naturally depend upon the identity of the anxiety-evoking stimuli. A good many relevant stimuli will already have been revealed by the history or by positive answers to items in the Willoughby schedule. In general, assertive responses are used for anxieties evoked in the course of direct interpersonal dealings, sexual responses for sexual anxieties, relaxation responses for anxieties arising from any source whatever but especially from stimulus configurations that do not allow of any kind of direct action (e.g., inanimate objects), and respiratory responses for pervasive ("free-floating") anxiety. As will be seen from case histories given below, special circumstances may dictate an unusual choice of therapeutic responses.

8 | *Reciprocal Inhibition in the Life Situation*

Systematic use of the reciprocal inhibition principle in the life situation has so far extended to three varieties of responses antagonistic to anxiety —assertive responses, sexual responses, and relaxation responses. Assertive responses are used against anxieties arising out of the patient's immediate relations with other individuals; sexual responses against the anxieties of sexual situations. Relaxation responses are theoretically applicable against anxieties from any source whatever; but, as will be pointed out, certain practical difficulties limit their use in the life situation.

Assertive Responses

The word *assertive* has rather a wide meaning here. It refers not only to more or less aggressive behavior, but also to the outward expression of friendly, affectionate, and other nonanxious feelings. It covers exactly the same ground as Salter's (1949) word *excitatory*, but is preferred because it is somewhat more specific: for even anxious behavior is excitatory in a way. Since the kind of assertive behavior that is most used in therapy is aggressive (anger-expressing) behavior, this will receive most of our attention. The two components of anger-expressing behavior referred to in Chapter 5—motor activity and a parasympathetic-dominated autonomic response pattern—probably both play a part in the inhibition of anxiety responses.

Assertive responses are mainly employed in situations that occur spontaneously in the normal course of the patient's life. Great prominence has been given to them by Salter, who, having independently come to their use by way of a different theory, seems to apply them almost universally. I have found them of value only for overcoming unadaptive anxieties aroused in the patient by other people during direct interchanges with them. In these circumstances assertive responses are extremely effective. To take a common example, a patient feels hurt when members of his family criticize him and responds by trying to defend himself, by sulking, or by an outburst of petulant rage. Such responses are expressive of anxiety and helplessness. But some measure of resentment is, understandably, almost invariably present at the same time. The patient is unable to express this resentment because, for example, through previous training, the idea of talking back to his elders produces anxiety.

Now, just because this anxiety inhibits the expression of the resentment, it might be expected that an augmentation of resentment motivation sufficient to procure its outward expression would reciprocally inhibit the anxiety and thus suppress it, to some extent at least. The therapist increases the motivation by pointing out the emptiness of the patient's fears, emphasizing how his fearful patterns of behavior have incapacitated him and placed him at the mercy of others, and informing him that, though expression of resentment may be difficult at first, it becomes progressively easier with practice. It usually does not take long for the patient to begin to perform the required behavior, although some need much initial exhortation and repeated promptings. Gradually the patient becomes able to behave assertively in progressively more exacting circumstances and reports a growing feeling of ease in all relevant situations. A conditioned inhibition of the anxiety responses is clearly developing, presumably on the basis of their repeated reciprocal inhibition—a process in all respects parallel to that involved in the overcoming of animal neuroses, as described in Chapter 4.

The operations involved in this method of therapy are closely analogous to the therapeutic procedure that succeeded in some of our neurotic cats (Chapter 4). These animals, having refused pellets of meat dropped in front of them in the experimental cage, did eat if the pellets were conveyed to them by the human hand. The explanation given was that the hand had become conditioned to evoke approach responses to food because food had been routinely given to them by the human hand in their living cages. These approach tendencies summated with the approach tendencies evoked by the food itself, achieving in some cases a total strength sufficient to overcome the anxiety-associated inhibition. Now consider the patient who has been chronically inhibited by fear from expressing resentment toward people who take advantage of him. When the therapist, having explained in a simple way the reciprocal inhibition principle, points to the need for assertiveness, he both instigates new behavior and counters old prohibitions, inducing in the patient an action tendency that, aroused on the next relevant occasion, summates with the resentment, so that assertive action may now take place. Such action leads to reciprocal inhibition of anxiety responses, and this results in conditioned inhibition of the anxiety-response habit in this particular kind of interpersonal situation.

The following are the details of procedure by which, typically, assertive behavior is instigated. It will previously have been established partly from the history and partly from the answers on the Willoughby schedule that the patient is fearful in at least some of his dealings with others. Other evidence of fears in interpersonal situations is elicited by asking how he behaves when, for example, (1) he notices after leaving a shop that he has been given short change, (2) he discovers that a garment bought two days previously is faulty, (3) someone pushes in front of him in a queue, (4) there is something wrong with the food he has ordered in a restaurant. If he has been ineffectual in such situations—unable, for instance, to return a faulty garment—I explain how unadaptive fears are at the bottom of this ineffectualness and draw the parallel between this and the child's fear of the chest of drawers in the illustration previously given (p. 111). I then make a small speech in somewhat the following words:

"These fears can be overcome if they are opposed by another, stronger emotion. I shall demonstrate this to you by means of an example or two. Suppose a university student goes to a meeting of a society that he has joined because of real interest in its field. A professor has been invited to lecture at this meeting, and afterward, at discussion time, the student wishes to get up and ask a question or make a criticism. Although he has no doubts about the good sense of what he has to say, at the very thought of saying it his heart thumps, his knees tremble, and his hands sweat. This fear is clearly unadaptive as, objectively, no dire consequences could reasonably be expected to ensue from his speaking. There are two possible outcomes— he may get up and speak in spite of his fear, or he may remain in his seat. He will in fact speak only if the motivation to speak is stronger than the fear. Just as fear tends to suppress the impulse to speak, this impulse, whenever it can be expressed, suppresses the fear to some extent and, through so doing, slightly weakens the habit of reacting with fear to this particular kind of situation. If the student should repeatedly speak on such occasions, this fear will be progressively weakened and eventually disappear. By contrast, another fearful student who at the same meetings has been frozen to his seat will not have improved at all.*

"My second example brings us nearer home, for it comes from the history of a patient. A university student of 19 came for treatment in a most unhappy state. For years he had been almost continuously tense and depressed, could make no friends, and although highly intelligent, had been unable to pass his examinations. I want to show you how, by expressing

---

* It is important to understand that the student's fear is weakened, not merely because he speaks, but because the speaking involves opposing to the fear another, contrary impulse of feeling. Other circumstances can be imagined in which the student might speak without being benefited. Suppose, for example, that before the meeting, somebody had threatened him with a thrashing if he did not speak. Motivated to speak by such a threat he would in effect be driven by fear into a situation itself fearful and this would if anything strengthen his fearful reactivity.

anti-anxiety feelings in his relationship with his stepmother he overcame some important fears. She was a most domineering woman who constantly criticized him. In a typical outburst she might say: 'Why can't you pass your exams? Johnny Jones next door always passes.' To this the patient would react in one of three ways—he would try to defend himself, or sulk, or have an outburst of impotent rage—for example, he once smashed the dinner plates on the floor and on another occasion pulled the electric bell out of the dining room ceiling.* These three patterns of behavior, although widely different in themselves, are all expressive of the anxious, helpless feeling that this woman aroused in him. In any situation where a person is unjustly attacked, he feels *anger and resentment*, no matter what other reactions he may be having at the same time. My young patient had no difficulty in recognizing this to be true of himself in his encounters with his stepmother.

"I told him that by giving outward expression to this anger, he would on each occasion simultaneously suppress some of the anxiety that she aroused in him. He soon became well able to express his anger against her, so that, for example, if he were *now* attacked on the theme of 'Johnny Jones next door' his response might be 'You say this sort of thing because you are jealous of Mrs. Jones. Isn't that so?' This was hitting back, expressing his resentment at the stepmother's attack. Practice of appropriate counterattack against her gradually led to a complete removal of all his fears of her, an increase in confidence with other people, a diminishing general level of anxiety. He became a very well-adjusted person, and mainly on the basis of this kind of direct action."

Ways of applying the lesson of this speech to the patient's own situation are now discussed in detail. As much pressure as seems necessary is applied to motivate the actual performance of the requisite behavior in appropriate circumstances. Not only is he told that it will result in his feeling better, but his attention is focused on the enormity of any injustices being perpetrated on him, and in addition he is shown how undignified and unattractive to others it is for him to behave in his accustomed spineless way. These pressures lead to the desired behavior in most cases, though not always immediately. In subsequent interviews he will be asked to recount his experiences in relevant situations, and his handling of them will be discussed and corrected.

Obviously, in advising assertive behavior, the therapist must be dis-

---

* Insofar as this third pattern of behavior (petulant rage) contains elements of assertiveness, it may in itself have some therapeutic effects, but only transitorily. Being misdirected, it not only fails to deal with the adversary but strengthens her moral position. Awareness of this, combined with remorse at the violence itself, reconstitutes the patient's original anxiety.

creet. He should advise it only when the anxiety evoked in the patient by the other person concerned is unadaptive—in other words, when the anxiety occurs even though no unpleasant repercussions can reasonably be expected to follow from making a stand. For nothing can be gained, and sensitivity may even be increased, if the patient's assertiveness should meet with a swift and sharp punishment. For example, however much a person may resent his boss's surly manner, it would in most cases be foolhardy to give frank expression to this resentment.

But it is quite frequently possible to express aggression indirectly, through gaining control of an interpersonal relationship by means subtler than overt assertiveness. One way of doing this is to play upon the other person's known or presumed sensitivities without seeming to intend to do so. Many of the "ploys" or gambits described in Stephen Potter's amusing books on *Lifemanship* and *Gamesmanship* are examples of this, and I do not hesitate to recommend these books to patients who seem likely to profit from reading them.

A journalist gave his reactions to the therapeutic use of assertive responses in the following words:

I have been given the assignment of winning emotional victories in daily life. To win them involves a new attitude on my part to people. It means that I no longer regard them as being more important than myself. It means that I am no longer overanxious to please them just because they are other people. Public opinion? I represent it just as much as any one person. This is the important discovery I made—and it is a satisfying one emotionally. Other people's opinions and feelings count—*but so do mine.*

This does not mean that I have become aggressive, unpleasant, or inconsiderate to other people. That would merely be putting myself in a false position. Emotionally I would gain nothing—unless, of course, it was a situation in which aggression was required. This new method of coping with interpersonal situations simply boils down to doing the things which, if you were an onlooker watching the situation, would seem fair and fitting.

A kind of "psychodrama" is employed in the consulting room with certain patients who find it unusually difficult to commence the practice of assertive behavior in their day-to-day relationships (patients who, as previously noted, tend to have low self-sufficiency scores). Unlike Moreno's original psychodrama, it does not consist of making the patient act out his *existing* attitudes in the relationships. Instead, with the therapist taking the role of some person to whom the patient ordinarily reacts with excessive anxiety, the patient is directed to behave in a new, usually aggressive manner, in the expectation that thereby the anxiety that tends to be evoked will be reciprocally inhibited. If the patient deals successfully with this relatively mild "play" situation, it is a steppingstone toward dealing with the real person. Another application of the idea of psychodrama is found with people who become very tense when "put under pressure" by the demands of others, as, for example, when being questioned. Tension from this source can often be diminished by giving the patient fairly difficult arithmetical problems and then "barracking" him while he is trying to work them out, *having told him beforehand that the more he is pestered the more he is to delay giving his answer.* It is easy to see how the new reaction pattern may inhibit the old.

It is interesting to consider what part assertive behavior plays in the therapeutic methods of other writers. The only one of these who has clearly realized its worth as a therapeutic instrument is Salter, whose book (1950), already mentioned, contains much of practical value, although its somewhat flamboyant style has dissuaded some from giving it serious attention. Herzberg (1945), in advocating the prescription of specific tasks in the life situation in opposition to individual neurotic tendencies, also refers to assertion as a useful "counteracting impulse" (p. 27), but understandably makes little use of it since the character of the tasks he assigns depends upon psychoanalytic interpretations. Some other psychoanalysts also use assertive behavior at times without being aware of its central curative role. One of these is Wolberg. He presents a detailed record (1948, Vol II., pp. 366–501) of his interviews with a man of 30 who complained of having persistent headaches and other symptoms since the age of 16. In the course of the 14 interviews there is clear evidence that the majority of the forward steps made by the patient are preceded by assertive acts (which the therapist persistently encourages, though often in a circumlocutory way, hedged around with psychoanalytic theorizing). Yet, "re-education utilizing psychoanalytic insight" is given the credit for the success of the treatment. Regarding another patient whom he has (pp. 197–98) enabled to behave assertively with the aid of hypnotic suggestions, Wolberg ascribes the "remarkable change in the patient's patterns of adjustment" that ensued not to the anxiety-inhibiting effect of assertion but to "the gradual realization [!] that he could ask for things and not be rejected, that he could get angry and show others that he was resentful without being hurt." Patients may easily *realize* that they can safely express anger but do not overcome their anxieties unless they actually *express* the anger.

There can be little doubt that even those analysts (and therapists of other convictions) who do not explicitly encourage assertion (and perhaps even oppose it) nevertheless owe some of their favorable therapeutic results to their patients behaving assertively either because this seems to be a logical implication of some of the discussions with the therapist or because of a feeling of support that the therapeutic relationship gives. Some illuminating examples of therapeutically effective assertiveness manifested in the face of strong prohibitions from the therapist are to be found in a paper by Seitz (1953) on the treatment of 25 patients with psycho-cutaneous excoriation syndromes. He encouraged his patients to express *during interviews* their hostile feeling toward other people. At the same time he discouraged them from expressing aggression in their life situations, i.e., "acting out," but 11 out of the 25 did so to some extent. *In these 11 alone the skin became clear*; in the remainder it was unimproved. It is of particular interest that when patients who had "acted out" were rapped on the knuckles by Seitz for doing so and in consequence became more restrained outside the consulting room, there was a tendency to relapse. Expression of aggression during the therapy hour was not an effective substitute. Clearly, declaiming to the therapist, however vigorously, about one's friends and relations can scarcely inhibit the anxieties they arouse as effectively as opposing these people in the flesh. It is indeed lamentable that Seitz should have been so preoccupied with psychoanalytic dogmas that the lessons of his excellent study entirely escaped him.

ILLUSTRATIONS OF THE PSYCHOTHERAPEUTIC USE
OF ASSERTIVE RESPONSES

It is not often that I use assertive responses on their own, but they play either an exclusive or a dominating role in each of the cases given below. The first of these cases will be presented in some detail, interview by interview, the others more briefly.

Case 1.

This case illustrates the use of two kinds of assertive behavior—aggressive and affectionate—in an insecure individual who had anxious obsessions as well as a specific reactive obsession (see Chapter 6). Relaxation under hypnosis was also used to a small extent. There were, as a rule, wide intervals between interviews, because the patient lived several hundred miles away.

First interview (August 24, 1950). Mr. W. was a commercial traveler for a textile firm. In the consulting room he was very tense and kept shifting in his chair. Nervous since childhood, he felt even now inferior to other people and anxious when dealing with them, going out of his way a great deal to do things calculated to win favor. He was given to brooding over unpleasant events, and dwelt particularly on the fact that while he was overseas on military service, his wife—then his fiancée—had had an affair with another man and had confessed to this only after their marriage. Since puberty he had had exceptionally strong pleasurable sexual feelings on watching buxom women and had indulged in fantasies about them as much as possible in spite of increasing feelings of guilt about doing so since his marriage.

The first session was devoted mainly to obtaining details of his early life. He was an only child who had been brought up on a farm. His parents hated each other and lived together only for his sake, divorcing as soon as he turned 21. He was quite fond of his father and used to go hunting with him sometimes. On these occasions, he would hear bitter complaints against his mother. His mother loved the limelight. She tried to give other people the impression that she was devoted to her child but was very short with him when they were alone. She was the center of some very unpleasant incidents. On one occasion she terrified him by threatening, knife in hand, to kill the three of them. On another occasion, when he was 12 years old, he had remonstrated with her when, at a wedding, she had been trying very blatantly to gain attention. She had snapped at him, "I hate you. You're not the sort of son I want," wounding him deeply. At the age of 8 he had been sent to a boarding school where he was even more miserable than at home. He was bullied a great deal, and the school was so badly run that it was closed by government order when he was 15 years old. He spent his last two high school years at a day school where he was quite happy and did reasonably well scholastically. After various short-lived commercial jobs, he obtained employment as a traveler for a leather firm and had a fair measure of success. Two years later, when World War II broke out, he enlisted in the South African army, became an air gunner, and saw a good deal of active service, which he invariably found fearful. Since his discharge from the army in 1944 he had been traveling for his present textile firm and had built up a very good clientele.

Second interview (September 5, 1950). In this session I took his sexual history. Although Mr. W. had from the age of puberty found erotic pleasure in staring at buxom women of all ages, he had not dated girls until he was 20. Thereafter he went out with many women, enjoying coitus with some of them. But the first buxom woman he ever took out was Jill, who was later to become his wife and whom he met at the age of 24. While he was in Italy on military service, he observed that he could not be excited by any prostitute who was not buxom. When he returned, this quality seemed to matter less. Jill had lost weight but was "still very well built." She attracted him only a little less strongly but he hoped that she would put on weight again. However, they got on very well together and their sexual relations were extremely satisfactory, although in the course of the years she became progressively thinner. In 1948, having largely completed the spadework of establishing commercial connections for his firm's goods, he had a good deal more free time and found himself reverting increasingly to his old habit of staring at buxom women. But there had been a growing reaction of guilt to this, so that now, if he saw one at a dance, his whole evening was disturbed.

Questioned about his mother's build, he said that she had been tall and slender. The only buxom females he could recall from his youth were three daughters of a family who lived on a farm a few miles away when he was about six years old. These girls were all in their late teens or older. The memory of them was a happy one. He had been much impressed by their warmth and had admired their family, which was all that his was not. The girls used to pay him some attention but did not in any way fondle him.

A year before coming for treatment he had had intercourse with a buxom girl, but had not found this as exciting or satisfying as intercourse with his wife. However, this girl was unattractive in other ways. He had not made any real effort to make love to really attractive buxom girls because he was very much afraid of being found out, despite the fact that his wife had told him that she would have no objection to his having intercourse with another woman.

Third interview (September 6, 1950). Mr. W. began by mentioning his social and political views, and much of our time was spent discussing them. He became very emotional about the need for a real brotherhood of man and was very vociferous on the iniquities of the capitalist system and racial discrimination, but with little real knowledge of the issues. Since in South Africa it is most unusual for a European to have strong leftist views unless he is in some way concerned in the labor movement or intellectually immersed in such matters, it seemed likely that in his case these attitudes were an expression of his general feelings of insecurity. The remainder of the session was taken up with the Willoughby schedule. It showed marked reactivity to many of the questions indicating social anxiety. His total score was 59. His self-sufficiency as shown by the Bernreuter questionnaire was satisfactory—53 per cent.

Fourth interview (September 7, 1950—double period). On sitting down, Mr. W. stated that he had remembered a time when he was seven or eight years old, that his mother's sister had stayed with them for two years. She was a beautiful, buxom girl who had given him very much more attention than his mother ever had. Often she told him that his mother did not treat him right. One day she said she was leaving to get married, and he had been struck with grief. He expressed surprise that he had not remembered his association with this aunt when on previous occasions he tried to think of buxom women in his life, but agreed that the probable explanation was that he had been concentrating on a sexual context.

His wife's "affair" during their engagement chiefly preoccupied him when he was depressed, and in these circumstances it caused him intense pain. But he also dwelt upon it whenever he had been to some extent unfaithful, and then the thoughts had had a comforting character—"After all, there is nothing sacred about our marriage." He felt that his wife had really always been in love with the other man and never really with him. She had expressed the view that it was possible to love more than one person and had shown great pleasure when, in 1949, he had agreed to her meeting this man for a few hours at a railway station. When, on another occasion, someone had brought the news that this man was married, she had shown great curiosity about his emotional reactions at the wedding. Mr. W. had then said in pique, but with an outward display of detachment, "Why don't you try to sleep with him?" and she, manifestly delighted, had commended him on his understanding, and had subsequently on more than one occasion said that she would have intercourse with this man again if the opportunity arose. Mr. W. went on to say that from the beginning of the marriage he had felt that his wife was not in love with him and had married him on the rebound. She had seemed more unreservedly affectionate in the early days of their engagement. Then he said, "As a matter of fact she had intercourse with him in January and again last week."

At this stage, I attempted to give Mr. W. a perspective on what he had told me and to indicate some implications of it. "We must not overestimate your wife's part in your unhappiness. You were a very anxious person long before you met her. It is likely, though, that if you had felt sure of her complete acceptance of you, your anxieties would have been lessened. In due course we shall consider how to improve your marital situation. But first we must apply ourselves to the main source of your anxieties— other people. You become anxious when they disapprove of you, or even if there is a possibility that they may, in all sorts of curcumstances in which their opinions cannot make any real difference to you. Suppose, for example, that while out visiting, you want to express a political viewpoint but do not do so because Mr. X. may think less of you. In reality you could not be harmed by his low opinion. In failing to express your view, however, *you are expressing anxiety*, and so keeping up the strength of your anxiety habit. If, on the contrary, you were to express it, the feeling behind it would force down the anxiety to some extent, weakening the anxiety habit."

I followed this by giving examples of the therapeutic use of assertive responses. He said that he had no difficulty in asserting himself with customers. I responded: "It is in the social sphere that your behavior is deficient and it is there that I want to see you make a start." We began to consider in more detail the kinds of social behavior in which he found himself disturbed. He almost invariably felt tense when out visiting. He was persistently disturbed at being watched from the side, and the more so the larger the audience and the less familiar to him the individuals who comprised it. Sometimes tension mounted so rapidly that after about an hour he felt that he wanted to go home. Similarly at business conferences he would be very anxious for the others present to approve of his remarks. I wound up the interview by saying, "What I expect from you is to stand up for your legitimate human rights, to express your views as clearly and as forcefully as possible no matter how critical of you other people may appear to be. Stop being on the defensive, and stop apologizing for yourself."

Fifth interview (September 30, 1950). Mr. W. reported that he was standing up to people better but nevertheless still felt tense most of the time in company. But there were exceptions. The previous Monday evening when several commercial travelers were congregated in the bar lounge of a hotel, one of them had become abusive and Mr. W. had called him to order. He had been very pleased with himself and felt quite buoyant afterward. He was feeling rather freer in some aspects of social activities, visiting only people whom it suited him to visit and departing when he felt so inclined.

When I broached the topic of his condonement of his wife's extramarital activities with her old boy friend, Mr. W. said that he did not like it but wanted his wife to feel that he was "too big" to be affected by that sort of thing. I replied, "If you had not been so passively permissive about the matter, your wife would have been less keen on her meetings with this man. You must tell her frankly that you dislike the association." He said, "As a matter of fact my wife has often complained that I don't really love her, because I don't display much affection or jealousy." Then after a pause he went on, "As we are on the subject, I suppose I'd better tell you that Jill has arranged to meet this man this very evening." I said, "This is an excellent opportunity to climb down from your pedestal of godlike superiority. Go now and tell her that your behavior has been dictated not by your true feelings but by some abstract principles that you now realize to be wrong. Tell her she's your wife, that you love her and are not prepared to share her."

Sixth interview (October 1, 1950). Mr. W. took action with his wife the way I suggested. He said to her, "I've been thinking things over and I've decided that your relationship with this friend of yours must come to a stop." To this she replied, "It's about time. You're jealous at last." She then canceled her arrangements with her friend and spent a happy day with her husband. Mr. W. said that he felt much relieved—happier than for years.

He said that for years he had had a fear of dropping off to sleep, so that it had usually taken him a long time to get to sleep, but in the past month, since the interviews had begun, his fear had decreased and he had fallen asleep much more easily.

He was now hypnotized by the light-fixation method. He entered rather a deep trance in which suggestions were given that he would feel very relaxed and that the relaxation would persist when he left the room. I also suggested that on future days he would automatically become relaxed whenever he wanted to be so. When he woke from the trance he said that throughout its duration he had been aware of nothing besides my voice and his bodily sensations, which were the most pleasant he had ever experienced.

Seventh interview (November 4, 1950). Mr. W. said that in the month past he had made consistent efforts to assert himself but had "slipped up at times." He was aware of far more peace of mind and self-confidence than before. In company he was pleasing himself to an ever-increasing extent, was feeling much less out of place, and less conscious of what other people might be thinking. Where in the past he would be "extra nice" to offensive people, he had now taken to ignoring them. At a party at his own house, for the first time, he had not run around in circles trying to help everybody, but had been casually pleasant and, he felt, a much more successful host. I commended him on his accomplishments.

He still looked at buxom women but had less "afterthought" about it and little consequent anxiety. He was enjoying his wife's company more than ever in every respect. Sleep had entirely ceased to be a problem.

At this point I was called away from the room and asked him to relax. When I returned ten minutes later, he was fast asleep. He woke feeling very pleasantly relaxed. I induced a medium trance by the light-fixation method and gave posthypnotic suggestions regarding continued relaxation in life situations. On waking he said that he felt very relaxed and contented.

Eighth interview (January 31, 1951). Mr. W. said he was feeling quite well and happy almost all the time. At a large conference in Cape Town which was attended by members of all the branches of his firm, he had felt much less nervous than ever in the past. At the beginning of the first meeting there had been some nervousness for which at first he had been unable to account, but had subsequently related it to the proximity of two men whom he knew to be hostile to him. His enjoyment of life was continuing to increase. In the past he had not dared to tell jokes at parties, but now he was able to do so with ease and with pleasure.

He said that the amount of agitation he felt before acts of assertiveness had progressively been declining in the past months, but had not quite disappeared. He was incomparably calmer than in the old days. The remainder of the interview was devoted to discussing methods of improved handling of some specific situations.

Ninth interview (September 10, 1951). Mr. W. said that he was "really getting a kick out of life." He was socially more liked and more in demand than before. However, there were still certain circumstances in which he was nervous—when he felt that he ought to attack people who were bigger and stronger than himself in circumstances where he might be physically attacked. I told him that these were circumstances in which to attack would be foolhardy, circumstances in which nervousness was perfectly adaptive. He had joined a lodge and was doing some public speaking with increasing confidence. In company he no longer minded displaying his attraction to plump girls, but when watching them from his car he still had some feeling of guilt, though much less than before.

At this interview, a year after his first visit, the Willoughby questionnaire was applied to him for the second time. His score had fallen from 59 to 26 and individual answers revealed that there was still appreciable excessive sensitivity to other people, though much less than in the past.

Tenth interview (September 6, 1953). Mr. W. had continued to improve since the last time he was seen, two years previously. He had no difficulty in expressing himself aggressively when necessary. He did not mind conferences in the least and expressed himself well and without anxiety. He still was attracted to buxom women but had at no time gone beyond mild petting. He felt that if he could have a thoroughgoing experience with one of them, it would remove that "mystery." He had fantasies about these women quite often but without any guilt feeling. If anybody watched him staring from his car at one of them, he felt very slight guilt. He was not uncomfortable in any other situation whatever. People continued to remark on how much he had changed. He regarded himself as a happy man.

He continued to get on very well with his wife in every respect. He no longer gave a single thought to her premarital or postmarital unfaithfulness.

His wife, who had been in the waiting room, was called in for a few minutes. She stated that in the past two years he had been a pleasure to live with.

Comment. This patient's over-all improvement was very striking indeed. The fact that distance imposed long intervals between visits made it particularly easy to judge how much improvement was related to assertive behavior in life situations and how much to the interviews as such. He felt better after each interview but related further degrees of improvement between interviews to successful assertion. The persistence of a strong positive attitude to buxom women continued to be a source of intrusion in his life but the secondary guilt feelings had greatly diminished and the intrusions had been less frequent and almost entirely pleasant. The guilt feelings could have been completely disposed of by systematic desensitization (see Chapter 9). The attraction these women held for him could have been removed only by some kind of aversion therapy (see Chapter 12), which not only seemed unwarranted in the circumstances but also harbored the danger of affecting through generalization his positive feelings toward his wife.

Case 2

Miss G., a very attractive woman of 28, came for help in acute distress at her lover's growing coolness toward her—following the pattern of numerous previous love affairs. Having gained a man's interest, she would at once abandon herself to him and adopt an attitude of extreme dependence and submission. He would become increasingly contemptuous and after a time reject her completely.

She had spent her childhood in an unstable, uneasy atmosphere with a younger sister and brother. Her father was an amateur philosopher who preached peace and brotherhood but gave vent to frequent unreasonable fits of violent temper sometimes with physical brutality toward his son. Her mother was very possessive and jealous, and nagged and shouted a great deal. Miss G. had always been at the top of her class at school, which she had greatly enjoyed and felt to be a haven from home. Financial difficulties had forced her to leave at 15 to become a shorthand-typist.

In general she lacked assurance, was very dependent, and practically never free from feelings of tension and anxiety. Her Willoughby score was 45, reflecting very considerable neuroticism. Her Bernreuter self-sufficiency score was 34 per cent—distinctly on the low side. A year previously she had terminated a two-year course of psychoanalysis, which had benefited her somewhat. She came to me only because her analyst was not available, and during the first few interviews she repeatedly expressed doubt regarding the value of my nonanalytic treatment.

At her fifth interview she stated that she "felt very good" for a few hours after each interview and then became very anxious, feeling that she had "no ability to take any kind of initiative." At this interview the unadaptiveness of her anxieties and the rationale of the reciprocal inhibition principle were explained to her, and she left feeling optimistic. At the next interview she was told how to behave with firmness and take independent courses of action with her lover. She was also shown how to counterattack her nagging mother and to deal with her boss and other people who easily upset her. Through appropriate action she gradually developed a feeling of mastery, both at home and at work.

Although her lover was obviously not genuinely interested in her, Miss G.'s emotional involvement with him was so great that it was difficult for her at first to behave toward him consistently according to prescription. Each failure upset her. The turning point came after the ninth interview when he approached her to lend him £10 ($28). *She refused without explanation and without permitting discussion,* and was left with a profound feeling of triumph. Within a week she was able to terminate the association finally—with dignity and satisfaction.

In the meantime, another beau had commenced to pursue her. She made an effort to be firm and to be guided by her own wishes, but one evening she permitted herself to be seduced although clearly aware that she was motivated by a fear of not pleasing. Recounting this at the eleventh interview, she expressed some disappointment, but I praised her for the measure of her success after so short a time under therapy.

During the week that followed, she did better. When she went out with her previous week's seducer, she did not let him make love to her at all and noted with surprise that this made him more keen on her. She also went out with a divorcé who took her to his apartment "to play music"—in vain! Taking her home, he apologized for treating her as "cheap"—also to her surprise. She was no longer upset by the tantrums and nagging of her mother, which had been greatly reduced in response to Miss G.'s assertiveness. However, she felt ill at ease when she had to spend "too many evenings" at home.

At her thirteenth interview she reported a further gain of control over minor sexual situations. She said that she was making more rapid progress than ever—felt increasingly constructive and decreasingly anxious. After this interview she went on holiday and returned six weeks later to say that she had made continued efforts to control interpersonal situations and was feeling much more stable emotionally. She was much better poised and had been a social success for the first time in her life. She no longer felt, as in the past, that it was important to go out a lot. On holiday she had met a man who attracted her, and now her feelings had an adult, independent character. After handling many difficulties admirably, she married him three months later. Her Willoughby score had dropped to 17. She had 14 interviews in all, and two and a half years later was reported to be a happily married mother.

Case 3

In May 1952 a 31-year-old clerk was referred to me for treatment of a severe stutter which had begun at the age of five. Almost every sentence was repeatedly interrupted by the stutter, and each interruption was marked by violent facial contortions. He was worse during any "unhappiness, worry, uncertainty, or work under pressure." The first three interviews were devoted to history-taking and personality inventories. A number of causally significant past events were narrated—without therapeutic benefit. His Willoughby score was 41. There were a great many interpersonal situations that could arouse anxiety, and it was hypothesized that to the extent that these lost their ability to upset him, the stutter would disappear.

At the fourth interview I described to him how neurotic reactions are conditioned and explained the reciprocal inhibition principle of therapy. He said that he frequently endured aggression from others for long periods and then exploded. I told him that he had rights as well as duties and pointed out the emotional tone of helplessness in his delayed rage reactions, emphasizing the need for insults to be rebuked as soon as possible if real mastery of situations was to be gained.

Three days later he reported that he had been less permissive to his assistants at work and had insisted on their getting things done without delay. However, he had found it difficult to be firm consistently. I assured him that practice would produce consistency. He had also for the first time asked his wife to help him with work he had brought home from the office.

Four days later he gave the following example of counteranxiety expressive behavior. While playing solo whist with some friends, he had made an error, for which his companions derided him, upsetting him so that he was left trembling. After a while he realized his inner annoyance and answered back sharply, soon to find that his trembling had disappeared completely. In the past he would have remained completely passive and downtrodden in such a situation. At work he had taken no nonsense and was conscious of a decreased level of tension. But there was one person at the office who had always particularly discomfited him—a spinster of 48, Miss P., who was in the approximate position of general foreman of the business. She was very bossy, often in a subtle way; sometimes she made him uncomfortable by criticizing his work, often placed him under stress to finish a given piece of work, and at times interrupted him with trifles when he was busy. He used to be greatly irritated by this behavior, but suppressed any outward manifestations of this irritation. I urged him to express his feelings to this woman, using discretion where necessary.

The next week he reported further improvement in his control of situations. He had made especially good progress with his boss, bringing all points of difference into the open and refusing to let himself worry about what the boss might be thinking. When the latter had querulously asked him whether he had sent off a certain routine letter, he replied, "I send this letter routinely once a week. If you want it sent more often, all you have to do is tell me." He observed that his speech was much better when standing up for his rights than when cringing. During this interview, he stated that his stutter was particularly bad on the telephone. This was suggested as a good situation for him to use the relaxation in which I had begun to train him.

During June and July, he came for interviews at fortnightly intervals. He had made further progress, although setbacks occurred now and then. He continued to find Miss P. particularly difficult to handle, and I suggested that he try to gain control by exploiting her anxieties. Meanwhile his speech on the telephone had improved a great deal.

Between August 1952 and January 1953 he came at monthly intervals. Apart from a few anxious weeks during October, bound up with the expense of necessary alterations to his house, he made steady progress. From September onward he was beginning to cope with Miss P. and in January said she was no longer any trouble to him at all. He then stated that he was "doing pretty well." He had dealt adequately with such few tension situations as had arisen. During the interviews there was very little stuttering indeed. His final two interviews took place in March and in May, respectively. He felt completely at ease with Miss P. and could speak to her without any stuttering. He had a general feeling of inner freedom and his speech was almost invariably good. Only with his boss did he sometimes stutter a little.

When I met this patient by chance in April 1955 he spoke rapidly and without the slightest suggestion of a stutter. He said that in the past two years he had had practically no trouble with his speech and had been happy in his relationships with others.

Sexual Responses

These responses, of course, are mainly of use when anxiety responses have been conditioned to various aspects of sexual situations. When very high degrees of anxiety conditioning have produced a complete inhibition of sexual responsiveness, other measures, such as systematic desensitization (p. 139) have to be employed. But very often the sexual inhibition is partial and varies according to variations in definable properties of sexual situations. The patient is told that he must on no account perform sexually unless he has an unmistakable, positive desire to do so, for otherwise he may very well consolidate, or even extend his sexual inhibitions.

There are occasional patients of either sex in whom so high a degree of anxiety has been conditioned to individual women (or men) or classes of women (or men) that the mildest embrace or even close proximity may produce great disturbance; and if there is pervasive anxiety, as may be expected in patients so sensitive, its level is raised. Such a patient is instructed to expose himself only to sexual situations in which pleasurable feelings are felt exclusively or very predominantly. The decision regarding the suitability of a situation is made *on the basis of the feelings experienced when the situation is in prospect.* The women who can still arouse the patient in a desirable way invariably have clearly definable characteristics. He is told to seek out such women and when in the company of one of them to "let himself go" as freely as the circumstances allow. If he is able to act according to plan, he experiences a gradual increase in sexual responsiveness to the kind of situation of which he has made use, with generalization to sexual situations of other kinds. The range of situations in which love-making may occur is thus progressively extended as the anxiety potentials of stimuli diminish, and at each extension these potentials diminish further. This may well be called a *virtuous circle.*

In cases of the above type the anxiety-evoking stimuli belong to other-than-sexual aspects of the sex object. In other much more frequent cases anxiety is evoked by specifically sexual stimuli. Although complete or partial impotence or frigidity is practically invariable in these patients, sexual feeling responses are evokable in them in suitable circumstances. The manner of use of these sexual responses varies, but when the anxiety is closely associated with coital performance, a typical procedure that is usually extremely effective is on the following lines.

The patient is told to inform his sexual partner (quoting the therapist if necessary) that his sexual difficulties are due to absurd but automatic fears in the sexual situation, and that he will overcome them if she will help him, i.e., if she will participate on a few occasions in situations of great sexual closeness without expecting intercourse or exerting pressure toward it. He is to ask her to be patient and affectionate and not to criticize. Assured of her cooperation, he is to lie in bed with her in the nude in a perfectly easy, relaxed way, and thereafter to do just what he really feels like doing *and no more.* He has no duty at any stage to reach any criterion of performance. It is found that from one love session to the next there is a decrease in anxiety and an increase in sexual excitation and therefore in the extent of the caresses to which the patient feels impelled. He has increasingly strong erections, and usually after a few sessions coitus is accomplished and then gradually improves.

ILLUSTRATIONS OF THE PSYCHOTHERAPEUTIC USE
OF SEXUAL RESPONSES

Case 4: A Case of Recent Impotence

This case of impotence due to anxieties related to the coital situation is of particular interest because a credible explanation of the upset is ap-

parent and because treatment by the method described above was entirely
successful after a single interview. The patient was a young doctor who
despite somewhat less than the average amount of premarital sexual experience had on several occasions had successful and pleasurable intercourse. When he had married three months previously, he had known his
wife for a year, during which time he had frequently made love to her,
invariably with strong erections, but had never attempted intercourse because of objections on her part which he accepted without quibble. On
the wedding night, partly because he had just recovered from an attack of
influenza and partly because of the strain and excitement of the wedding,
combined with rather excessive alcohol consumption, he had felt "washed
out." Alone at last with his wife in the bridal suite, he had not had his
usual erection, and even when intercourse was imminent his erection was
poor and became even worse after he had rushed out of bed to get a con-
dom. Ejaculation occurred the moment his penis came into contact with
the vulva. He was greatly embarrassed, slept poorly, and the next day felt
very low. He was very worried at what had happened and made no further
attempt at intercourse for two days. At his next attempt, he again failed
to get a satisfactory erection and again ejaculated very prematurely, becoming as a result even more alarmed. The next day he made two attempts
at intercourse of which the second was fairly satisfactory and broke the
hymen. During the rest of the honeymoon, coitus was sometimes successfully performed and sometimes not, but he had some feeling of uncertainty
on each occasion. In the meantime, his wife was responding very well,
sometimes having orgasms even when he failed to perform well. On returning from the honeymoon, the patient found that at every attempt at
coitus ejaculation was very premature. After a fortnight, he saw his family
physician, who diagnosed nervous strain. The patient said that this did
not seem reasonable to him as he felt very fit, and except for the sexual
problems, which did not occupy his mind for much of the day, he was particularly calm and unharried. The physician, apparently, was convinced
by this argument and recommended a course of testosterone injections,
which merely made the patient feel quite flat sexually. He visited the
physician again, who this time put him on a mixture of androgens and
estrogens together with a general tonic and said, in effect, "Don't worry."
Since then his sexual performance had improved a little but was still far
from satisfactory, and on each occasion he was "on tenterhooks in case
his erections should fail." On several occasions, his penis had, in fact,
become flaccid before entry, and usually he had no erection at all during
preliminary love play.

I discussed the physiology of coitus with him and pointed out the interfering effects of anxiety upon performance. Since erection depends pri-

marily upon parasympathetic activity and ejaculation upon sympathetic activity, it is easy to see that anxiety may both inhibit erection and cause ejaculation to occur prematurely. I instructed him to lie in bed with his wife in a relaxed way and to attempt intercourse only if he had an unequivocal positive impulse to do so.

A week later he telephoned to say that the plan suggested had "worked like a charm" and that his sex life had become entirely normal. Six months later he told me that he had had no further trouble whatever in the sexual sphere.

Case 5: A Case of Long-Standing Impotence

Mr. V. was a 40-year-old architect who complained of very premature ejaculations. He had first become sexually aware at about 14 and had masturbated to an average extent, with no feelings of guilt. At 16 he began to be attracted by girls, and at 17, in his first year at the university, he had taken out a large number of them without any emotional involvements. At the age of 22, just after graduating, he had formed his first intimate association with a woman of his own age with whom he had got on very well and had frequent satisfactory sexual intercourse. The association had ended three years later when he left his employer to start his own practice in another town. There he had soon met another girl of whom he became very fond and began an association which lasted about seven years. He had at no time attempted coitus with this girl because he was certain that he was never going to marry her on account of religious differences. In this period Mr. V. had casual intercourse with other women fairly often and quite satisfactorily. He had felt rather glad when his special girl friend decided to marry someone else.

In the years that followed, Mr. V. continued to have only casual sexual relations. Coitus on these occasions would at first last between half a minute and one minute, but when he got to know a girl better there could be up to four minutes of continuous movement. At the age of 36, four years before he came for treatment, he had no coitus for a year because he knew nobody who interested him enough. Then, one evening he attempted intercourse with a girl he met at a party and ejaculated before intromission could occur. Ever since, this had been Mr. V.'s invariable reaction in the coital situation. Two months before coming to me he had met Anne. He was strongly attracted to her and felt sure that he wanted to marry her. He had made love to her, but because of his premature ejaculations had used various excuses to avoid intercourse.

There were no other noteworthy features in his history. He was good at his work, and his social adjustment was good. The latter was reflected in a Willoughby score of 17.

At the fourth interview the reciprocal inhibition principle of psycho-therapy was explained to Mr. V. He was told that the coital situation itself could be put to therapeutic use, provided that he obtained Anne's coopera-tion. He was to tell her that whenever in the past after a long period of abstinence he had tried to resume sexual intercourse, he had had initial failures; thus, if she was patient, after putting up with a few intimate situa-tions without fulfillment she would find that everything would work out all right.

To enable him to reduce anxiety in the sexual situation, I now went on to show Mr. V. the first steps in progressive relaxation. Training in this occupied part of each of the six interviews of the next four weeks. During this period he was unable to summon the courage to make the prescribed approach to Anne on the subject of intercourse. I then increased my efforts to instigate him, giving examples of other cases, and telling him that even if there was complete failure during the first two or three attempts at inter-course, it would make no difference to the eventual outcome. He was not to make another appointment with me until he had something definite to report.

A month passed before I saw Mr. V. again. A fortnight earlier he had told Anne of his sexual difficulties, and since then had been in intimate sexual situations with her on three occasions. He had attempted inter-course on the first of these occasions, had been very nervous and failed. On the two subsequent occasions, he had had no sexual feeling and no erection. I pointed out that on the first occasion there should have been no thought of intercourse and that nothing more should have occurred than fairly mild caressing, and instructed him to confine himself to this at the next two or three occasions. When he returned a week later, he reported that they had several times made love in a mild way, fully clothed, and that there had been a progressive improvement in his sexual feeling and responses. On one occasion he had developed quite a good erection, but when, encouraged by this, they got into bed, it had weakened so that no attempt at intercourse had been made. I said it was clear that there was still far too much urgency about having successful intercourse. The idea of intercourse should be put into the background and he should just try to enjoy Anne and let things happen.

The following week Mr. V. reported having twice lain in bed with Anne in the nude without intercourse being intended. He had had several erec-tions of varying quality lasting about five minutes at a time. He felt rather less worried about the situation. I told him that if he were to get a good erection he should now try the effect of an increasing amount of manual stimulation from Anne. At the next week's interview, he stated that he had found Anne could handle his penis without causing ejaculation. On three nights sexual activity had been limited to this. He found that his erections now lasted very much longer and for short periods were really good. On the fourth love-making occasion, he had felt his erection sufficiently good after such handling to warrant attempting coitus. Intromission having succeeded, coitus lasted a minute and a half with movement most of the time. The previous night he had again made love but not having had a sufficiently good erection, had desisted from coitus. I praised him for this and suggested that the apparent retrogression was probably due to his trying too hard again on the basis of his successful coital act. He felt much happier about the whole situation and was convinced that he was well on the way to overcoming his anxiety about sexual failure.

I next saw Mr. V. a month later. He had been on a seaside holiday with Anne and had had successful intercourse with her on repeated occasions. Since their return a week previously they had thrice had intercourse. On the first occasion, there had been a slight degree of premature ejaculation, but on the other two, intercourse had lasted several minutes and was enjoyable to both. He announced his intention of marrying Anne the following month.

Eight months later, Mr. V. reported to me that he was happily married and the sexual situation was entirely satisfactory.

Relaxation Responses as Used by Jacobson

Reference has been made (p. 72) to the fact that deep muscle relaxation has autonomic effects antagonistic to those of anxiety. Jacobson (1938) was the first to make a careful study of the effects of deep relaxation and of the techniques by which it may be achieved. He reported its application to a large number of clinical cases. If we abstract from his tables (pp. 417, 419) those diagnoses indicating a neurotic basis—anxiety neurosis, cardiac neurosis, compulsion neurosis, phobia, tic, esophageal spasm, stammering, tremor, neurosis of bladder, and functional tachycardia—we find 23 cases, of which 21 were improved either "very markedly" or "markedly."

The essence of his method is to give patients intensive and prolonged training in the practice of relaxation, and then to get them to keep relaxing all muscles not in use (*differential relaxation*). His own words are worth quoting (pp. 81–83):

The use of relaxation in the recumbent position obviously is limited in its possibilities, if, when the patient is up and about for the day, we make no attempt to avoid continual symptoms of nervous hypertension. But how can this be accomplished? I faced the question, Is it possible for the ambulant patient to remain at his daily duties and affairs while at the same time something is being done to replace irritability and excitement with nervous quiet? . . . Can he learn to do essentials, yet omit non-essentials? make necessary movements, yet omit those which reveal irritability and excitement? . . . Investigations justify the belief that some degree of differential relaxation commonly takes place during reading, writing, and other customary activities, and can be specially cultivated, if desired, in patients. . . . *Differential relaxation accordingly means a minimum of tensions in the muscles requisite for an act along with the relaxation of other muscles.*

It can scarcely be doubted that Jacobson's good results must in some way be related to the extension of relaxation into the life situation, for, in contrast, physiotherapists who misguidedly give "relaxation sessions" as an end in themselves usually fail to produce any worth-while improvement in their tense and anxious patients. Jacobson did not realize the central importance of the anxiety-countering effects of relaxation in the treatment of neurosis, and explained his success on the theory that ". . . an excess of slight or incipient tensions or movements, some coordinated and with well marked function and some not, involving in many instances small but in others great caloric expenditure, seems from one standpoint to constitute the very essence of what is commonly called nervous disorder. From this standpoint, the effect of differential relaxation is to eliminate such elements of motor disorder" (pp. 99–100).

Apart from the nonspecific therapeutic effects of interviewing (p. 193) (from which Jacobson's patients are doubtless not immune) it would seem that his method succeeds because if a person can maintain differential relaxation all the time, he will obtain some measure of reciprocal inhibition of the effects of any anxiety-evoking stimuli he happens to encounter; and the repeated occurrence of such inhibitions will enable conditioned inhibition of the anxiety responses gradually to develop.

I give training in relaxation to the great majority of my patients, frequently including differential relaxation. The number of sessions in which I give actual training rarely exceeds seven, in contrast with the 100–200 sessions that Jacobson is prepared to allot to this end (1956). Nevertheless a small number of my patients learn to relax sufficiently well to be able to counter anxieties that arise from stimuli they come upon in the course of day-to-day living. The history of one such patient is given below. No doubt a greater number would benefit from more thorough training. The reason why I have not resorted to Jacobson's intensive program is that by the desensitization method described in the next chapter I have been able to overcome anxieties in far less than 100 sessions, on the basis of such relaxation as is attained by my brief method of training.

In teaching patients how to relax, I follow Jacobson's procedures in all essential respects. On the first training occasion, I explain to the patient that he is to learn relaxation because it has emotional effects directly opposing anxiety, which can be applied therapeutically both in life situations and in the consulting room. I then direct him to grip the arm of his chair with his left hand and to observe what sensations appear in his hand and his arm. The difference between muscle tension and other sensations is brought to his notice. Next, he successively pushes and pulls against me while I grip his left wrist, so that he becomes aware of muscle-tension feelings in biceps and triceps. I ask him, after this, to maintain tension in the biceps for about thirty seconds, giving the feeling his fullest attention, and then he gradually reduces the tension while I decrease my countertraction correspondingly. He is instructed to continue the "untensing activity" even after he has ceased to feel tension, for ten minutes or more. Most patients soon grasp the idea, and these then spend 15 to 20 minutes relaxing the forearm and arm muscles on both sides. Sensations of numbness or tingling in the hands are often reported spontaneously and are regarded as indicative of commencing relaxation. The patient is then asked to practice what he has learned for at least half an hour a day. At the next session I draw his attention to the muscles of his forehead and give him 10 or 15 minutes to "smooth it out," enjoining him to persist in trying to "let go further," even when it seems impossible to do so. Then we proceed to relaxation of the muscles of the other parts of the face. The apparent capacity of the patient decides the number of muscle groups to be covered at a session. The remaining groups are dealt with in the following order— jaw muscles, tongue and pharynx, extrinsic eye muscles, neck, shoulder, back, abdomen, and legs and thighs. Usually I also make use of the muscles of respiration, pointing out that with normal expiration there is an automatic relaxation of the muscles of inspiration and that awareness of this makes it possible to add a "quantum" of relaxation to other muscles in rhythmic coordination with expiration. Some patients find this very helpful. As a rule, instruction in relaxation is completed in five to seven lessons, devoting about half of a session to each lesson.

As stated above, relaxation after the manner of Jacobson, in the life situation, is therapeutically effective insofar as it comes into opposition with unadaptive anxiety responses. Since it would be plainly absurd in most day-to-day contexts for the patient to slump down in a state of complete bodily relaxation in order to inhibit anxiety, he has to be taught differential relaxation, the selective relaxation of those muscles that are not in use. Thus, while walking it is possible to relax arms and facial muscles; while sitting and talking, the muscles of the arms and legs. Very considerable autonomic effects can be obtained with the efficient relaxation of even limited muscle groups. The patient is encouraged to keep all muscles not in use relaxed all the time and to augment their relaxation when he is exposed to specific anxiety-evoking stimuli. For example, a patient who reacted with anxiety to churches and associated stimuli was told to relax as much as possible whenever she encountered such stimuli.

Although some very good individual results come from use of relaxation in the life situation, there is a theoretical limitation to its value, that is borne out by my experience. This is that there is not control of the relevant anxiety-evoking stimulus constellations. On the one hand, the patient may without warning be subjected to such strong evocation of anxiety that his available "relaxation power" is insufficient to inhibit it; on the other, the relevant anxiety-connected stimuli may simply not arise often enough at times convenient for optimal inhibition through relaxation. These disadvantages are avoided by the method described in the next chapter.

ILLUSTRATION OF THE USE OF RELAXATION
BY JACOBSON'S METHOD

Case 6

Early in 1951 a divorcée of 39 stated that from as far back as she could remember she had been nervous and hypersensitive and perpetually worried about the future. Many ordinary situations, such as overhearing others quarrel, constituted stresses for her, made her anxious and left her fatigued, and sometimes produced epigastric pain. For seven years she had persistently suffered from fibrositic backaches. Her symptoms had improved somewhat after her divorce, two years previously.

Her Willoughby score was 30.

She was encouraged to be more assertive and less subservient to the wishes of her friends. But her severest tensions arose from situations in which no direct action was possible, e.g., having visitors for dinner, hearing people shout, thinking about the future. From her seventh interview onward she was given lessons in relaxation. Her response was excellent. Through learning to relax she became acutely aware of tension and was "constantly pulling herself up." She was astonished at how easy it was for her to become calm through muscle relaxation. She deliberately calmed herself in an increasing range of situations, and their anxiety-evoking power waned and eventually disappeared. The patient had 13 interviews over four months, during which she entirely overcame her neurotic nervousness, and her Willoughby score dropped to 12. She was functioning well in all areas. Her fibrositis had disappeared completely after the first month. In a five-year follow-up there has been no recurrence, but, instead, consolidation.

9 | Systematic Desensitization

Based on Relaxation

Of the methods of therapy considered in this book the present parallels most closely the experimental procedure of feeding cats in the presence of increasing "doses" of anxiety-evoking stimuli (described in Chapter 4).

An anxiety hierarchy is a list of stimulus situations to which a patient reacts with graded amounts of anxiety. The most disturbing item is placed at the top of the list, the least disturbing at the bottom. These hierarchies provide a convenient framework for systematic desensitization, through relaxation, to increasing amounts of anxiety-evoking stimuli.*

The theory may be summarized like this: If a stimulus constellation made up of five equipotent elements $A_1A_2A_3A_4A_5$ evokes 50 units of anxiety response in an organism, proportionately less anxiety will be evoked by constellations made up of fewer elements. Relaxation that is insufficient to counter the 50 units of anxiety that $A_1A_2A_3A_4A_5$ evokes may be well able to inhibit the 10 units evoked by A_1 alone. Then if the anxiety evoked by A_1 is repeatedly inhibited through being opposed by relaxation, its magnitude will drop, eventually to zero. In consequence, a presentation of A_1A_2 will now evoke only 10 units of anxiety, instead of 20, and this will similarly undergo conditioned inhibition when opposed by relaxation. Through further steps along these lines the whole combination $A_1A_2A_3A_4A_5$ will lose its power to arouse any anxiety.

The raw data for a hierarchy are obtained in several ways. The patient's history frequently reveals a variety of situations to which he reacts with undue disturbance. Further areas of disturbance may be revealed by perusal of his answers to the Willoughby questionnaire. Then he is given the "homework" task of making up a list of everything he can think of that is capable of frightening, disturbing, distressing, or embarrassing him in any way, excepting, of course, situations that would frighten anybody, such

* A basic assumption underlying this procedure is that the response to the imagined situation resembles that to the real situation. Experience bears this out. People are anxious when they imagine stimuli that are fearful in reality. This is in keeping with Stone's observations (1955) in another context.

as meeting a hungry lion. Some patients bring back extensive inventories, others very scanty ones; and with the latter a good deal of time may have to be spent during interviews eliciting further items.

Confronted at last with anything between about 10 and 100 heterogeneous items, the therapist peruses them to see whether they belong to one or more thematic categories. If there is more than one theme, the items of each are grouped together. For example, one patient had a subdivision into enclosement, death, and bodily-lesion themes; another into social disapproval, disease, and aloneness; a third into trauma, death, and being in the limelight; a fourth into rejection and scenes of violence.

The subdivided list is now handed to the patient, who is asked to rank the items of each sublist in descending order according to the measure of disturbance he would have upon exposure to each. The rearranged list constitutes the hierarchical series that will be used in treatment. Modifications or additions may of course be made later.

At the first desensitization session the patient, already trained in relaxation, is hypnotized and in the trance is made to relax as deeply as possible. He is then told that he will be required to imagine a number of scenes which will appear to him very vividly. If he feels disturbed by any scene, he is to raise his hand as a signal. The weakest scenes from the hierarchical series are now presented in turn, usually for between two and three seconds each in the beginning. The raising of the left hand or any manifestation of increased bodily tension leads to the immediate curtailment of the ongoing scene. When it is judged that enough scenes have been given, the patient is roused from the trance and asked how clear the scenes were and whether any of them were disturbing. Even if he has not raised his hand during the trance, he may report having been very slightly to very considerably disturbed by one or more of the scenes. (Patients almost never raise their hands to a disturbance that is only slight.)

At the second desensitization session, a day or more later, the procedure is largely determined by what happened at the first. A scene that produced no disturbance at all is omitted and the next higher item in the hierarchy presented in its place. A scene that was slightly disturbing is presented again, unchanged. If there was considerable disturbance to the weakest scene from any hierarchy, a still weaker stimulus must now be substituted. Suppose, for example, that the disturbing item was seeing a funeral procession. Typical weaker substitutions would be the word "funeral," seeing the procession from a distance of 200 yards, seeing an isolated and presumably empty hearse, or a *very brief* presentation of the original scene. The verbal substitution would usually be the weakest of these and would therefore be preferred. No harm is ever done by presenting a stimulus that is too weak. A stimulus that is too strong may actually increase sensitivity, and, especially during early experiments with the method, I have occasionally produced major setbacks in patients by premature presentation to them of stimuli with a high anxiety-evoking potential.*

In most patients, when the same scene is presented several times during a session there is a weaker reaction to each successive presentation. When this occurs, it accelerates therapy.† In other patients there is perseveration of anxiety responses, so that the anxiety produced by a second presentation summates with that from the first, the repetition tending thus to have a sensitizing effect rather than a therapeutic one.

With suitably cautious handling some headway will be made in the hierarchies at each session, and *pari passu* with this the patient will report a progressive decrease of sensitivity to the relevant kinds of stimulus situations encountered in the normal course of his life. The total number of sessions required varies greatly but is usually between 10 and 25.

The introspections of a clinical psychologist who was treated by this method are of interest:

> Most typically the emotion associated with a situation tended to diminish or disappear between one session and another. On three or four occasions, however, the desensitization seemed to occur quite suddenly in the course of a session. On these occasions the change was subjectively a dramatic one: I would feel, all at once, a sense of separation, or apartness, or independence of the situation; a feeling that "I am *here*, it is *there*." To say simply that I attained greater objectivity, or more simply that the emotional component of the image disappeared, would be accurate but not quite as descriptive of my subjective experience as the preceding sentence.
>
> The change, even when sudden, never seemed to constitute an "insight." My insight into my difficulties was perhaps fairly good initially, and was not altered one way or the other by the desensitization process *per se*. It might be said, however, that my "perception" of situations changed.

Patients who cannot relax will not make progress with this method. Those who cannot or will not be hypnotized but who can relax will make progress, although apparently more slowly than when hypnosis is used.

---

* When sensitivity is increased as a result of an error of this kind, no scenes must be presented at the next session or two, and during these the hypnotic trance should be utilized merely to relax the patient as deeply as possible. At subsequent sessions scenes are introduced very cautiously from far down in the hierarchy whose subject matter produced the setback.

† I frequently inquire whether the reaction is weakening or not by saying after, say, the third presentation of a scene, "If your reaction has been decreasing, do nothing; if not, raise your hand." If it has been decreasing, I present the same scene two or three times more.

The method necessarily fails with a small minority who are unable to imagine the suggested scenes. A few, perhaps about 5 per cent, do not make progress because although they can visualize clearly, they do not have the disturbed reaction to the imagined scene that they would have to the reality. Experience has shown that most of these can arouse the relevant emotions by *verbalizing* the scenes, and they then progress in the same way as other patients.

Occasionally, one comes across a patient who, having been desensitized to a hierarchy list, reveals a range of further, previously unrecognized sensitivities on a related but distinct theme. After desensitization to the latter, a third theme may become evident, and so on. It is surmised that this profusion of variations is due to unusually numerous and severe past stresses having brought about a conditioning of anxiety responses to an extraordinarily large number of aspects of certain situations. In these cases, abreaction is sometimes a valuable adjuvant because it involves the whole of the original conditioning situation (see pp. 195–98).

The Conduct of Desensitization Sessions

An account will be given of the exact details of procedure at one patient's desensitization sessions—her first session and two successive sessions when therapy was well under way. This patient had the following anxiety hierarchies (the most disturbing items being on top, as always):

Hierarchies

A. Fear of hostility
1. Devaluating remarks by husband
2. Devaluating remarks by friends
3. Sarcasm from husband or friends
4. Nagging
5. Addressing a group
6. Being at social gathering of more than four people (the more the worse)
7. Applying for a job
8. Being excluded from a group activity
9. Anybody with a patronizing attitude

B. Fear of death and its accoutrements
1. First husband in his coffin
2. At a burial
3. Seeing a burial assemblage from afar
4. Obituary notice of young person dying of heart attack

5. Driving past a cemetery
6. Seeing a funeral (the nearer the worse)
7. Passing a funeral home
8. Obituary notice of old person (worse if died of heart disease)
9. Inside a hospital
10. Seeing a hospital
11. Seeing an ambulance

C. Fear of symptoms (despite *knowing* them to be nonsignificant)

1. Extrasystoles
2. Shooting pains in chest and abdomen
3. Pains in left shoulder and back
4. Pain on top of head
5. Buzzing in ears
6. Tremor of hands
7. Numbness or pain in fingertips
8. Dyspnea after exertion
9. Pain in left hand (old injury)

First Desensitization Session (12th Interview) *

Before this interview the patient had learned to relax most of the muscles in her body. At our last meeting hypnosis had been discussed, and as she was afraid of it, I had tried to reassure her.

After some discussion about other matters, I told her that we would now try to have a hypnotic session. As she was comfortably seated, I said, "Rest a hand on each thigh. In response to suggestions that I shall give you, you will notice various things happen to your hands. However, if at any time you feel anxious at what is happening, you will be able to interrupt the proceedings immediately. You will at no stage lose consciousness."

Her hands having settled comfortably on her lap, I went on, "Look at your hands and keep on looking at them. At the same time I want you to give your fullest attention to the sensations in your hands, whatever they may be. At this moment you may be aware of the texture of your skirt, of the warmth between your fingers and in your thighs, of tingling sensations, perhaps an awareness of your pulse, or the movement of air over your fingers. There may even be other sensations. Concentrate on your sensations, give them your complete attention, no matter what they are, and continue to do so. As you go on watching you will notice small movements appear-

---

* The hypnotic induction procedure follows Wolberg (1948).

ing in your fingers. It will be interesting to see which finger moves first—maybe the thumb or little finger or index finger or the middle finger or even the fourth finger. (*Right index finger moves.*) There, your right index finger moved, and now, as you go on watching, you will notice other fingers move, and the general effect of these movements will be to spread the fingers farther and farther apart. (*Movements appear in other fingers of the right hand.*) Now you begin to notice that as the fingers spread apart, a feeling of lightness appears among the other sensations in your hand and soon you will observe that your right hand begins to rise. Your right hand will become lighter and lighter and it will begin to lift. There, we can already see some slight arching of the right hand. Your hand goes up higher and higher. (*Hand rises.*) As it rises you will notice that the palm begins to turn slowly inward, because it is going to rise to your face. When your hand touches your face, you will be aware of a profoundly pleasant, heavy feeling throughout your body. Then, or even before then, your eyes will close. (*Her hand slowly rises to her face and her eyes close.*) Now you feel so pleasantly heavy and drowsy, you become heavier and heavier.

"Now let all the muscles of your body relax. Let relaxation grow deeper and deeper. We shall concentrate on the various zones of your body in turn. Relax the muscles of your forehead and those of the rest of your face. (*Pause.*) Relax all the muscles of your jaws and of your tongue. (*Pause.*) Relax the muscles of your eyeballs. (*Pause.*) Now relax your neck. (*Pause.*) Let the muscles of your shoulders and your arms relax. (*Pause.*) Relax the muscles of your back and your abdomen. (*Pause.*) Relax the muscles of your thighs and your legs. (*Pause.*) Let go more and still more. You become so calm, you feel so comfortable, nothing matters except to enjoy this pleasant, calm, relaxed state. (*Pause.*)

"Now I am going to give you some scenes to imagine and you will imagine them very clearly and calmly. If, however, by any chance anything that you imagine disturbs you, you will at once indicate this to me by raising your left hand two or three inches. First I am going to give you a very commonplace scene. Imagine that you are sitting alone in an arm-chair in the living room of your house. It is a very pleasant sunny day and you are sitting in this chair perfectly at ease. (*Pause of about 5 seconds.*) Next I want you to imagine the printed word 'Dentist.' (*Pause of about 3 seconds.*) Stop imagining this word and concentrate on relaxing your muscles. (*Pause.*) Now imagine that you are reading the newspaper and that your eye falls upon the headline 'Prominent citizen dies at 86.' (*Pause of about 3 seconds.*) Stop imagining those words, and again concentrate on your muscles. Let them go completely. Enjoy this calm state."

After a minute or two, I said to the patient, "In a few moments, I'll count five and then you will wake up feeling very calm and refreshed. (*Pause.*) One, two, three, four, five."

She now opened her eyes and to my "How are you?" said that she felt quite calm. Replying to further questions, she said that all three of the scenes had been clear and the only one that had disturbed her was the third one and the disturbance had even in this case been very slight. It may be noted that the first scene had nothing to do with the items on the hierarchy list. It was inserted as a kind of control, and a street scene or a flower or almost anything else which has no obvious relevance to the hierarchy items could equally well have been used. The word "dentist" was used as a kind of sensitivity test because of its vague associations with hospitals and illness.

17th Desensitization Session (32d Interview)

Since desensitization to the fear of hostility (sublist A) had progressed much more rapidly than the others, at the last few sessions this sublist had been set aside and our attention concentrated on the death fear and fear of symptoms. Six sessions before, we had begun to deal with funerals (B-6) on the hierarchy list. On the first occasion, the word "funeral" had alone been presented, and thereafter actual funerals had been presented, starting from two blocks away and then at decreasing distances as her reaction declined. At the previous session she had been made to imagine a funeral passing in the street in front of her and this had caused slight disturbance. Imagining a pain in her left shoulder had been just perceptibly disturbing. A scene of a woman in a film weeping had also been introduced because of its association with the idea of death and she had reacted very slightly to it.

At this session she was hypnotized in the same way as in the first session, but, as would be expected, the procedure took much less time. When she was deeply relaxed, I spoke as follows: "I am going to present a number of scenes to your imagination which you will imagine very clearly. It goes without saying that, if by any chance any scene should disturb you, you will indicate it by raising your left hand. First, I want you to imagine that you are standing at a street corner and a funeral procession passes you. You may have some feeling of sadness, but apart from this you are absolutely calm. (*Brief pause.*) Stop the scene. (*Pause of about 4 seconds.*) Now I want you to imagine the same scene of the funeral passing in the street before you. (*Pause of 6 or 7 seconds.*) Now just relax. Think of nothing but your muscles. (*Pause of about 15 seconds.*) Now I want you to imagine the same scene of the funeral again. (*Pause of about 8 sec-*

onds.) Stop imagining that scene and just relax. If the last presentation of that scene disturbed you even to the slightest degree I want you now to raise your left hand. (*Hand does not rise.*) Good. Now let yourself go still further. (*Pause of about 15 seconds.*) Now I want you to imagine last time's scene of the woman in the film weeping bitterly. (*Pause of about 4 seconds.*) Now stop imagining this scene and just relax. (*Pause of about 15 seconds.*) Now I want you again to imagine the scene of the weeping woman. (*Pause of about 8 seconds.*) Stop that scene and again think of nothing but relaxing. If the last presentation of that scene disturbed you in the slightest, please raise your left hand. (*Hand does not rise.*) Good. Relax. (*Pause of about 15 seconds.*) Now I want you to imagine that you have a pain in your left shoulder. (*Pause of about 10 seconds.*) Now stop that pain and think only of relaxing. (*Pause of about 15 seconds.*) Now again imagine you have a pain in your left shoulder. (*Pause of about 10 seconds.*) Stop that pain and think of your muscles only. Soon I'll count five and you will wake. (*Pause.*) One, two, three, four, five."

The patient was not asked during the trance to indicate if she had been disturbed by the shoulder pain, because I assumed—wrongly, as it turned out—that there would be no disturbance. (As stated earlier, patients usually do not spontaneously signal *mild* disturbances.) On waking, she stated that there had been a very slight disturbance to the first presentation of the funeral scene, less to the second, and none to the third. The weeping woman had not disturbed her at all, but each presentation of the pain in the shoulder had been very slightly disturbing.

18th Desensitization Session (33d Interview)

The hypnotic session was, as usual, preceded by a discussion of the patient's experiences of the past few days.

At this session the funeral scene and the one of the woman weeping were abandoned because it had been possible to present them without any disturbance whatever at the previous session. They were replaced by two new scenes, slightly higher on the hierarchy. The pain in the left shoulder was again presented because its presentation had not been completely free from disturbance last time. Having hypnotized the patient and made her relax, I spoke as follows:

"First we are going to have something already well familiar to you at these sessions—a pain in your left shoulder. You will imagine this pain very clearly and you will be not at all disturbed. (*Pause of about 4 seconds.*) Stop imagining this pain and again concentrate on your relaxing. (*Pause of about 15 seconds.*) Now again imagine that you have this pain in your left shoulder. (*Pause of about 10 seconds.*) Stop imagining the pain and again relax. (*Pause of about 15 seconds.*) Now I'd like you to imagine the pain in your left shoulder a third time, very clearly and calmly. (*Pause of about 10 seconds.*) Now stop this pain and focus your attention on your body, on the pleasant relaxed feeling that you have. If you felt in the least disturbed by the third presentation of this scene, I want you now to indicate it by raising your left hand. (*The hand does not rise.*) Go on relaxing. (*Pause of about 15 seconds.*) Next I want you to visualize the following. You are in your car being driven by your husband along a pleasant road in hilly country. On a distant hillside you can clearly see the gray stones of a cemetery. (*Pause of 2 or 3 seconds.*) Now stop imagining this scene and think only of relaxing. Let yourself go completely. (*Pause of about 15 seconds.*) I want you again to imagine the same scene of the distant hillside cemetery. (*Pause of 4 or 5 seconds.*) Now stop imagining the scene and again think of your muscles and of letting them go still more. (*Pause of about 15 seconds.*) I want you to imagine that while you are standing in a queue at a drugstore you begin talking to the woman next to you and she tells you that her husband has been very short of breath since he had his heart attack. (*Pause of 2 or 3 seconds.*) Now cut that scene short and relax. (*Pause of about 15 seconds.*) Now I want you to imagine the same scene again very clearly and calmly. (*Pause of about 4 seconds.*) Stop imagining this scene and relax."

On waking, the patient reported that the first presentation of the pain in her left shoulder had been very slightly disturbing but by the third presentation it had not disturbed her at all. The first presentation of a distant cemetery had been fairly disturbing but the second much less so. The woman in the drugstore whose husband had had a heart attack had disturbed her considerably the first time and somewhat less the second time.

Two remarks must be made here. First, it was not imperative to present the two new scenes only twice each, but experience with this patient had shown that new scenes did not entirely lose their power to disturb at the first session at which they were given, so that to force the pace would have taken up time and gained nothing.

Second, it will have been noticed that although the scenes presented follow the general idea of the hierarchy list, they do not conform to it absolutely and the therapist may introduce variations according to his discretion and his knowledge of the case.

Cases Illustrating Systematic Desensitization to Anxiety-Evoking Stimuli on the Basis of Relaxation

The cases given below have been selected to illustrate (*a*) the practically limitless range of stimuli in relation to which this method can be used and (*b*) that no matter what the character of the neurotic *responses* may be, they disappear when the power of the stimuli to evoke anxiety is removed.

Case 7: Desensitization to a Broad Spectrum of Social Stimuli Resulting in Apparent Cure of Duodenal Ulcer

Miss T., a 46-year-old unmarried dressmaker, was referred for psychotherapy by her physician on June 7, 1955. A year previously she had begun to have epigastric pain and other digestive symptoms which radiology had shown to be due to peptic ulceration. Medical treatment had relieved the pain but there was still radiological evidence of activity in the ulcer and she complained of nausea at the slightest emotional disturbance. Since she was exceedingly sensitive to other people in many contexts, such disturbance was very frequent. Her social neuroticism was reflected in a Willoughby score of 56. History-taking was complete at the end of the first interview.

Miss T. was the fifth child in a family of ten. During a pleasant and uneventful childhood, she had got on well with her parents and siblings. Her father had died in 1944; her mother was still living. She had not liked going to school because it was difficult for her to learn and she was always near the bottom of the class. She had made friends quite easily but no intimate friendships, feeling that there was a sufficiency of these within her family circle. When 14 years of age, Miss T. had left school to help her mother at home, and at 19 had taken up dressmaking, at which she had been steadily employed ever since.

Sex had played but a small part in Miss T.'s life. She had never masturbated. In her adolescence and early adult life she had found the company of men pleasant, but since she was practically always ignored by them and asked out only very rarely, she gradually developed a sense of inferiority and became increasingly nervous in male company.

At the age of 33 she had her first relationship with a man. He began to court her, and she, attracted especially by his lively personality, grew fond of him. A love affair developed which Miss T. found satisfying in many ways. Very prolonged preliminary lovemaking was necessary to excite her sexually, but occasionally she had orgasms. Miss T.'s lover had promised to marry her when his financial circumstances improved, but after four years he returned one day from a three months' absence on business to tell her that he was engaged to another woman. She was deeply shocked by this news. Since that time there had been no other men in her life, and she had neither sought nor wished for them.

As always in such cases, efforts were made to get her to stand up to people in relevant situations, but in the first month of treatment she failed to rise to the few opportunities for direct assertion that occurred. Meanwhile, during seven interviews, training in relaxation was given and a hierarchy on the theme of her sensitivity to people was constructed. This is given below, not in its original form, but with all later additions included. It should be noted that though most of the items refer to specific situations, other situations of the same general structure could be substituted, and sometimes were.

Hierarchy A

1. Having an interview with any doctor or lawyer (her own doctor was the stimulus figure used in the desensitization)
2. Unexpectedly finding a strange man when visiting at her brother's house
3. Being phoned by a man to whom recently introduced
4. Speaking, in company, to a man to whom just introduced
5. Meeting her girl friend's boy friend
6. Making a speech to the employees at her firm at the end-of-the-year party
7. Going up to receive a prize at end-of-the-year party
8. Having an interview with the representative of the Industrial Council because of sick pay not received from employer
9. Telling her employer that an error of which she has been accused is due to someone else's wrong instruction
10. Being told by her employer that a hem she has made is not straight
11. Criticisms from members of her family
12. Criticisms from fellow workers
13. Being at a party with other girls who work with her

The items of the above hierarchy were presented to the patient, hypnotized and relaxed, on the dates given below.

July 1. Neutral item of standing at a street corner in Johannesburg; and then item 13—at a party with the other girls from her place of work. No disturbance.

July 5. Scene 13 repeated; 12—the girl next to her unjustly says, "You have taken my thimble"; 10—being told by her supervisor that a hem she has made is not straight. No disturbance.

July 8. Scene 9—she tells her employer that she did certain stitching incorrectly because of someone else's wrong instructions; 8—she has an interview with a representative of the Industrial Council because she has not received sick pay due from her employer; 7—she goes up to receive a prize for good performance at the annual Christmas party. On waking from the trance she reported very slight disturbance to scenes 9 and 8.

July 12. Scenes 9 and 8 were presented again and also 5—being introduced by her special girl friend at work to the latter's boy friend. She reported no disturbance this time to 9 or 8, but quite considerable disturbance to 5.

July 15. Item 7 was again presented in view of its poor visualization on July 8, and scene 5 was presented thrice. She reported considerable disturbance to 7 and slight but decreasing disturbance to the successive presentations of 5.

July 22. Scene 7 was presented three times and scene 5 twice. She reported that the disturbance to 7 had initially been very slight and had not been present at all at the third presentation. Scene 5 had been slightly disturbing each time.

July 27. Scene 5 was presented thrice; 6—making a speech to the employees at the Christmas party; 4—speaking to a man to whom she has just been introduced at a party. There was no longer any disturbance to scene 5, but 4 and 6 each evoked a slight amount of disturbed reaction.

August 5. Two presentations of scene 4 and two of 6, followed by 3—speaking on the phone to a man to whom she has recently been introduced. The introduction of scene 3 at this stage may seem unduly bold in view of the fact that the patient had not been asked to indicate her reactions to scene 4. However, I had for some time been aware that she made very slight finger movements when she was disturbed even to a very small extent and she had made no such movement to the presentations of scene 4 on this occasions. On waking from the trance, she reported that scenes 4 and 6 had not been disturbing but there had been a very slight disturbance to 3.

August 19. Scene 3 alone was presented, thrice. She reported slight but decreasing disturbance to it.

September 9. Scene 3 was again presented twice, followed by 1—consulting her own physician—also given twice. She was not disturbed by 3, but considerably disturbed by the first presentation of the scene with her physician and somewhat less by the second.

September 23. She was given scene 1, thrice; and then scene 2—unexpectedly finding a strange man when visiting at her brother's house (five times). She reported afterward slight disturbance to the first two presentations of scene 1 and none to the third. There was a considerable degree of disturbance to the first presentation of scene 2 but this had decreased slightly by the fifth presentation. It may be noted that the giving of as many as five presentations was determined by the presence of the small finger movements mentioned above.

On September 30, Miss T. reported that on September 27 she had been upset at the lady supervisor at work shouting at her when she had asked for certain information. The characteristic sick feeling in her stomach had come on and had persisted until the end of the following day. She said she had never been able to stand being shouted at or even witnessing shouting. Since the incident of the 27th, Miss T. had felt continuously nervous. As this nervousness seemed to me to consist of pervasive ("free-floating") anxiety, I now subjected her to two doses of carbon dioxide–oxygen by the method of La Verne (see p. 166). Rising from the couch she said that she felt much better.

Because of Miss T.'s strong reaction to shouting, we had a discussion on the subject, and from this Hierarchy B emerged.

Hierarchy B

1. Men across the road punching each other with Miss T. the only witness
2. Men across the road punching each other in the presence of other people besides Miss T.
3. A man across the road punches another one with whom he is quarreling without being punched in return
4. Men across the road engaged in argument

The following were the details of subsequent hypnotic sessions.

September 30. Scenes 1 and 2 from Hierarchy A were repeated and scene 4 from Hierarchy B—waiting for a bus she sees men across the road arguing. No disturbance.

October 10. Miss T.'s general nervousness had decreased markedly after the carbon dioxide treatment. Scenes A-1 and B-4 were presented again and also B-3—one of the quarreling men punches the other without being punched in return. There was no disturbance.

October 28. Scenes 4 and 3 thrice (scenes from this date on were all from Hierarchy B). There was slight disturbance to 3, which decreased with successive presentation, and very slight to 4.

November 11. Scenes 4 and 3 twice, and 2—the two men across the road hitting each other. There was just noticeable disturbance to 4, very slight to 3, and slight to 2. (Because Miss T. continued to have a small amount of "free-floating" anxiety, she was now given two further doses of carbon dioxide–oxygen and felt completely calm afterward.)

November 25. Two continuous sequences of items 4, 3, and 2. Slight disturbance to the first series, very slight to the second. (She said that since the last carbon dioxide treatment her general nervousness had completely disappeared.)

January 6. The sequence 4, 3, 2 was presented twice and 4, 3, 1—the men fight while Miss T. is the only witness—once. There was slight disturbance to the latter sequence only.

February 24. Sequence of items 4, 3, 1 twice and then the same items viewed not from across the road but from the first floor of a building adjacent to the fighting men. There was no disturbance to any of these sequences.

Miss T. was seen for the last time on April 13, 1956. She had been on a month's holiday at the seaside until April 3 and enjoyed it greatly despite some bad weather. In her hotel she had spoken freely to everybody and had not had any of her old shyness. Nothing had upset her emotionally at any time. She had been happy and had eaten and slept well. A week before there had been a fight between a European and an African outside her workroom which had gone on for about an hour but left her completely unruffled. On April 8, her mother had had a heart attack late at night (cardiac asthma). Miss T. had given her a tablet and then gone back to bed. She was undisturbed, in contrast with the past when she would have been greatly upset. The Willoughby test now yielded a score of 13.

She had had no gastric symptoms for three months, and there was no longer any radiological evidence of duodenal ulcer.

In December 1957 her physician reported that she had remained well.

Case 8: Cure of Impotence Following Desensitization to Situations Involving Injury and Suffering

First and second interviews. (The content of these two interviews has been rearranged to make a more or less consecutive story.) Mr. L., a tall, thin man of 22, consulted me for the first time on August 23, 1953. He had suffered from impotence for three years without seeking treatment, but was now very anxious to overcome his disability because he had recently fallen in love with a very attractive girl (Irene) who reciprocated his feelings.

His sexual history was as follows. He had first become aware of sexual impulses at the age of 13 when he started noticing girls and occasionally managed to kiss them. At 15 he began to masturbate in accompaniment with sexual fantasies—about once a week, without any feelings of guilt. He began to meet girls in the course of various social activities, and at 16 he became interested in Eve, a pretty, intelligent, and lively girl with whom he "went steady" for the next two years, though they quarreled a good deal because she was moody. They frequently petted, but he never went further than to fondle her breasts through her clothes.

While he was still friendly with Eve, he met Nina, who pursued him with great determination, although he neither felt nor displayed any particular interest in her. Nina was quite easygoing sexually and one day when he visited her in her parents' absence they had coitus. He ejaculated prematurely on the first occasion but later performed very successfully. This was the beginning of a sexual relationship which went on very satisfactorily for a year, in the course of which Mr. L. also had a few casual experiences with other girls.

Then in 1950 when he was 19 years old he found himself strongly attracted to Alice in the same pharmacy class. After a platonic phase of a month or so, they began mild petting which gradually grew warmer until by the fourth month they had begun to lie in bed together. Mr. L.'s sexual responses to Alice were extremely powerful and he invariably had strong erections even if they were only flirting in the mildest way. On the third occasion on which they lay in bed together, Mr. L. suggested intercourse but Alice, a virgin, was afraid. But she yielded at last to his insistent pressure, and then he found that his erection had vanished and could not be reinstated, even though they spent the night together. From that time onward, although he had innumerable opportunities to make love to Alice, he never had another erection with her. At no time since then had he had anything like a full erection with anyone. However, his *general* responsiveness to sexual objects was only slightly reduced.

Mr. L.'s association with Alice continued for nine months after this incident, when it was ended by a trifling argument. He had a severe reaction and kept away from people as much as possible for about three months. Then he began casual associations with women, avoiding physical contact. One day late in 1952 when an easy opportunity to make love to an attractive girl arose, Mr. L. made the necessary advances but failed to get an erection. He was very upset at this but went on seeing the girl until February 1953 when she went to live in a distant city. From April to July he went out with another girl whom he found quite attractive, but he never had the slightest semblance of an erection.

Early in July he met and became strongly attracted to Irene, who bore some physical resemblance to Alice but was better looking and shared more of Mr. L.'s important interests and attitudes. He was finding it pleasant to fondle her and was noticing a trace of an erection. Caressing her also increased the rate of his breathing and made him perspire to some extent, and sometimes after very prolonged lovemaking he had orgasms despite the virtual absence of an erection. A pleasurable feeling accompanied the orgasm but much less so than when he had been able to experience it in a normal way.

Other details of Mr. L.'s life were as follows. He was the eldest of three boys. Both parents were living. His father, pleasant, sociable, and unpractical, had always treated him kindly and rarely punished him. He described his mother as "nervous, often depressed, somewhat vicious, and very belligerent." She displayed a certain amount of affection and throughout Mr. L.'s childhood was constantly asking him to tell her how much he loved her. She did not often give beatings but kept shouting and nagging, so that from the age of six onward, Mr. L. felt an increasing dislike of her. He became so sensitive to her bullying that once when he was eight years old and his ear was cut by a stone he delayed returning home as long as possible because he feared her tongue. She quarreled endlessly with her husband mainly over trifles, so that the atmosphere in the house was one of perpetual discord.

Mr. L. recalled two occasions on which he could overhear his parents having intercourse in the next room when he was about seven years old. On each occasion he heard his mother shout, "No, stop" and then weep. He was greatly upset by this, felt his father was being brutal, and hated him for it. Until he was 12 years old, he thought that sexual intercourse was painful, and this idea had recurred when he was trying to seduce Alice.

He had been happy at school and a good deal above the average as a scholar. He was a good sportsman, representing his school at cricket and rugby football. Making friends was easy for him and there were always one or two who were especially close. He had done well in his pharmacy studies and was happy in his present job.

Until the age of 12 he had felt extremely unhappy and insecure but had become increasingly confident in relation to most aspects of life—and this confidence had continued to develop even in the past three years despite the onset of sexual impotence.

Third interview (September 12, 1953). At this interview I gave him the Willoughby questionnaire to answer. His relatively low score of 26 confirmed his statement of relative confidence in most social situations. However, he gave the maximum positive answer of 4 to question 23—"If you see an accident, does something keep you from giving help?" When, as usual, I went into the reasons for this, it turned out that he had very strong disturbed reactions to pain or suffering or evidence of tissue damage to other people. These reactions were sometimes so marked that it became very difficult for him to concentrate on his work for a day or two afterward. He said that he had been aware of the traumatization that would have occurred if he had deflorated Alice.

He then stated that on the evening of September 9, lying in bed with Irene, he had had a partial erection and had attempted intercourse. She, being a virgin, told him that it was beginning to be painful. At this, his erection subsided completely. On the evening of the 10th, they made another attempt at intercourse, but this time Mr. L. had no vestige of an erection. Both of them were greatly depressed at this.

Pointing out that his experience of September 9 had increased his sexual inhibition, I advised him to desist for the time being from further attempts at coitus.

Fourth interview (September 13, 1953). Mr. L. stated that he had been giving a good deal of thought to his sensitivity to pain and tissue damage in other people, and had been surprised to realize how many of his experiences in the shop were colored by it. He recalled also that he had had such a strong reaction at the age of five when a gang of boys attacked a slightly older friend of his; he had remained upset for days after and for years had avoided the street in which this had happened. When he was seven years old he had become involved in a fight with a bigger boy. Hitting the latter in the solar plexus and seeing the reaction, he had run home in terror. He was not disturbed by injuries to his own person. Watching a boxing match was intolerable to him. He found quarrels a shade less disturbing, but if he was one of the participants, they disturbed him scarcely at all.

I discussed muscle relaxation with him and instructed him in relaxation of the muscles of his arm and forehead. Before he left I asked him to bring me next time a list of everything he could think of that could possibly disturb him.

Fifth interview (September 14, 1953). The earlier part of this interview was devoted to training Mr. L. to relax the muscles of his face and jaws. After this, taking the list of disturbing items he brought me and adding to it items from his history and others that arose during discussion, we constructed the following three hierarchical lists of anxieties (in descending order).

Hierarchies

A. Injury and suffering

1. Idea of uterus being scraped
2. An untreated fractured limb (what is most disturbing is the idea of the broken ends scraping together)
3. A raw wound bleeding (worse if large; worse on face than on trunk and not so bad on a limb)
4. A person being injected (would be worse if Mr. L. had to give the injection himself)
5. A very small facial wound with much bleeding
6. Dissecting an animal
7. Injecting a drug into an animal
8. The sight of a dead human body
9. Watching someone else dissect an animal
10. Seeing a patient propped up in bed short of breath
11. An old unhealed wound: the worse the larger
12. Seeing an animal that has just been killed by a car
13. Seeing an animal that has died evidently of disease
14. A small facial wound with slight bleeding

15. Traumatic epistaxis
16. A schoolboy being caned

B. Vocalizing of suffering
1. An unseen hospital patient groaning
2. His father groaning
3. A child crying
4. A customer comes in groaning and says he has abdominal cramps
5. A kicked dog howling

C. Vocal violence
1. A quarrel in his family
2. A quarrel anywhere else
3. A child being shouted at

Sixth interview (September 16, 1953). Mr. L. said that there was no significant change in his reaction to Irene, but perhaps his sexual arousal was slightly quicker. He had observed in himself numerous examples of reacting unpleasantly to trauma-associated stimuli. For example, he had been upset for many minutes after hearing somebody in his shop mention a uterus being scraped.

He was instructed in relaxation of the muscles of the tongue, eyes, pharynx, and neck.

Seventh interview (September 19, 1953). Mr. L. reported that on the evening of the 16th while petting with Irene he had had a rather better erection than before.

He recalled that at school he had had a private game with a friend in which they used to twist other boys' arms. One night Mr. L., then aged eight, had had an overwhelming sense of guilt about this and the next day had apologized to all the victims. He had always been somewhat unhappy about this game.

He was shown relaxation of the shoulder muscles and then a hypnotic trance was induced by the light fixation method. He was made to relax all the muscles he had learned to relax, and then the following scenes were presented: a neutral scene of standing at a busy street corner; C-3 (see list)—a mother shouts at her child because he is dirty. On waking, Mr. L. reported the scene to have been very clear and that C-3 was slightly disturbing initially only.

Eighth interview (September 20, 1953). The previous evening Mr. L. had seen a film about a man wrongly committed to a mental institution, being depressed but not insane. In the past he would have been considerably disturbed by such a film but this one did not affect him at all.

After instruction in relaxation of the muscles of the back and abdomen a hypnotic trance was again induced by the light fixation method and the patient was made to relax as deeply as possible. The following scenes were presented: C-3 (see above); A-16—standing outside the door of the headmaster's office at his old school, Mr. L. hears the sound of caning; A-15— a customer comes in with a slightly bleeding nose. On waking, Mr. L. reported a slight initial disturbance to A-16 but none to the other scenes.

Ninth interview (September 23, 1953). Mr. L. reported that when making love on the 21st he had again had no erection at all.

On the 22d he had seen a doctor treat a collapsed patient for three-quarters of an hour in his pharmacy. He had been aware of occasional muscle twitches but had not been really badly disturbed on the whole. He also had a feeling of interest in the procedures that the doctor had used and thought that he would like to see more now.

After training in relaxation of the muscles of the inferior extremity a hypnotic trance was induced as on previous occasions. The well-relaxed patient was made to visualize scene A-16 twice; A-14—a customer comes in with a small facial wound slightly bleeding, twice; A-13—dead laboratory rat. Mr. L. reported afterward that none of the presented scenes disturbed him at all, but after the last of them he had a spontaneous image of a mangled rat and this disturbed him considerably. He still felt rather shaky.

Tenth interview (September 27, 1953). Mr. L. reported that he had had a row with Irene the previous evening, and that in the past week or so they had had several arguments over trivialities. On questioning it turned out that the reason for the previous evening's argument was that Mr. L. had refused to go to a party because he knew that one of Irene's old boy friends was there and he feared the competition—as he was so inadequate sexually.

He was also depressed because his mother had seen a psychiatrist who had said that he could do nothing to remove her highly emotional behavior, her nagging, and her tantrums. This meant that the unpleasantness at home would persist. He always had a feeling of anxious anticipation when going home.

Under hypnosis the scenes presented were A-3—a man comes into the shop with a half-inch bleeding cut on his hand; A-12—a dog killed in an accident seen from a distance of 50 yards; A-11—a man in his shop removes a bandage to reveal an old unhealed wound on his forearm about one inch long. None of these scenes disturbed him.

11th interview (September 30, 1953). Mr. L. had overcome his differences with Irene and the relationship was sailing smoothly, but he was seeing little of her as she was studying for an examination. He had had no real anxiety in the past two weeks despite some arguments at home. Even the arguments with Irene had not provoked him as much as he would have expected. The scenes presented under hypnosis were A-3, modified—a one-inch bleeding wound on a man's forearm; A-12, modified—a dog killed in an accident seen from a distance of about 20 yards; A-10—an old man ill in bed and slightly short of breath; C-2—while waiting for a bus, he sees two men quarreling across the road; A-7—he sees a dog being injected against distemper. A-7 alone was slightly disturbing.

12th interview (October 3, 1953). Mr. L. was getting on better with Irene but still having small arguments at times. On September 30 they made love and he "came near to full erection." He had been upset the previous day by hearing a puppy's prolonged howling.

The scenes presented under hypnosis were: A-7, twice; A-16, modi-fied—a boy receives three strokes with a cane in Mr. L.'s presence; A-11, modified—a man has an old three-inch wound on his forearm; B-5—a kicked dog yelps, thrice. Mr. L. reported slight disturbances to the first presentations of A-7 and B-5 only.

13th interview (October 7, 1953). As Mr. L. came very late, there was just time for a hypnotic session. The scenes presented were A-7, four times; B-5; A-11, second modification—the old wound is five inches long; B-4—a customer comes in groaning with abdominal pain. None of these scenes disturbed the patient.

14th interview (October 11, 1953). Mr. L. reported having felt un-usually contented. He had been getting on well with Irene and had had no arguments with her at all. He was aware that her parents disapproved of him but didn't mind this in the least. During the weekend there had been a violent quarrel at home between his mother and one of his brothers but for the first time this had not worried him.

Under hypnosis the scenes presented were E-3—walking past a house and hearing a child crying within; A-3, modification 2—a man comes into his shop with a three-inch bleeding wound on his forehead; A-9—seeing a frog with its abdominal organs exposed by dissection, twice. He was slightly disturbed by the first presentation of A-9 only.

15th interview (October 14, 1953). On October 12, Mr. L. had en-gaged in prolonged petting with Irene. He had been quite excited and experienced some erection but had rightly abstained from intercourse. I now told him not to abstain if his erection should become really strong as part of a powerful general sexual excitation.

The scenes presented under hypnosis were A-9, twice; B-2—the sound of his father groaning at night in the next bedroom; C-1—overhearing his parents quarreling in another room; A-9, modified—watching the incision made in the animal. There was a very slight disturbance to A-9, modified, only.

16th interview (October 17, 1953). Mr. L. had nothing to report. During hypnosis, he was presented with A-9, modified, three times; and B-1—standing in a hospital corridor and hearing the groaning of an unseen patient. There was moderate disturbance to the first presentation of A-9, modified, decreasing with repetition, but none to the other scenes.

17th interview (October 20, 1953). On October 18 Mr. L., finding that he had quite a good erection while making love to Irene, attempted coitus and succeeded in deflorating her. He ejaculated after about half a minute with normal feeling. On the 19th Irene began to menstruate and, having severe dysmenorrhoea, groaned in his presence persistently. In a few minutes Mr. L. found himself growing tense and this increased until he left her about an hour later.

The scenes presented under hypnosis were B-1, modified—the patient groans with every exhalation (Mr. L. was made to imagine this continuously for about a minute, and then after a pause it was presented to him again for another minute); A-9, modified, three times. There was no disturbance.

18th interview (October 22, 1953). Mr. L. reported that as he lay in bed the previous night a dog outside howled for a very long time. He had felt slightly disturbed initially but then relaxed, becoming only dimly aware of the still-continuing sound.

Scenes presented under hypnosis were B-1, modified; A-7—making a prick on the skin of an animal, twice. There was no disturbance.

19th interview (October 28, 1953). Mr. L. said that he had had entirely satisfactory sexual intercourse on the 22d. Irene had had her first coital climax—simultaneously with his. In the past week he had noticed a great increase in the general level of his sexual reactivity. He perceived all women in a more sexual way. Kissing Irene was sufficient to produce an erection.

The scenes presented were A-7, modification 1—scratching the animal's skin; A-3, modification 3—a customer comes into the shop with a profusely bleeding cut on his forearm; A-3, modification 4—profusely bleeding wound on his forehead. There was no disturbance.

20th interview (November 15, 1953). Mr. L. had had intercourse on four occasions, each perfectly satisfactory.

He had felt slightly uncomfortable when a student who had failed an examination broke down weeping in the shop. He had also been deeply affected at a film in which a deaf and blind person gave evidence in the witness box, and particularly at sequences of him as a child groping around and being roughly treated by his harsh and impatient mother. However, this was not an anxious feeling, but a "lump in the throat" affair.

The scenes under hypnosis were A-3, modification 4; A-7, modification 2—he gives an animal an injection, the syringe entering easily. There was slight disturbance to the last of these scenes only.

Mr. L. had always loathed doing dissections and giving injections during his training as a pharmacist. He had kept away from such tasks as much as possible and had always tried to get his friends to do them for him when they were impossible to avoid entirely.

21st interview (November 18, 1953). Mr. L. was well pleased with life. The scenes presented under hypnosis were A-7, modification 3—he pricks the animal's skin so as to draw blood; A-6—he moves aside with forceps a frog's liver so as to expose the kidney. There were no disturbances.

22d interview (November 21, 1953). The scenes presented were A-7, modification 4—he pricks the skin of a friend so as to draw blood; A-2— a customer comes in with a fracture of his wrist. Mr. L. reported a considerable disturbance to the first presentation of A-2 and somewhat less to the second. There was no disturbance to the other scene.

23d interview (November 29, 1953). Under hypnosis the scenes presented were A-2, thrice; A-1—a young man comes in with an abrasion of the knee and says that he fell and scraped it on concrete, twice. There was some disturbance to the first presentation of A-2, but this decreased to very slight by the third presentation. The first presentation of A-1 produced a very slight disturbance, the second none at all.

This patient was encountered from time to time and on each occasion stated that his sexual performance was excellent. He was last seen in July 1956.

Case 9: Cure of an Intense Jealousy Reaction (Paranoid Obsession) by Means of Desensitization Based on Relaxation

Because the number of interviews required for this patient was large, it is not possible to follow his treatment interview by interview, and the case will be presented more or less in narrative form.

Mr. E., a 28-year-old insurance agent, consulted me on August 22, 1951, because his "suspicious nature" was threatening to wreck his engagement to Celia. For Celia to point out any virtue in any other man was enough to produce in him a strong feeling of jealousy that would "gnaw within him" for days afterward, causing him to be quite unreasonably irritable and very unjustly critical of almost anything Celia might do. Whenever in the past he had had a close relationship with a girl he had reacted in the same way.

He was an only son, with two elder sisters and two younger ones. His mother, who died four years previously, he had regarded as "wonderful," having felt always very close to her. In his childhood she had been very good to him and taught him from an early age to do things for himself. Punishments from her were rare and just. His father, a businessman who had made and lost fortunes, was still living. He was very generous and had treated his children well, except on the frequent occasions when he was drunk. He then became excessively touchy and quarrelsome and displayed extreme jealousy and possessiveness—traits present in much milder form when he was sober.

At school Mr. E. did moderately well, being always very neat and systematic. He showed little prowess at games. He made a few friends but no very intimate ones, never exerting himself to be friendly. He spent two years working for a degree in commerce at the university, enjoying the life there and forming two very close friendships. When he failed his second year he was glad to leave. At the age of 21 he joined his father's business in which he was given a great deal of responsibility. He was so successful that after about five years his father gave him virtually complete control of the business. At first, setbacks would upset him badly, but he had become able to weather them well.

He started going out with girls at 16, always preferring steady girl friends to casual dates. Nevertheless he was 23 before he became emotionally involved with anyone. This was a very pretty girl called Edith with whom he had an affair lasting three years, becoming engaged to her after a year. He had numerous baseless fits of jealousy during the engagement, causing Edith to hesitate to marry him and finally to leave him. Such fits had not occurred in earlier relationships because he had never before regarded a girl as "his."

At 26 he developed a highly satisfactory, mainly sexual, relationship with Joan. She often aroused his jealousy by telling him about dates with other men. He would respond by being nasty, which would upset her without comforting him.

Eighteen months previously, while still associating with Joan, he had met Celia. For a year he took her out as a platonic friend. Then she went away for three months on holiday and on her return told him that she was about to become engaged but would still be glad to go out with him. One night Mr. E. thought, "What am I looking for? This is just my type of girl. I have never felt jealous about her." He promptly telephoned her and asked whether she would marry him. After a few days' hesitation she broke her engagement to her fiancé and became engaged to Mr. E. At this stage he did not find her very exciting sexually, but as the months went on, his feelings increased gradually to a high level. His first jealous reaction in relation to Celia occurred about a month after the engagement, when he felt that she was too attentive to a male friend of his who had come to congratulate her on the engagement. Since then his sensitivity had increased beyond all bounds. He reacted if any young male who could possibly be regarded as competition praised Celia or even looked at her. By contrast, if a woman, an old man, or a "safely" married man were to praise her, Mr. E. was pleased. He felt that she was too warm toward other people and wished her to be more "standoffish." Typical occurrences which upset Mr. E. were these: (1) One day, as they sat in a café with a group of friends, Celia tapped one of the men on the arm in order to tell him something. (2) He overheard Celia ask a bachelor at a party whether he was tired. (3) Celia made an appointment with a hairdresser for 5:30 in the afternoon. Mr. E. felt that she must have an ulterior motive for having the appointment so late.

Outside the context of his close sexual relationship, Mr. E. was not particularly jealous. He felt slightly irritated and annoyed if his friends did not give him sufficient attention, but this feeling would quickly pass off. He was not jealous of people, even friends, who had more worldly goods or achieved greater eminence. He did not mind losing at games. He was very impatient and became extremely irritated if kept waiting, but could persist in trying to solve a problem for a long time without irritation.

Mr. E. usually came for treatment at weekly intervals. At his third interview he was found to have a normal Bernreuter self-sufficiency score of 55 per cent and a Willoughby of 34, largely made up of high scores on questions suggesting feelings of inferiority. From the fourth interview onward he was given training in relaxation. At his seventh interview he remarked that he always used to be hurt when a girl broke a date with him or even refused to accept his invitation. He recalled an incident that occurred when he was eight years old. With a small sister of his and another little girl he was playing a game involving the use of cups. When the other little girl used *his* cup, he became very upset and annoyed and quarreled with her.

At this interview, the following hierarchy was constructed.

Hierarchy A

1. Celia shows interest in another man or is nice to him
2. Celia is playfully embraced by (*a*) Peter, (*b*) Paul, (*c*) James, (*d*) John*
3. She engages in an animated conversation with a man
4. She is late for an appointment with Mr. E.
5. Celia says, "Mr. X. who used to give me lifts has been having an affair with a married woman"

* Peter, Paul, James, and John were friends of Mr. E., of whom Peter was conceived to be the greatest potential competitor and John the least.

6. Celia says, "Mr. X. has such a nice way about him"
7. Celia says, "Peter has such a nice way about him"
8. Celia says, "Paul has such a nice way about him"
9. Celia says, "James has such a nice way about him"
10. Celia says, "John has such a nice way about him"

As will be seen below (e.g., item 11), many variations on the themes indicated by the items of this hierarchy were used in the course of desensitization.

The first desensitization session occurred at the eighth interview. The only significant scene presented, 10—Celia says, "John has such a nice way about him"—produced no disturbed response.

At his ninth interview (November 18, 1951), Mr. E. reported that he felt annoyed whenever Celia said that such-and-such an actor was good-looking. The reaction was a momentary one only. He was hypnotized and made to relax and the following scenes were presented: 9—Celia says, "James has such a nice way about him"; 11—Celia says, "Marlon Brando is very good-looking." Each scene produced some disturbance, but the second presentation of 9 considerably less than the first.

At the 10th interview (November 25, 1951), when Celia and two other girls who accompanied them were away too long during the interval at a concert one evening, Mr. E. had an unhappy feeling that they were saying something about him—something mocking. It was the same feeling he would have if somebody were to put his arm around Celia. He said, "When anybody looks at Celia, I at once get a feeling of having to be on guard. If we have planned to go dancing with friends, I have a fear about it and will try to get out of the arrangement. Once actually there, I feel rather better." Under hypnosis, scene 9 was presented four times and scene 11 once. On waking, he reported a fair amount of disturbance to the first and second presentations of 9 and then a big decrease at the third. At the fourth presentation he felt "he couldn't care less." There was a just noticeable disturbance to scene 11.

During the next two months some progress was made in desensitization to the items of Hierarchy A with the use, in addition, of many variations. At the beginning of 1952, Mr. E. could accept without disturbance scenes of the general status of 7—Celia says, "Peter has such a nice way about him." He was aware of a slight but definite decrease in his sensitivities and, on the strength of this, decided to get married at the end of January.

On returning from his honeymoon he reported that he had been upset relatively little since the wedding. The worst occasion was during a discussion of the wedding photographs when Celia said, "I wish one was taken with Bill [a cousin of Mr. E.'s] next to me. He's so good-looking."

By the end of March desensitization to the hierarchy had gone so far that Mr. E. did not mind Celia speaking animatedly to another young man at a party. On March 31 he had no reaction at all during the session to scene 2—Celia being playfully embraced by John. But he reported that at a café one evening he and Celia had found themselves sitting near a rather drunk and rowdy group of people, mainly men. A familiar feeling had come upon him that somebody there might have designs on Celia and might come forward, fight and defeat him, so that Celia would afterward scornfully reject him as an inadequate protector. I said, "Objectively, it is not incumbent upon you to be the best fighter in the world, and if you were attacked by a hoodlum your proper course would be to appeal for help or to threaten legal action." It was obvious that awareness of the possibility of this kind of action would be helpful to Mr. E. in an actual altercation, but I did not expect that this awareness would remove the automatic fear responses related to such situations. Consequently, on the basis of further discussion the following hierarchy was constructed.

Hierarchy B

1. Celia sees Mr. E. trying to avoid a fight
2. Alone with Celia at a public dance hall
3. Alone with Celia in a hotel lounge
4. Alone with Celia in a restaurant
5. Alone with Celia in a café
6. Alone with Celia window-shopping while an after-theater crowd mills around them

(Situations 2–6 were also disturbing, but less if he were accompanied by a sister instead of Celia, still less if he were alone, and not at all if he were there with male friends.)

In the months that followed, desensitization proceeded to both hierarchies with the addition of some scenes that emerged from Mr. E.'s week-to-week experiences—for example, Celia saying, "Peter reminds me of Ronald Colman." By the end of 1952 these hierarchies had been almost completely covered, and Mr. E. felt much better. He was unaffected by many things that would surely have disturbed him in the past, such as Celia talking of previous male associates, or dancing with other men. Being with her in crowds scarcely bothered him at all.

It was decided at this stage to establish *a clear line of demarcation between situations that would give legitimate grounds for jealousy and those in relation to which jealousy would be abnormal.* The essence of the distinction made is indicated by the following. If at an evening garden party Celia were found kissing a man on a bench in a dimly lighted spot, there would be cause for jealousy; but not if she were merely talking to him.

In the meantime it had become evident that there were many situations in direct line with those of Hierarchy A that would disturb Mr. E. if they were to occur. A third hierarchy was thus assembled in January 1953. This is given below with a number of high-level items that were incorporated at various later dates.

Hierarchy C

1. Celia says she went to the movies with Peter while Mr. E. was away on business
2. Celia is brought home from a meeting at 11:00 P.M. by Peter but stays in the car for a few minutes before she comes in
3. Same as 2, but Celia comes in at once
4. Celia talks to a man at a dimly lit spot at a garden party
5. As Mr. E. enters a restaurant where he has arranged to meet Celia, he sees a strange man sitting with her at her table
6. Celia tells Mr. E. that a man she met at a party is pestering her to go out with him
7. At a party in a large house Mr. E. finds Celia sitting alone with a man at a table in a small reception room
8. A "wolf" openly grabs Celia and kisses her
9. A man talking to Celia at a gathering grasps her hand while trying to drive home a point
10. Celia is held close by her partner at a dance
11. A long-lost male acquaintance rushes up to Celia and hugs her, saying, "Where have you been all my life!"
12. A man jocularly pats Celia on the buttock
13. A man draws his chair closer to Celia's

Treatment continued at weekly intervals, and progressive desensitization under hypnosis to the hierarchy items was correlated with decreasing reactivity to similar situations encountered in life. Mr. E. had a total of 124 interviews, the last in December 1954, at which he expressed the view, "I think I'm a hundred per cent now," and gave a Willoughby score of 10. He could think of no reasonable situation that could possibly arouse his jealousy. Numerous occurrences that would previously have been unbearable had left him completely unruffled. For example, he had not minded when one evening at a party at his house Celia had gone away with Peter for half an hour to get supplies; or when a good-looking neighbor had given her a lift in his car to and from a town 30 miles away—even when she said afterward, "We had tea at a roadhouse on the way back. I wonder what gossip would have resulted if we had been seen!" A year later he was as well as ever.

10 | *The Treatment of Pervasive Anxiety*

by Respiratory Responses

In 1947 Meduna reported that in many cases neurotic reactions are ameliorated or even overcome after inhalations of high concentrations of carbon dioxide. His usual technique was to make the patient breathe a mixture of 30 per cent carbon dioxide and 70 per cent oxygen until consciousness was lost, repeating the procedure on a varying number of occasions. In terms of statistics there were good results about as often as with heterogenous psychotherapeutic methods (see Chapter 14). A similar impression is obtained from a recent study by Harris (1954) in which a group of patients treated by Meduna's method did not do either better or worse than a comparable group treated by psychotherapy. It would be easy to conclude from this that such favorable results as were obtained were due to the same nonspecific emotional responses to the therapeutic situation that operate in more conventional interviewing. But because certain unpleasant incidental aspects of the treatment, such as feelings of suffocation and loss of consciousness, produce anxiety in a good many patients, the possibility exists that the treatment as such has favorable effects in more than the usual number of patients but that this is concealed by the negative effects of the anxiety that is incidentally evoked in some of them.

A method that almost completely does away with the more alarming aspects of carbon dioxide therapy was described by La Verne in 1953. He tentatively claimed results superior to those of Meduna from the administration to patients of *single* full-capacity inhalations of 70 per cent carbon dioxide and 30 per cent oxygen, these producing no more than a very brief stupor. The single inhalation was repeated several times during a session at intervals of about three minutes. In his first paper La Verne gave no figures, but La Verne and Herman (1955) in a recent comparative clinical study of the methods of Meduna and La Verne, found the latter to be distinctly more effective: 50 per cent of neurotic cases were "improved" as against 22 per cent, "and maintained improvement up to 18 months." The standards of improvement are not stated. A number of additional cases improved for limited periods and relapsed. These patients, the authors say, "must receive the weekly administration of carbon-dioxide in order to remain in relative remission" (p. 110). No details are given, but from my own investigations, recorded below, it seems likely that these were people whose neuroses included a great deal of pervasive ("free-floating") anxiety.

Because of its simplicity I began, late in 1953, to experiment with a slightly modified La Verne technique and have continued to use this ever since. The details are as follows. First the patient is shown how to empty his lungs completely and then fill them to capacity. He then lies on his back on a couch where he is shown how to apply the anesthetic mask to his face. Unless he happens to have specific fears related to anesthetics or suffocation, the crucial sequence now begins. He shuts his eyes and, responding to commands from me, in turn empties his lungs, places the mask on his face, and inhales the gas mixture (usually 70 per cent carbon dioxide and 30 per cent oxygen). When his lungs are full, he removes the mask from his face. He breathes heavily, gradually subsiding in 5–15 seconds. After the hyperpnea he is left to relax undisturbed for half a minute or more. On being questioned he usually reports that while dyspneic he also felt flushing of his face and neck, tingling in the extremities and genital organs, visual phenomena such as flashes, colored lights, or blackness, and sometimes momentary loss of consciousness. Usually, between one and four inhalations are given at a session.

I did not obtain any important therapeutic effects in the first four patients on whom I used this method, but the fifth benefited markedly. This was a case of war neurosis of ten years' standing. He displayed, almost continuously, a high degree of "free-floating" anxiety and had a special sensitivity to all situations involving explosions or low-pitched rumblings like thunder. Desensitization under hypnosis could not be attempted because, when asked to imagine a scene, the patient could never visualize anything but irregular black and white blotches. He had three treatments, each consisting of two full inhalations of the mixture of 70 per cent carbon dioxide and 30 per cent oxygen. There was a week between treatments, and he felt persistently better after each. After the third treatment he said he felt perfectly well. Three months later he was still well and reported that thunderstorms had left him quite undisturbed.

Since this experience, I have used the method exclusively for the treatment of pervasive anxiety, with results that are almost uniformly good and often dramatic. One or two inhalations may transform the misery of a long-lived state of pervasive anxiety, leaving the patient comfortable until exposure to a specific stimulus conditioned to neurotic anxiety re-establishes it. A skilled biologist who had suffered from severe pervasive anxiety for at least ten years described the consequences of a single full-capacity inhalation of 65 per cent carbon dioxide and 35 per cent oxygen four days afterward in the following words:

I lay down comfortably on the couch at 4:30 on Thursday afternoon. Having emptied my lungs, I put the mask on and inhaled the gas through my mouth as deeply as I could. It had the flavor of soda water. For a second or two nothing happened. Then I noticed rapid breathing, and for a moment everything became brilliant and detailed. I had a brief feeling of apprehension. I remember shutting my eyes and holding the cover of the sofa as the gasping for breath became more intense. Then I felt tingling in both arms and legs and a very odd feeling, which is hard to describe, of being affected all through. When my breathing returned to normal, I felt somewhat more calm and relaxed than usual. I went on lying on the couch for a minute or two and, when I got up, felt slightly languid. I walked to my car and found that I had difficulty in keeping my mind on the job of driving. At home I lay down to relax and discovered that I was already more relaxed than I could ever remember having been before. I felt removed and sleepy. After dinner I became increasingly sleepy and went to bed at 8:30, falling asleep at once and sleeping continuously until 7:00 A.M. This was most unusual, since for years I have slept badly, taking an hour or two to fall asleep and waking at about 5:00 A.M.

That morning [Friday] we went to a city 30 miles away. My wife drove, and I hardly noticed the heavy traffic which in the past has always kept me on edge. We went to consult a lawyer on income tax, and whereas normally I would have been nervous all morning, on this occasion I was relaxed. My wife says she has never seen me in such a good mood on a similar occasion. On returning home I found that I could relax at once. I went to bed early and slept well without the half grain of phenobarbital I usually take.

On Saturday the great relaxation and sleepiness had gone, but I felt very well and could relax at will. My feeling on Sunday was similar except for a brief period when my wife was upset. Today [Monday] I still feel able to relax at will and find that the world is in proportion, not dominated by minor events of an annoying nature.

The patient remained completely free from tension for nearly three weeks until a specific disturbing experience reinduced the continuous anxiety. However, this fluctuated at levels varying, according to the patient's estimate, at between 20 per cent and 50 per cent of his accustomed level. Two weeks after its reinduction he was given another solitary dose of the gas mixture, which again brought down the level of pervasive anxiety to zero. During the next two months he was fortunate enough to avoid any major disturbing experiences and he was aware of nothing more than minor tension now and then.

I do not use carbon dioxide therapy in every case that has pervasive anxiety, usually excluding those whose encounters with *specific* stimuli conditioned to neurotic anxiety reactions are relatively frequent; for in them the effects of the treatment are rapidly undone. For example, a patient who had rather severe pervasive anxiety generated by a love affair full of conflict repeatedly experienced marked amelioration after carbon dioxide therapy, but each time relapsed when he met his lady friend a few hours later, or even if he allowed his thoughts to dwell on the relationship. This patient insisted on having a "dose" every two or three days for some weeks, but, generally speaking, the treatment is hardly worth while under such circumstances.

Because of exclusions on the basis of the above consideration, the number of cases on whom the method was used has been small—20 in all. In 16 of these, pervasive anxiety has been markedly diminished by each treatment (comprising one to four inhalations) and in four it has been unaffected. Two of the latter were patients with anxiety states of about 12 years' duration, originating in the stress of battle.

Meduna and his followers have assumed that the effects of carbon dioxide therapy are due to the depressing action of carbon dioxide on nerve structures. Gellhorn (1953, p. 462) has criticized Meduna's theory and has gone on to suggest another explanation of these effects, also in terms of gross physiology. But from a psychological point of view any such theory is untenable, because the treatment apparently affects only *neurotic* anxiety responses. If the effects of carbon dioxide were due to its action on some chemical factor in certain nerve cells, all cells containing this factor would be influenced; and since the relevant cells are those that in one way or another subserve anxiety responses, all anxieties, even those aroused in response to real threats, would be similarly diminished by the treatment. Neither Meduna's case histories nor my own personal experience reveals any indication of this happening. Anxiety responses, as such, are by no means removed from the repertoire of the patient, who continues to have and display normal anxieties. It is therefore to be concluded that a specific unlearning of the connection between certain stimuli and the anxiety responses has occurred.

It is not difficult to see how reciprocal inhibition may be responsible for this unlearning. Neurotic anxiety-producing stimuli are acting on the patient continuously if pervasive anxiety is present. (Specific stimuli are also sometimes brought forth as imagery during the stage of the treatment at which consciousness becomes clouded.) Processes antagonistic to anxiety can be found both in the excitation that goes with intense respiratory stimulation and in association with the complete muscle relaxation that high concentrations of carbon dioxide produce. It is not possible at present to say which of these processes is the effective one. Perhaps each plays a part. But because even the most profound relaxation obtained by Jacobson's method or by the use of tranquilizing drugs does not seem to have comparable profound and lasting effects on pervasive anxiety, one is inclined to believe that it is the respiratory excitation that is mainly relevant.

Case 10: Illustrating Removal of Pervasive ("Free-Floating") Anxiety by La Verne's Carbon Dioxide Therapy After Each of Repeated Precipitations by Exposure to Specific Stimuli to Anxiety

I first met Mr. Q., a 29-year-old shopkeeper, in September 1953. Owing to some unpleasant childhood experiences, he had for many years been unhappy about illness and tended to keep away from sick people. In July 1952, after a cold he had developed a severe cough and lost weight, with the result that tuberculosis was suspected. Investigations turned out to be negative, but because some small amount of cough persisted and he did not regain his previous weight, he kept on worrying about the state of his health. In November 1952, he had bleeding hemorrhoids which greatly intensified his anxiety. Although the bleeding stopped in a few days, he began to think almost incessantly about illness and found it hard to concentrate on business problems. His anxiety became gradually more severe, and for some months he had the greatest difficulty in falling asleep in spite of the use of barbiturates and other drugs. Awareness of his anxiety made him still more anxious, for he feared it was an indication of mental abnormality. Seeing anybody not quite normal or hearing of anybody's insanity greatly upset him.

In March 1953 a psychiatrist had given him a number of "narco-analysis" sessions with pentothal, and in June another psychiatrist had given him eight injections and also "nerve tablets." None of these measures had had any effect.

His history revealed many sources of neurotic conditioning. His Willoughby score was 68 and he had the low Bernreuter self-sufficiency percentage of 20. Some headway having been made with training in relaxation, the following anxiety hierarchy was constructed on September 30, 1953. (A few of the items given were inserted at later dates.)

Hierarchy

1. Seeing anybody whose behavior suggests insanity
2. The word "insanity"
3. Seeing anyone with a gross deformity
4. Seeing a person having a fit
5. Blood, especially if it comes from a hand (the more, the worse)
6. A patient lying sick in bed (the more sick, the worse)
7. Entering a hospital
8. The sight of physical violence

9. Overhearing a quarrel
10. The sound of weeping
11. The sound of screaming
12. Symptoms of illness in himself
13. The word "fear"

From the next session onward, attempts were made at systematic desensitization under hypnosis, but very little progress was made because the patient had a high level of pervasive anxiety. Toward the end of October 1953 I decided to try carbon dioxide therapy on Mr. Q. He received three inhalations on October 30, three on November 2, and two on November 5. Each treatment diminished the pervasive anxiety to a very noticeable extent. On November 9 it was reinduced to a high level by a quarrel between two men in front of Mr. Q.'s shop in connection with the parking of an automobile. Three carbon dioxide inhalations on November 11 improved his condition, and after four more on the 14th, he reported feeling less anxiety than for a very long time. This made it easier for him to carry out certain behavior that I had assigned to him in his life situation, and a week or two later, desensitization under hypnosis was resumed and progressed more rapidly than was possible when pervasive anxiety was high. By the end of December, Mr. Q. was feeling so much better that he made up his mind to stop coming for treatment, against my advice.

I next saw him on April 29, 1954. His pervasive anxiety had been brought back again by the occurrence of a bloody murder two blocks away from his shop, at a time when he was already feeling anxious as the result of complications in business and in his social life. Three inhalations of carbon dioxide reduced the pervasive anxiety very markedly, and I then resumed treatment of specific anxiety-evoking stimuli. He came for his weekly appointments quite regularly until the end of September, making a fair amount of improvement in all directions. Although there were increments of pervasive anxiety now and then due to minor exposures to relevant stimuli, these were at no time severe enough during this period to require the use of carbon dioxide therapy.

I did not see Mr. Q. from October until the end of the year. He returned on January 3, 1955, stating that he had been feeling much better until two weeks previously, since when he had had some rather severe social stresses. One of these was related to an inability to deal adequately with a new assistant who walked around reading a book while at work. Mr. Q. had boiled inwardly and said nothing. There had been a gradual mounting of pervasive anxiety. Ways of dealing with his assistant and with other problems were discussed at this interview and he was then given three carbon dioxide inhalations. On January 6, Mr. Q. reported

that his pervasive anxiety had largely disappeared after the last session
and that he had dealt adequately with his assistant. He came again on
January 13 and was then lost sight of for seven months.

He returned on August 10, 1955. He had felt quite well until two weeks
previously when a good deal of pervasive anxiety was precipitated by the
realization that the son of his partner who at times assisted in the shop was
appearing to develop insane behavior, such as staring into space and making remarks that made no sense. After a few days the youngster had been
removed to be treated for schizophrenia, but, as always in similar circumstances, this had not lowered the level of Mr. Q.'s anxiety. This anxiety
was further increased on August 7 after Mr. Q. visited a relative with heart
disease in a hospital. Three inhalations of carbon dioxide brought about
a marked improvement. I emphasized, as I had done several times in the
past, how foolish it was for him to continue to be vulnerable to these chance
occurrences when with a little persistence he could be entirely desensitized
to their effect. Until November 9, 1955, he made regular weekly appear-
ances at which desensitization proceeded. Further carbon dioxide inhalations were required on September 9 and November 2, on each occasion
after pervasive anxiety had again been precipitated by his partner's son
visiting the shop and again manifesting behavior suggesting mental abnormality.

From November 1955 until March 1956, the son of Mr. Q.'s partner
appeared to be normal. Except for some anxieties in relation to the business, Mr. Q. had felt quite happy. But in the middle of March the young
man relapsed and Mr. Q. was again disturbed but not as badly as on past
occasions. On March 23 he was given three carbon dioxide inhalations
with very good effect. From this time until the beginning of July he attended regularly for treatment. There were two further occasions, late in
April and early in June, when carbon dioxide inhalations were necessitated
by further outbreaks of irrational behavior on the part of the partner's
son. However, by July desensitization to all the items in the hierarchy list
was completed and now Mr. Q. was able to withstand any amount of exposure to other people's insane-seeming behavior without being disturbed
by it. He still had a certain degree of excessive sensitivity to social situations as reflected by a Willoughby score of 30.

11 | *The Use of Special Conditioning*

Procedures in the Consulting Room

In a strict sense all learning is conditioning. The present heading is used to denote formal procedures by which a definite stimulus is connected to a definite response. Apart from methods applied to obsessive behavior and to hysteria (discussed in the next chapter), the only report of the use of conditioning in neurosis appears to be that of Jones (1956), who in a neurosis characterized by severe frequency of micturition gradually conditioned an inhibition of the feeling of urgency, and with it some inhibition of the abnormal bladder tension—employing false manometer readings as the unconditioned stimulus.

Reciprocal Inhibition of Anxiety Through a Dominating Motor Response

Motor activity in the form of work or play has long been thought to be of use in the alleviation of neurotic disturbances. It can certainly be effective as a distraction, removing or diminishing the impact upon the patient of anxiety-evoking stimuli, as already noted in Chapter 6. Whether or not it is ever therapeutic in a more fundamental way has never been convincingly shown despite the widespread prescribing of occupational therapy, exercises, and games. Nevertheless, therapists can point to individual cases of neurosis in which one or other kind of motor activity seems to have been beneficial in a lasting way; and in keeping with this there is experimental evidence of an inhibitory effect of motor responses upon autonomic responses. Undirected motor activity speeds up the return of the galvanic skin responses (GSR) to its initial level (Freeman and Pathman, 1940) and directed activity accelerates it even more (Haggard and Freeman, 1941).

That particularly marked effects are obtainable with very highly specific motor responses is suggested by an experiment reported by Mowrer and Viek (1948). They showed that among rats exposed to a continuous electric shock, those animals which were able to learn a definite motor response (jumping into the air) as a precursor to the termination of the shock soon lost their anxiety at being placed in the experimental cage *minus* the shock, whereas animals given exactly the same amount of shock without the opportunity to learn a specific motor response did not tend to lose their anxiety at all. (See also p. 89).

This experiment suggested a new therapeutic method. It was postulated that if in the presence of a stimulus evoking neurotic anxiety a mild shock were repeatedly to be applied to the limb of a patient, and if this shock were also each time to produce a well-defined motor response, the neurotic anxiety would gradually be weakened. In only two cases, so far, have I made systematic use of this method. One was a girl whose hands trembled if she used a cup and saucer or knife and fork in company. She improved markedly after three sessions and was then lost sight of. The other was an exceptionally severe case of agoraphobia in whom the method was spectacularly successful. A very summary account of this (incomplete at the time) has already been published (Wolpe, 1954). The fuller account that follows only does bare justice to this outstandingly instructive case.

CASE ILLUSTRATING RECIPROCAL INHIBITION OF ANXIETY
BY A DOMINATING MOTOR RESPONSE

Case 11: A Case of Social Inadequacy and Extreme Agoraphobia

Miss K., a good-looking 23-year-old university graduate, was first seen in July 1952 at her parents' home. Three years previously she had had two fairly violent falls in the street within a few weeks and thereafter had been apprehensive of walking outside unaccompanied lest she should fall. As is apt to happen in such cases, her range of activity had then gradually become more and more circumscribed. At one stage she would walk in the street only if her mother held her arm; later she entirely refused to leave the house, and by the time I first saw her, she was practically bedridden, apart from very tense wall-hugging journeys between her bed and a couch in the drawing room, where she would sit with her legs up. If she tried to sit with her legs down, she became dizzy and nauseous, and reading even a few lines had the same effect. Sitting on the couch tired her, so that she always returned to bed by 4:00 P.M.

An only child, during her childhood and adolescence she had been incredibly overprotected by her mother who insisted on standing perpetually in attendance on her. She was permitted to do almost nothing for herself, forbidden to play games lest she get hurt, and even in her final year at high school was daily escorted over the few hundred yards to and from the gates of the school by her mother, who carried her school books for her. In her 23 years, Miss K. had not been allowed to make a cup of tea. Though very shortsighted, she never wore glasses or even mentioned her myopia because her mother was of the opinion that for a girl to wear glasses is worse than to be crippled. She found her mother's solicitude and inter- ference very irritating. Anything associated with her mother would lose its pleasantness. For example, when her mother came to listen with her to a new phonograph record it was less pleasurable to her afterward.

Her father was a studious man who spent all his spare cash on books. When she was a little girl, he was kind to her and often spent hours talking to her and telling stories. But through preoccupation with reading he had lost his friends so that hardly anyone ever visited the house.

At school she did very well, but disliked most of the teachers because of their "aggressiveness." She maintained one rather close friendship from her 12th to her 16th year, and later became one of a group of "cynical types." On entering the university she had a great sense of freedom, since she was no longer accompanied by her mother. She liked university life, but became bored with it after completing her B.A.

She had not often been asked out by men though they appealed to her both socially and sexually. In any event, her mother frowned upon her going out. She had once fallen in love with a man who was quite unre- sponsive to her. She said, "I never seemed to succeed socially. I was always the one to make the advances, although because of my shyness it wasn't easy. My shyness was often interpreted as aloofness. I wondered what was wrong with me!"

Her Willoughby score was 61.

I visited Miss K. about six times a month. During the first few months my efforts were aimed mainly at overcoming her social anxieties and in- creasing her control of interpersonal situations. I gave great emphasis to showing her ways of freeing herself from her mother's heavy hand, and she was only too eager to put them into effect. She became able to express herself freely, so that, for example, she could, without remorse, ask her mother to leave her alone. She was also encouraged to be more assertive with friends, acquaintances, and tradesmen (chiefly in telephone conversa- tions). In the course of about nine months she greatly improved her handling of other people and felt a marked increase in self-confidence. She was able to read for a few minutes in the morning and to stay up until 6:00 P.M.

Her mobility had meanwhile increased to a small extent. She could now walk to any part of the house, and for fetching things this made her relatively independent of her mother. While walking she still had to be always within a few inches of a wall or similar support, but it was no longer necessary to maintain practically constant touch therewith. It was noted that any social failure, such as letting her mother foist unnecessary help upon her, would produce a setback in her ability to move about, lasting for hours or days. An example of this occurred when Miss K., having spent some days happily clearing some bookshelves, discovered that her mother had secretly cleared the bottom shelf at night.

When during the second month I tried to give her a lesson in relaxation she reacted with some agitation. I therefore gave up the attempt, but soon after managed to connect a reaction of calmness to the sound of a metronome by conditioning an eyelid closure response to this sound. She purchased a metronome thereafter and found that it gave her a good deal of symptomatic relief from tension. During the seventh month of treatment (January 1953) she expressed willingness to receive training in progressive relaxation. After her third lesson, she said that she could achieve a deeper state of calmness by relaxing than by the use of the metronome.

It seemed clear that, notwithstanding its origin in anxieties arising from social relations that still influenced its intensity, Miss K.'s agoraphobia had some measure of autonomous existence. There was a fear of falling and of "empty" space itself that needed treatment in its own right. During March and April 1953 attempts were made to obtain desensitization by means of relaxation under hypnosis, making her visualize crossing spaces slightly greater than those she could actually cross. Although Miss K. was a fair hypnotic subject who could relax well, she made little progress with the space difficulty, apparently because even mild tasks sometimes produced a "queer feeling," and she became rather unhappy about the method. However, in the two months of its use she felt an increase in confidence, and came to be able to read for an hour or more at a stretch in the morning.

In April 1953 I decided to try to apply the lesson of the Mowrer and Viek experiment (pp. 173–74), employing the following procedure. Silver electrodes were attached to Miss K.'s left hand and forearm. She was instructed to close her eyes and imagine a relatively easy (though to her, slightly disturbing) fall and to signal at the beginning of the imagined movement. At this signal a mild electric shock (secondary of Palmer inductorium at 8.0 cm. with a 6-volt dry cell in primary) was passed into her forearm, being stopped only upon the occurrence of a brisk flexion of the forearm, which the patient had been instructed to make. This movement soon became the instant response to the shock. She found that the shock was not uncomfortable (as it would be at other times) and the *shock-cum-flexion* "vanquished" the disturbed feeling. When the whole sequence had been repeated a number of times (usually between 15 and 40), she reported that imagining the fall was becoming less unpleasant and disturbing and, after further repetitions, that she could imagine it with ease. Thereafter she was able to attempt this particular fall in actuality and, after practicing it a good many times a day, could do it easily after a few days. Then she was ready for a slightly more difficult fall.

The first fall to be dealt with in this way was sideways onto a mattress on which she was sitting. The next was standing next to a bed and falling forward onto the mattress. In subsequent months, until January 1954, increasingly "difficult" imaginary falls were used during the sessions and practiced in the interim. In September 1953 she was able, with her knees straight, to fall on her hands onto a hard chair; in December onto a cushion on the floor; and by the end of January directly onto the carpet. She could also fall on her knees onto a cushion on the floor. This seemed to be as much falling as could reasonably be expected, and she could do it all without the slightest fear even though she sometimes bruised herself.

During the months of overcoming the fear of falling Miss K. improved in many ways. She could walk freely within the house and on the porch at arm's length from a support, go down the four porch steps onto the gravel path while carrying a light straw chair, jump into the air, take a normal bath (impossible during the previous three years) excluding her mother from the bathroom (which had never happened before in all her life), and make her own bed. Her bedtime had advanced to 9:00 P.M. She could read at length at any time, was doing phonograph record reviews for a journal, and was handling people with increasing confidence.

These advances taken together gave me the impression that she was ready for another kind of step toward liberation. In all her life she had never spent a night without her mother under the same roof. Early in February 1954 I asked Miss K. how she would like to have her parents go on holiday for a week or two while some friends of hers moved into the house to keep her company. She was delighted at the idea, and we had little difficulty in overcoming her parents' resistance (because by this time they clearly understood the role played by overprotection in the illness of their daughter). They agreed to go away for ten days early in April. In the interim Miss K. found a good deal of pleasure in making arrangements for the time of their absence.

During the first two days of her parents' holiday Miss K. was slightly weepy. Thereafter it was "wonderful." She felt she was making progress every day. She walked about the house with almost normal unconcern for the details of her surroundings. She took her meals with her three guests, sitting at the table with her legs down, and went to bed when they did—usually at 11:00 P.M., but once at 12:45 A.M. She enjoyed doing the cooking during the day while her friends were away at work. All these gains were maintained when her parents returned.

Meanwhile, by February 1954 it had also become evident that the fear of falling was only one component of Miss K.'s fear of space. There seemed to be also *a conditioned fear reaction to the very awareness of distance from support.* I resolved to treat this in the same way as the fear of falling. Almost completely covering the floor of the lounge where our interviews took place was a Persian carpet. She stood at the bookshelves along one wall, and then advanced on the carpet to the farthest point at which she felt perfectly comfortable (about 18 inches from the bookshelves). She noted the marking on the carpet at the tips of her toes. When she sat down, I applied the electrodes and, having asked her to signal in the usual way to the idea of advancing one inch beyond this marking on the carpet, presented, at the signal, the forearm-lifting shock. On the first occasion (February 17, 1954), after ten shocks, anxiety to the image of standing at this advanced point was markedly decreased and, after seven more shocks on February 22, 1954, completely eliminated; so that she could now practice standing there in actuality. At subsequent interviews the imagined standing position moved slowly nearer to the center of the carpet. It was found necessary at each position to "do" it facing different directions. At the middle of May she was able to stand comfortably at a mark on the carpet about halfway to its center. This mark was about two arm's lengths from the bookshelves. The ability to stand at increasing distances from this support in the lounge was, as might be expected, at every stage generalized to other supports. Thus, at the two-arm's-length stage she could make her way along a ledge to the front garden gate and then walk along the sidewalk either to left or to right, staying always well within two arm's lengths of the neighboring garden fences and stopping only when confronted by the wide gap of an open garage gate. At this time it had also become possible for her to go across the sidewalk to the open door of a car; and on April 26 she went out with a male cousin on an hour's drive— her first for years—which she greatly enjoyed.

The progression from the halfway zone on the carpet to the middle of the central medallion was extremely slow, and the more so because from June 1954 onward I saw her only once a week. It became necessary to do each half-inch or so in three stages: (a) standing about twelve inches back and placing the left foot on the carpet marking to be "conquered"; (b) bringing the right foot alongside the left, and (c) standing with both feet at the marking for increasing durations. It was not until October that she was able to pass across the center of the carpet and then only quickly with a kind of "curtsey" during the middle step, making it part of a ballet step. (Since June she had been taking lessons in ballet.) This "curtsey" was also useful for negotiating space elsewhere. In November, at the forearm-lifting shock sessions, I began to give her, in addition to imagined positions on the carpet, a series of scenes of walking from the front gate toward the curb (with no car waiting). On February 28, 1955, she reported that *she could stand indefinitely anywhere in the lounge.* She could also stand as long as she wanted at a point halfway between the gateway and the curb.

During the next three or four months the imagined content of the forearm-lifting shock sessions was confined to going from the gateway to the curb. Progress was very slow. A note of April 18 reads, "41 shocks were given before she could comfortably 'do' 4 normal paces from gateway to curb." Toward the end of April, having one day walked a distance of three blocks with a girl friend (whose arm she could have clutched if necessary), she expressed the desire to go and live on her own in an apartment—a possibility I had brought up some time previously. As no apartment was obtainable, she arranged accommodation in a hotel.

When she moved into the hotel on June 1, 1955, she had still not accomplished the full six paces from the garden gate to the curb and, correspondingly, could advance alone only five paces across the sidewalk from the door of the hotel. Crossing this sidewalk now became the objective of the shock sessions. At the second weekly session at the hotel she reported having walked the 12 paces from the *side* of the hotel to the curb parallel to it. Since the street which this curb lined was a narrow one, it was decided to make crossing this street a second objective of the sessions. On July 12 she reported having gone nearly half way across this street (12 paces), and on August 1 well over halfway (16 paces) but without being able to cross. At the session of August 1 she required 10 shocks for the 17th pace, 27 for the 18th, and 8 for the 19th.

At 10:00 A.M. on August 2 she telephoned to say in jubilation that she had crossed the street four times. Two hours later she arrived at my consulting room for the first time, having walked the 12 blocks from the hotel—alone!

There were loose ends—crossing a street at the middle of a block, crossing very wide streets and open squares, and riding on trolley cars and buses—and these were fairly rapidly overcome in the next few months by the same arm-flexion technique. At the end of August, she returned to her parents' home, and in September began to work in a bookshop, having had spectacles made for her myopia. She became increasingly at ease and confident in all activities and all relationships and gradually extended her range of social contacts.

In February 1956 interviews were put on a rather loose basis of two- to four-week intervals. Miss K.'s few remaining minor difficulties with space were easily cleared up. She felt "marvellously free." She was very happy at her work and was much appreciated by her employers. In June she said that she had never before been so happy. She was slightly disturbed when anybody tried "to look after" her, but this reaction was diminishing and she was "not at all worried about it." Her Willoughby score was 10. She had had a total of 185 interviews.

The Conditioning of "Anxiety-Relief" Responses

The possibility that "anxiety-relief" responses might be directly conditioned to convenient stimuli and subsequently used to counter anxiety was suggested by an observation in a recent experiment by Zbrozyna (1953). This observation was that if a stimulus is repeatedly presented to an eating animal just before withdrawing the food, that stimulus acquires the property of inhibiting feeding even when the animal is in the middle of a meal. By analogy with this it might be expected that a stimulus that consistently coincides with the termination of a noxious stimulus might acquire anxiety-inhibiting effects. There are, in fact experiments that point in this direction. Coppock (1951), Goodson and Brownstein (1953), Smith and Buchanan (1954), and Barlow (1956) have all shown that approach responses are conditioned to a stimulus repeatedly presented at the moment of termination of an electric shock—in contrast to the avoidance that is conditioned to a stimulus that precedes the electric shock.

On the strength of these observations it seems reasonable to expect that if an uncomfortable induction shock is administered to a human subject for several seconds and then made to cease immediately after a signal, that signal will become connected to such bodily responses as follow cessation of the shock, these responses being the negative of the anxiety produced by the shock.

I have put this idea into practice in the following manner. Silver "cardiac" electrodes are attached by means of rubber bands of the kind used in electrocardiography to the patient's left forearm and the palm of his left hand. The electrodes are connected to the secondary circuit of an induction coil whose primary is fed by a six-volt dry battery. Tests are then made to determine a level of shock that is very uncomfortable without being unbearable—usually at an inductorium setting of 7.0–7.5 cm.

This intensity of shock is now administered to the patient. He has been told beforehand to endure the shock until the desire to have it stop becomes very strong, and then to say aloud the word "calm." The moment he says the word, the current is switched off. After 30–60 seconds the shock is again administered under the same conditions as before. It is necessary to inform the patient that he will never be shocked without warning, and such warning must be given each time, since some patients otherwise become very anxious between shocks. Most patients report a feeling of relief at the cessation of the shock, and this sometimes seems greatly out of proportion to the discomfort that went before.

The whole procedure is repeated 10–20 times at a session. Many patients find after one, two, or three sessions that using the word "calm" can diminish the intensity of anxiety evoked in the course of day-to-day experience. In a small minority of patients (perhaps 15 per cent) the effect is very marked indeed. Others report smaller effects and some none at all.

The reason for this great variability is not obvious, but it seems that the greatest conditioning occurs in those in whom the shock produces considerable *emotional* disturbance (as distinct from sensory discomfort). This would be in keeping with our theoretical expectation. It is interesting to note that Eysenck and his co-workers (1956) have recently found that in some subjects in whom they failed to condition "anxiety-relief" reactions initially, these reactions could subsequently be conditioned if the subject was given dexedrine before the conditioning session. Eysenck has attributed this to an improvement in learning ability that the dexedrine accomplished by decreasing reactive inhibition. But the possibility does not seem to have been excluded that the drug had its effect through increasing the intensity of the *emotional* (autonomic) reactions evoked by the shock.

My own use of "anxiety-relief" responses has had primarily a symptomatic aim. In one patient, by chance, some desensitization effects apparently followed their use. This was a woman in whom the word "calm" did not become the effective conditioned stimulus to the relief reaction; but she found herself automatically picturing the inductorium against the background of the consulting room whenever she experienced anxiety rising within her. This would bring on "surges of relief," under which the anxiety would melt away. Gradually, according to prediction on the reciprocal inhibition principle, with repeated occurrences of this experience the amount of anxiety produced by relevant stimuli became less and less.

It seems likely that much more use will be found for "anxiety-relief" responses in fundamental psychotherapy. Meyer (1956) at the Institute of Psychiatry, Maudsley Hospital, has employed them in a systematic way to overcome phobias, by getting the patient to evoke the "anxiety-relief" reaction in himself (by means of a conditioned verbal stimulus) when exposed to controlled amounts of phobic stimulation. Some cases of agoraphobia have apparently lent themselves particularly well to this method.

12 | *Treatment of Neurotic Responses*

Other Than Anxiety

Avoidance Conditioning of Obsessions

The treatment of those obsessions not removed by measures against anxiety is an instance of the application of the reciprocal inhibition principle to a response other than anxiety, for here it is an intense and excessive approach response that is being overcome. The essence of the method is to subject the patient to a very unpleasant electric shock in the presence of the obsessional object. It seems that the first to report the use of such a method was Kantorovich (1934), who employed it in the treatment of alcoholics—with considerable success. The technique was first applied to an obsessional patient by Max (1935) a good many years ago and was then apparently ignored. Max administered to his patient an unusually severe induction shock in the presence of a fetishistic object. By doing this repeatedly and then reinforcing at intervals when required, he produced a persistent avoidance reaction to this object, which alone, it seems, very greatly ameliorated the patient's emotionally disturbed state. More recently, Raymond (1956) has described how he overcame a sex-connected fetish toward handbags and perambulators by showing these objects to the patient "after he had received an injection of apomorphine and just before nausea was produced." The treatment was repeated every two hours day and night for a week, and boosters were given eight days later and six months later. Nineteen months after the first administration of the treatment there was no recurrence.

I have occasionally attempted to remove obstinate obsessions by conditioning to them an attitude of "avoidance" using a modification of the method of Max described above. Instead of presenting the actual objects or situations that form the substance of the obsession, I ask the subject to imagine them. When he indicates by signal that the image is clear, a severe shock is passed into his forearm. This is repeated five to 20 times at a session.

A very good result was apparently obtained in the first patient to be treated in this manner, whose case is briefly given below. In three later cases on whom it was tried the method failed in one (who suffered from an inability to make any movement unless certain "good" thoughts were in his mind); it was partially effective in the second (a case of exhibitionism who had greatly improved with the overcoming of neurotic anxieties but had a residual impulse at the sight of schoolgirls in uniform); and seemed to be having an increasing effect in the third (a man of 68 with an obsession about the possible dangers to children of razor blades and other objects he might have left lying about). His treatment was interrupted by my departure overseas, but on my return 16 months later the improvement, rated by the patient at 75 per cent, had been maintained.

Case 12: Treatment of a Food Obsession by Avoidance Conditioning

Miss H. was a very intelligent woman of 36 who had for 16 years suffered from a severe neurosis dominated by a food obsession which had resisted numerous modes of therapy including electroconvulsive therapy and psychoanalysis. The foods that were so irresistibly attractive were all undesirable in one of two ways. Either they had a high salt content and were forbidden because of a long-standing cardiac insufficiency with edema, or they were fattening, and she had a horror of getting fat.

Certain other very distressing neurotic reactions had improved considerably after about a year of treatment by the more usual reciprocal inhibition techniques. But the obsession was still present almost always and was worse when the patient was reacting to any persistent anxiety-producing stimulus. She would have visions of various items of "delectable food" and would be tortured by a conflict as to whether to eat or not. If she did eat, she soon felt a rising guilt (anxiety about something done) which would lead back to the obsession. Thus, a vicious circle of eating and anxiety would be started, which, within a few days, would leave her in a desperately helpless and exhausted state.

Avoidance conditioning was carried out as follows: The electrodes having been attached to her left forearm, Miss H. was told to raise her right hand as soon as she had formed a clear imaginary picture of some desirable foodstuff. An almost unbearable current from the inductorium at 7.0 cm. (6 volts into the primary) was then instantly delivered and continued until she lowered her right hand as a signal that the shock could no longer be borne, as she usually did after a second or two. About ten reinforcements were given at each session, and two to three days were allowed to elapse between sessions. After the first session the "nagging" of the obsession was already markedly reduced. It was further reduced in four more sessions, which implicated the whole range of items of "delectable food." Miss H. reported that on imagining any such food she immediately had a feeling of fear and revulsion, accompanied by an image of the shock situation. (At an earlier stage this feeling was occasionally preceded by a momentary feeling of pleasure.) Within a few seconds she was able to turn her attention to whatever she had been doing before the food image came up—a tremendous gain as contrasted with the old misery of hours spent debating, "Should I eat; should I not?" After her fifth and last session she stated that her tendency to think of food was also diminishing. Unfortunately, but not unexpectedly, there was also some generalization of the avoidance to permitted foods, i.e., nonfattening, sodium-free foods eaten only at mealtime. This was a very considerable difficulty, but Miss H. regarded it as trivial in comparison with her obsession. The overall lightening of the burden made it much easier to return to the usual procedures for overcoming the anxiety reactions. Gratifying progress was made, only to be brought to an end a few weeks later by her sudden death from ventricular fibrillation due to chronic rheumatic heart disease.

The Treatment of Hysteria Without Anxiety

In discussing the etiology of hysteria in Chapter 6 it was noted that out of a small group of 22 hysterical patients there were 13 whose hysterical symptoms were associated with a good deal of neurotic anxiety as reflected by the Willoughby schedule, whereas the other 9 showed relatively little neurotic anxiety. In those in whom much anxiety was present its successful treatment was accompanied by disappearance of the hysterical symptoms. But in patients who had little neurotic anxiety, treating it did not affect the hysterical symptoms. For example, the "writer's cramp" of one case did not improve though his Willoughby score dropped from 24 to 13 after 23 interviews. The presumption is that because in these cases the hysterical reaction has been conditioned independently of anxiety (see Chapter 6) its treatment is a problem distinct from the treatment of anxiety.

In low-anxiety hysteria a variety of procedures have proved to be curative in different cases. It seems clear that to be effective a procedure must bring about a reversal of the conditioning that underlies the hysterical reaction. In other words, positive hysterical responses (e.g., the compulsive mimicry of Case 13) must undergo conditioned inhibition, while negative types of reaction (e.g., anesthesia, paralysis, amnesia) require positive reconditioning.

From the standpoint of the above hypothesis it is instructive to survey some of the methods that others have used successfully.

a) Conditioning Methods

The course of therapy is particularly clear where *conditioning* has been used to overcome sensory or motor hysteria. In 1933, Sears and Cohen treated a case of hysterical anesthesia, analgesia, and astereognosis by establishing conditioned responses to stimulation of anesthetic areas, and complete recovery of sensation resulted. No relapse or other adverse effects were noted in a six-month follow-up (Cohen, 1953).

Hilgard and Marquis (1940, pp. 297–98) reported the equally successful treatment of a woman of 32 who, since a motor car accident six years previously, had a completely paralyzed and anesthetic left arm. In the procedure which led to the recovery of sensation, a shock to the anesthetic hand was used as the stimulus to be conditioned to the withdrawal of the normal hand evoked by shock to a finger. Distinct conditioning occurred, and with it sensitivity gradually returned to the anesthetic hand and arm in the course of several sessions held daily. Thereafter, "the conditioning procedure was reversed for purposes of developing voluntary control." The conditioned stimulus was now a light shock to the normal hand, and the response to which it was to be conditioned was movement in the paralyzed limb, using a more severe shock to the hand on that side as the unconditioned stimulus. "Presently, movement began to occur in the paralyzed hand at the signal given to the normal hand. This was the beginning of control, and voluntary movement was gradually restored." Two years later the symptoms had not returned, nor had any new ones appeared. (Some of the above details are due to Hilgard [1957].)

Malmo, Davis, and Barga (1952) overcame total hysterical deafness of 3½ months' duration in a 19-year-old girl by a method similar to the above, following a brief 1,000-cycle tone by a shock producing finger withdrawal. About 50 per cent conditioning was achieved in the last 20 of 140 presentations of the combination. Hearing returned the next morning, when a car driver who narrowly missed her blasted his horn and shouted at her. (The therapist had suggested that hearing would return on the morning after the treatment.)

The successful treatment of several cases of writer's cramp by a conditioning technique has recently been reported by Sylvester and Leversedge (1955).

b) *"Reliving" Traumatic Experiences*

In Chapter 6 some cases of Freud's were noted in which the cure of hysteria followed upon the patient *relating the story of the distressing events that started the hysteria.* Other therapists have had similar experiences. Fodor (1946) produced partial recovery in a case of hysterical color blindness, when, becoming for the first time aware of the color blindness at the 26th session, he made the patient recount the highly emotional circumstances of its onset 20 years earlier, previously a well-kept secret. Awareness of green alone failed to return. After the 28th session the patient did not come back and Fodor was unable to re-establish contact.

Dicks (1939, p. 96) hypnotized a girl who had for four years suffered from hysterical fits and, noticing during the trance that she became flushed and rigid, commanded her to recall what she was experiencing and then woke her. She related with horror the scene of a sexual assault in a barn during which the boy's face "changed to that of her father." After a spell of great emotional excitement that necessitated her admission to a mental hospital for a few weeks, she made a rapid recovery and became free of fits, according to follow-ups over three years.

MECHANISMS OF THERAPY IN HYSTERIA*

In those of the above cases in which hysteria was cured by a deliberate conditioning procedure, a possible explanation (illustrated by Figure 10) is the following. By stimulating, in relation to a new stimulus-response sequence the pathways "blocked" by conditioned inhibition, there is the possibility of some of the blocked synapses being activated as the result of spatial summation (p. 11). For example, in treating an anesthetic limb, impulses from stimulation of the limb summate, at the "blocked" synapses, with impulses from the unconditioned stimulus to the normal limb so that at some of them transmission occurs. Lasting "unblocking" effects may now be produced there in consequence of the drive reduction due to cessation of the electric shock. These effects are probably quite minute at first and increase with repetition. Repetition "wears down" the block until at last stimulation of the anesthetic limb is itself able to produce the response originally evoked by the unconditioned stimulus. The block to consciousness is overcome in the same way, though evidently at a slower rate. Thus are sensory impulses from the anesthetic limb reintegrated into the body's reaction systems.

Treatment of the reverse situation, where an undesirable positive conditioning has to be overcome, is demonstrated by Case 13 (below) in

---

* The cures by conditioning quoted above, together with those described below, contradict the repression theory in the context of the theory's origin—hysteria. A psychoanalyst, if asked before the conditioning treatment of any of these patients what outcome his theory would predict, would have said, "You are unlikely to benefit the patient in any important way. You may remove the symptoms, but if you do they will recur or be replaced by other symptoms, because the repressed complexes will not be affected by your treatment." *His prediction would have been falsified in every case, for in no patient did the old symptoms reappear or new ones arise.* Either, then, the "repressed complexes" never existed, or they were rendered lastingly inert by conditioning. The first possibility would negate the repression theory, the second would require it to be modified beyond recognition.

("Resistance" on the part of psychoanalytically orientated individuals to evidence such as the above is almost invariable. See Eysenck's excellent discussion [1957, p. 271] of the irrationality of this "resistance.")

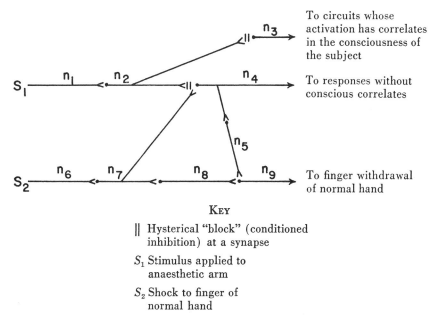

KEY

|| Hysterical "block" (conditioned inhibition) at a synapse

S_1 Stimulus applied to anaesthetic arm

S_2 Shock to finger of normal hand

Fig. 10. Diagram illustrating hypothetical mechanism of cure of an inhibitory hysterical state, on the paradigm of the case of Hilgard and Marquis (p. 185). The figure depicts the state of affairs before treatment has begun. Impulses from S_1 are blocked at the $n_2 \cdot n_3$ and the $n_2 \cdot n_4$ synapses. Impulses from S_2 that produce finger withdrawal pass directly along n_6–n_7–n_8–n_9. But impulses from S_2 are also *delivered* at numerous other synapses, e.g., $n_7 \cdot n_4$, probably without transmission occurring. Even if the synapse $n_7 \cdot n_4$ does transmit some impulses, the block at $n_2 \cdot n_4$ will not be affected if n_2 is not delivering impulses to the synaptic zone. But if impulses from n_2 arrive at the zone at the same time as impulses from n_7, the $n_2 \cdot n_4$ block may be rendered susceptible to change. It seems likely that such change will occur only if the post-synaptic neurone (n_4) is activated, and will be driven home by the drive reduction that ensues upon cessation of the electric shock (see Chapter 2). The neural relations that would undo the $n_2 \cdot n_3$ block are not shown in the figure but are conceived to be parallel to those affecting $n_2 \cdot n_4$.

which, through achieving a partial inhibition of single responses in pathways in which responding had been "unbridled," a conditioned inhibition of the excessive and undesired responses was built up. It is important to realize that in such a case as this it is not a particular movement whose conditioning has to be reversed, but a manner of responding to a class of stimulus conditions, a conditioning at a "higher" level of organization; but it is only through inhibiting an individual response of the pattern that an inhibition of the general tendency can occur.

In those cases in which cure of hysteria is associated with re-experiencing the causal situation, the mechanism would seem to be that which appears to account for abreactive cures in general (p. 196). All the stimuli that were present at the time of conditioning are again present. But now, in addition to the responses that were then evoked, there are others, attributable to factors in the therapeutic situation. These responses inhibit the older (hysterical) set of responses (just as they might inhibit anxiety) and so weaken the hysterical habit—rapidly in circumstances highly charged emotionally, more gradually otherwise (e.g., Case 14).

CASES ILLUSTRATING THERAPY OF
LOW-ANXIETY HYSTERIA

Among the five cases of hysteria with low anxiety that I have successfully treated, the cure was related to the use of special procedures in three. One (Case 13) was treated by suggesting, under hypnosis, a new response that brought about an inhibition of the hysterical response. The second (Case 14) was repeatedly "exposed," under hypnosis, to the original situation which had led to the hysterical reaction. In the third, who had suffered from "feelings of unreality" following a traumatic experience nine years previously, this method failed. An excellent result was achieved with carbon dioxide–oxygen inhalations, for, apparently, the hysterical symptom was evoked by pervasive stimuli.

Case 13: Hysterical Compulsion Treated by Hypnotic Suggestion of a Response Inhibiting the Compulsive Behavior

A 47-year-old married male nurse, employed in an industrial first-aid room, was sent for psychiatric treatment by the medical officer who had observed him during the previous four years. For 17 years he had never been free from an uncontrollable impulse to mimic any rhythmic movements he saw, e.g., waving of arms or dancing. He would also automatically obey any command, no matter from whom, unless it was to do something grossly improper. A command, though, could not stop a rhythmic movement. The workmen frequently exploited his compulsion, to amuse themselves, often exhausting him and distressing him sometimes so much that he was left trembling. His Willoughby score was 18.

No anxiety component could be observed in this behavior. Although it had features of a compulsion, its essential stereotypy suggested a greater kinship with hysteria. I resolved to employ hypnosis to try to break the compulsion by attaching to the cues to its occurrence new and incompatible behavior. The patient was a good hypnotic subject, and six inductions were done in the course of three interviews. Two were done at the first interview. At the first induction he was made to recall the first occasions of compulsive mimicry and obedience, and was then given the direct suggestion that he would stop imitating. At the second he was simply hypnotized and wakened, as a control experiment. No change followed either of these trances.

At the second interview the posthypnotic suggestion was made that after waking he would copy only alternate movements of my right arm, but on being wakened, he still copied every movement, as before. He was then hypnotized again and told that on waking he would find that he would move only his hand when I moved my whole arm rhythmically. This posthypnotic suggestion was obeyed. A third trance was induced in that session and the posthypnotic suggestion given that he would decrease his hand movement as I continued to wave my arm rhythmically, and also a general suggestion that he would move only his right hand when impulses to mimic anybody arose. When he woke and was tested, the excursion of his hand was seen to be lessening.

At his third interview, two days later, the patient reported that he had entirely stopped being affected by other people's movements or commands. He showed no reaction at all when I beat my fist on the desk. He said that he was sleeping much better and was no longer startled at being awakened, and his fear of the dark had vanished. He was hypnotized again and told he would continue to be unaffected by people's movements or commands. During this trance, at my instigation, he told how the onset of his condition had followed a violent wakening by a nurse early one morning when he was in a hospital with pneumonia.

Four years later the patient was perfectly well and had not relapsed in any respect.

Case 14: Hysterical Paresis of Right Forearm Treated by Repeated Presentation of the Causal Experience Under Hypnosis

Mr. J. was an electrician, 34 years old. One day in February 1953 when he was pulling hard upon some cables, they suddenly came away so that he struck his right elbow quite hard against the wall behind him. The impact was not painful but he was startled. From that moment, he invariably felt a "tired" pain and stiffness developing in the region of his right elbow (especially over the insertion and belly of the brachioradialis) whenever he gripped a tool for more than a minute or two or if he repeatedly opened and closed his hand. In the course of the next two months he noticed a gradual weakening of the grip of that hand. Frequent procaine injections and faradic stimulation had no effect. On April 19, 1953, ostensibly because X-rays had revealed the presence of a minute spicule of bone near the right lateral epicondyle, but really as a "psychological measure," an operation was performed on the elbow under general anesthesia. There was slight improvement during the first few days after the operation and then the patient was put on exercises. Soon the condition reverted to its previous state. Nevertheless Mr. J. returned to work on May 19, 1953, and thereafter observed an increasing tendency for the second and third digits of his right hand and the fourth and fifth digits to "stick together." Meanwhile his grip was becoming weaker and weaker, so that on June 19, 1953, he was again off work. Faradism and novocaine injections were again tried, again without effect.

On June 29, an orthopedic surgeon reported as follows:

There is a healed operation scar three inches in length over the external epicondyle of the right elbow. The excursion of movement in the shoulder, elbow, wrist, and all finger joints is normal. However, he holds the ring and little fingers of the right hand closely approximated to each other all the time. His grip is poor in the right hand, but this seems to be due to poor cooperation on the part of the patient. There is no wasting of forearm muscles or in the interosseous spaces and no objective sensory changes in the right arm or hand. Circulation and sudomotor activity are normal. There is no organic cause for his complaint; the manifestations appear to be of psychoneurotic origin.

I first saw Mr. J. on July 1, 1953. He was a pleasant-looking person whose history revealed nothing of significance. He stated that he enjoyed his work and was happily married and that there were no circumstances in his life that he found unpleasant. His Willoughby score was 22.

At his fifth interview on July 14, I showed him how to relax his arm. After relaxing for ten minutes, he found to his surprise that he could make considerably more gripping movements than before without pain. On July 16, he reported that the stiffness in the elbow was worse but he could get some relief by relaxing. I showed him how to relax the muscles of his forehead and, when he had practiced for a few minutes, hypnotized him and made him relax as far as possible. On waking he stated that there was some diminution in the stiffness of his right forearm.

At the next interview, the following day, he reported that he had had no stiffness on waking that morning but it had gradually come on later while he was walking in the street. There was no change in the functional capacity of the hand. I made him reproduce as exactly as possible all the movements associated with the precipitating incident. It was quite clear from his demonstration that there could not have been much pain or damage. I then hypnotized him and asked him to imagine in as much detail as he could the whole sequence of events at the time of the incident. On waking from the trance he said that imagining the sequence had not disturbed him.

On July 20, five days having elapsed, he said that there had been somewhat less tension since the previous session and a slight improvement in function. Again, under hypnosis, I asked him to visualize the sequence of events of the precipitating occasion. On waking he said that he had had a queer desire to use the right arm after the sequence—"Like when fingers have gone to sleep and you want to move them." At this moment he still felt a desire to move the arm. This had never happened before. Later that day he performed minor acts with that hand in a normal way—for the first time since his operation in April. Between July 20 and August 12 Mr. J. was given 12 more hypnotic sessions in which, as before, he relived in imagination the details of the traumatic incident. Twice there was a recurrence of the "peculiar feeling"; on several occasions there was twitching of his fingers, but usually nothing special was noticed. After each session there was some improvement in the feeling and function of his hands. The strength of the hands gradually returned and on August 11 Mr. J. went back to work. On August 14, he stated that his hand had reverted to its original, normal state. His only complaint was a slight pain in the elbow upon extending it to the full, but this too was gradually disappearing. There was no longer any suggestion of the pairs of fingers "sticking together." The grip of the right hand seemed normal when I tested it.

Mr. J. was followed up through the agency of his industrial medical officer for about two years. During this period he went on working without any difficulty and did not complain of his hand.

The following two of my five cases are interesting because of the rapid disappearance of hysterical symptoms even before formal therapy was attempted. One (Case 15) recovered during the taking of the history, and the other (Case 16) improved markedly after taking a tranquilizing drug on my advice before I had as much as seen her. It seems possible that despite their low Willoughby scores, anxiety reduction was at the bottom of their cures, but this is not certain; and they are described here because, by definition (p. 88), they belong to the low-anxiety group of hysterics.

Case 15

A woman of 42 had suffered from intermittent paraesthesia and coldness of her left hand for 17 years. This had rather suddenly become much worse and now had been almost continuous for six months. There was no individual occurrence with which she could associate the worsening, and the only circumstance of possible relevance was that her husband had a mild manic-depressive psychosis about which she had become increasingly concerned. Her Willoughby score was 10. At the first two interviews all I did was take her history and make a few reassuring remarks. At the third she reported that since the first interview the unpleasant sensation in her left hand had gradually been waning and she had been less nervous and more herself. A week later, coming for the last time, she said that she had hardly been aware of her left hand at all and had felt only very slightly nervous despite her husband having had one of his most severely psychotic weeks; for, she said, she now recognized that she had to accept his illness. The only time she had felt considerably upset was when he had criticized her for not giving enough attention to the children; but this had not affected her hand. Three months later there had been no relapse. It seems likely that in spite of the low Willoughby score, this was an anxiety-connected hysteria, and was overcome when conditioned inhibition of the anxiety was produced by nonspecific emotional factors due to the interview situation itself (see Chapter 13). (Compare Case 17.)

Case 16

One day a young physician telephoned to say that his mother had recently acquired a very bad tic. Three months previously she had developed a painful alveolar ulcer. The next morning she woke to find her jaw trembling and her face making contortions of its own accord. These symptoms had gone on ever since and, besides being most grotesque, had caused her difficulty in eating and in falling asleep. Since I was unable to see her at once, I suggested that he try the effects of Atarax. A week later when she came for her first and only interview, all that I could see was slight tremor of the lower jaw and occasional grimacing. She stated that the first Atarax tablet had controlled her movements for four hours; then she had taken another. Since that time, all week, she had been at least 75 per cent improved. I spent the period taking a brief history and administering the Willoughby schedule, to which her score was 20. Six weeks later she telephoned to say that she had been perfectly well and was leaving on holiday. The relevant process is obscure. The fact that Atarax played a part suggests that, as in Case 15, this hysterical reaction was bound up with anxiety. See also pp. 201–3.

13 | *Therapy Without*

Reciprocal Inhibition Procedures

Interview-Induced Emotional Responses

Cures of neuroses appear to be obtained by all kinds of therapists, even though, owing to their different theories, they devote the interview period to procedures that differ in a large variety of ways. Such studies as have compared the success of various kinds of interviews have shown no important differences either in the percentage of cures or in their quality. Wilder (1945), for example, found that the psychotherapeutic results achieved by hospitals, mental hygiene clinics, psychoanalytic institutes, private psychoanalysts, and private psychotherapists were much the same. This finding strongly suggests that the various special points of procedure that the different therapists regarded as vital to success were not vital at all, and that the effective factor must have been something that all the therapeutic situations generated in common.

The only feature common to all the therapies seems to be that there is a private interview in which the patient confidentially reveals and talks about his difficulties to a person he believes to have the knowledge, skill, and desire to help him. This kind of situation undoubtedly excites emotional responses in many patients, and both the character and the strength of these responses vary as functions of many factors, of which the personality and attitude of the therapist and the individual reactive potentialities of the patient are presumably the most important. If, in a patient, the emotional response evoked by the interview situation is (*a*) antagonistic to anxiety and (*b*) of sufficient strength, supposedly it will reciprocally inhibit the anxiety responses that are almost certain to be evoked by some of the subject matter of the interview, and therapeutic effects will occur. They will not occur if the emotional response to the interview is too small. If the interview arouses much anxiety, the patient may well be made worse. (Some instances of this would correspond to the "negative transference" of the psychoanalysts.)

This hypothesis requires systematic testing. Some studies have been made of autonomic changes in relation to occurrences in the interview by Coleman, Greenblatt, and Solomon (1956), DiMascio, Boyd, and Greenblatt (1957), and Lasswell (1935, 1936). However, what interests us most—the relation between specific kinds of emotional response and clinical improvement—is not elucidated by these studies. In the absence of systematic information I may mention that I have a strong clinical impression that patients who display strong positive emotions toward me during the early interviews are particularly likely to show improvement *before* special methods for obtaining reciprocal inhibition of anxiety are applied.

Occasionally, one comes across strikingly clear evidence of the therapeutic effects of interviews quite automatically, when the therapist has done nothing active at all. Such a case is given below (Case 17). It seems, on the face of it, virtually certain that any therapist would have obtained the same changes (at any rate, if he did nothing to upset the patient).

Case 17: Demonstration of Automatic Interview-Induced Therapeutic Effects

Mr. U., a 30-year-old machinist, gave the following history. Four years previously, while having afternoon tea at work, he was discussing politics somewhat heatedly with a confrère who suddenly said, "A person like you who can't look a man in the eye should have treatment." Mr. U. had always been a little unsure of himself, but from this time onward he had become increasingly nervous on looking people in the face. At first this reaction had been confined to people in authority, then it had spread to strangers, and in the past six months it had come to involve his friends as well. He had reached a point where it was impossible to look anybody in the face except his wife and children, and even the very thought of a possible need to do so gave him a scared feeling and made his heart beat faster. The reaction was extremely disabling, as may be imagined: for example, he would be unable to answer a knock at his front door.

Two years previously he had consulted a psychiatrist who had spoken to him very little and had proceeded to give him several treatments of carbon dioxide therapy by Meduna's method. He had felt better for a few hours after each treatment but at the end was unimproved.

Four days before coming to see me, he had had a long talk about himself with the general practitioner, a woman, who referred him to me, and since then *his looking phobia had been slightly but distinctly diminished.* During his third interview with me, he averted his gaze only about half the time and explained this by saying that he knew I wanted to help him and would understand him.

Since there obviously had been a pre-existing sensitivity to enable the precipitating event to affect him so profoundly, I asked him at the third interview whether he could recall any incident earlier at which he might have been greatly distressed by the gaze of other people. He said that when he was eight years old, at a picnic the fruit had consisted of one large orange and many small ones. He had agreed with a friend to take and share the large one. Everybody had stared as he took it out of the basket and he had felt intensely ashamed.

Interviews occurred at approximately weekly intervals. The patient's attitude was one of eagerness and cooperativeness. The first three interviews and part of the fourth were devoted entirely to taking his history. There was nothing unusual either in the content of the history or the manner in which he gave it. From one interview to the next, he reported increasing improvement. At the third interview he reported that he had made a direct request to his engineer face-to-face without feeling in the least afraid. In the past he had been afraid even to look at this man. The Willoughby questionnaire, administered at the fourth interview, yielded the fairly high neurotic score of 49. I explained to him, with examples, how unadaptive fear originates and outlined the reciprocal inhibition principle that is applied to overcoming such fears.

At the fifth interview Mr. U. said that he no longer had any difficulty in looking anybody in the face. This applied even to his boss of whom he had previously been more fearful than anybody else. He said he could feel his whole life changing. Nevertheless it was quite clear from his high Willoughby score that a great deal of neuroticism remained. Consequently I continued to develop the reciprocal inhibition theme with special reference to behavior in the life situation. A week later this patient telephoned to cancel his next appointment, saying that he felt well able to carry on on his own and expressing gratitude for what I had done for him. While it is obvious that this man's neurosis could by no means be said to have cleared up, it is equally obvious that *certain anxieties of great importance in his life had been overcome, apparently merely as a result of the patient having subjected himself to psychotherapeutic interviews, without deliberate measures on the part of the therapist contributing in any way to the improvement.* I found confirmation of the improvement he reported in the fact that throughout the last two interviews he looked me steadily in the eyes, in a way that would be expected of any normal person.

Abreaction

Abreaction may be defined as the emotional re-evocation of a fearful past experience. It is a special case of the interview-induced emotional reactions considered under the previous heading. It may occur under thiopental (Pentothal), hypnosis, or deep relaxation, or even in the course of an ordinary interview. The emotion is of considerable intensity, and beneficial effects seem to be positively correlated with its intensity. But, as Grinker and Spiegel (1945*b*, p. 81) have pointed out, if unrelieved terror is the only emotional component of the abreaction, the patient makes no progress. It is only when the patient can feel the impact of the therapeutic situation, e.g., the therapist's sympathetic acceptance of him, that beneficial abreaction can occur. This is emphasized by Grinker and Spiegel's observation (1945*a*, p. 392) that "abreactions that occur spontaneously under alcohol are nontherapeutic." Thus here too benefit apparently depends on the evocation of other emotional responses in association with the fearful situation, so that, presumably, reciprocal inhibition of anxiety occurs. The specially dramatic changes sometimes produced by abreaction are in line with the experimental finding that modifications of response are likely to be more marked when there is a higher level of drive to be reduced.

If the above interpretation is correct, it would follow that the uprooting of "repressed memories" is not essential to the therapeutic effects of abreaction, although the ventilation of forgotten material often provides the subject matter. Many of Grinker and Spiegel's patients (1945*a, b*) were improved by abreactions in which the battle experiences concerned were well-remembered ones. On page 94 a case is described that illustrates in another way the lack of a relationship between neurotic anxieties and forgotten memories. In this case the neurotic anxieties were overcome by other means while painful memories remained forgotten; and the patient was quite unaffected when the memories were later restored.

Generally speaking, abreaction is not easy to obtain in civilian neuroses even though, in addition to such usual aids as hypnosis and thiopental, facilitation may be sought by the use of ether or Methedrine. But even when abreaction does occur it is not always followed by beneficial effects, either because the opposing emotions fail to inhibit the anxiety adequately or because the memories that are evoked have little or no relation to the stimulus constellations central to the neurosis. Sometimes abreaction is harmful even in the consulting room. For example, I once saw an abreaction provoked by Methedrine arouse intense anxiety and leave the patient far worse off than before.

Because the techniques that are specifically aimed at obtaining reciprocal inhibition of neurotic reactions give the therapist rather detailed control of the processes of change in the patient, I do not often either desire or need to procure abreaction, with all its uncertainties. But sometimes it occurs unbidden in the course of interviews, and if it happens to benefit the patient, I am, naturally, glad of it and, if necessary, try to induce further abreactions later. In an occasional case, such as the one that follows, abreaction has greatly accelerated the recovery of a patient whose progress has previously been slow.

Case 18: Illustrating Marked Acceleration
of a Patient's Progress
by Repeated Abreactions

In November 1952 I began treating Mr. D., a young man with very severe neurotic reactions which had originated chiefly in appalling experiences with a stepmother who easily outdid most of the wicked stepmothers of the storybooks. There were a great many stimuli that could arouse his anxieties, and a very important group of them were related to social situations implying rejection or criticism. Besides a direct attack on these anxieties by means of assertive behavior where it was relevant, hierarchies were constructed and dealt with by desensitization under hypnosis. Every now and then, while the treatment of an apparently comprehensive hierarchy was under way, Mr. D. would report an experience showing that a new angle of things had to be taken into account. We started off with a hierarchy of situations on the theme of social disapproval such as might be threatened if Mr. D. had a dirty mark on his jacket or if there was some minor imperfection in his work; but in the course of three years hierarchies on the following interrelated themes had to be added: loss (of affection or goods), encounters with symbols of "the law" (e.g., policemen), being "responsible" (e.g., meeting creditors), and hostility from others (e.g., customer's making complaints). As these anxiety hierarchies (and others too involved for the present account) were overcome, Mr. D. gradually improved, but late in 1955 there was still a material degree of neurotic anxiety, and progress near the top of the current hierarchies was slow.

In November 1954, I had, for the sake of experiment, given Mr. D. a single inhalation of carbon dioxyde–oxygen (see p. 167). This had caused an abreaction, but a nonbeneficial one. He had had a vivid image of an incident at the age of 14—he knelt at the feet of his stepmother saying, "I do love you," and she kicked him in the face. Mr. D. had been profoundly disturbed by this image, and had a setback from which it took him about three weeks to recover.

After this experience, I had carefully avoided any allusion to the content of this image. But in October 1955, because of the slow progress, I decided to introduce this image during a hypnotic trance. Mr. D. became greatly agitated, sobbed, and woke from the trance. At his next visit he reported that he had felt "completely drained" during the next two hours, but had afterward improved so his general level of anxiety was distinctly lower than that of the previous week. The kneeling incident was presented to him on two subsequent occasions, with a slight initial reaction at the first and none at all at the second.

Other traumatizing past incidents were treated along the same lines, some requiring five or six presentations, and by January 1956 none of them could disturb him. Reactivity to many hierarchy items disappeared in correlation with these abreactions, and desensitization to the remaining items proceeded at a much faster rate. In three months Mr. D. made more progress than in the whole of the previous year.

A possible explanation for this course of events is suggested by the very fact that so many facets of a single situation could, as it were, independently arouse anxiety in Mr. D. (perhaps as a result of the great number and severity of the traumata that he suffered in his early years). Desensitization along a separate "dimension" for each facet was a long and perhaps interminable task. On the other hand, abreaction to images of traumatic situations involved desensitization to all aspects of the situations.

Fortuitous Therapeutic Effects in Life

If habits of neurotic response can be overcome through inhibiting neurotic responses by simultaneous antagonistic responses, it might be expected that sometimes in the ordinary course of life there will be emotional arousals that inhibit neurotic anxiety responses. These will be no less therapeutic than similar arousals during deliberate efforts at psychotherapy. It was pointed out on pages 97–100 that the impact of daily experience continually changes the habit patterns of neurotic response constellations (as well as of others). A particularly favorable succession of experiences may entirely eliminate given neurotic sensitivities.

There are several kinds of evidence in favor of this presumption. To begin with, the overcoming of unadaptive "nervousness" and its attendant gaucheries is a commonplace process in our culture during adolescence and early adulthood. Then, in the life histories of neurotic patients it is frequently found that various unadaptive anxieties have gradually lessened in the course of the years without the help of formal therapy. Some quantitative evidence of improvement in neurotic patients on a hospital waiting list has been reported by Barron and Leary (1955).

It is likely that *low-intensity* anxiety can be inhibited and consequently weakened in habit strength through the competition of emotional responses aroused by relatively unexciting experiences. Evidence of this is to be found in an experiment by Berkun (1957) in which rats made mildly anxious by an approach-avoidance conflict in an alley overcame their anxiety when repeatedly run in the same alley (or, in some cases, at first in a somewhat different alley) even if there was no food reinforcement.

A typical and not infrequent example of very marked benefit to neurotic reactions is that in which a highly nervous, diffident person becomes progressively more self-assured after some favorable change in his life, such as a successful marriage. The emotional impact of his marital relationship is such as to inhibit the unadaptive anxieties evoked in him in many situations, so that the neurotic conditioning to these situations is gradually overcome. Even the neurotic dependency with which the marriage began may be cured by the marriage itself; and the person then retains his newly gained confidence even if he should later be deprived of his wife.

An experience I had with my little son when he was four years old affords a compact illustration of the therapeutic process outlined above. He was in the habit of jumping on the lawn from a wall three feet high. But having on one occasion fallen and hurt himself, he was for months after afraid to jump again even though he watched younger children cheerfully do so. One day I persuaded him to jump while I held his hand. At the next three or four jumps my grip became lighter and lighter, and thereafter I did not hold him at all. Then I gradually increased the distance between us when he jumped. By about the 12th jump he did not care whether I was there or not, and was never again afraid of jumping from this wall. Such experiences are undoubtedly very common. They parallel quite closely the therapeutic experiments described in Chapter 4 in which a neurotic cat, inhibited by fear from eating in the experimental cage, eats if the food is given to him by the human hand, and is enabled thereby to eat in the absence of the hand.

Systematic studies of the influence of life events on neuroticism would obviously be of great interest, but it would be singularly difficult to carry them out without automatically creating a therapeutic situation.

Subsidiary Methods

A. CORRECTING MISCONCEPTIONS

Erroneous meaning that words and other phenomena have acquired for the patient frequently prompts attempts at correction by therapists of almost every kind. It is often important to remove a patient's misconceptions whether they relate to simple items of misinformation, such as the idea that masturbation weakens the body and the mind, or to complex mistaken attitudes to society, to other people, or to the patient himself— for example, the mistaken belief that it is *for his good* that his elder sister subjects him to arduous duties. Successful correction of wrong ideas that seem important is sometimes labeled "insight," although it must be said that the "insights" given by some therapists are further removed from reality than the beliefs that they purport to correct.

It is necessary to point out that changing meanings does not constitute an example of fundamental psychotherapy as it is understood in this book. Fundamental psychotherapy involves detaching neurotic responses (usually anxiety) from stimuli that are objectively harmless; and changing meanings does not do this. Here is an illustration: A man is afraid to cross a quiet suburban street. If when I ask him what he fears he says, "I do not know. It's quite irrational. I just feel afraid," therapy will consist of removing the power to evoke this irrational fear in the idea of crossing. But if he says, "I'm afraid because Mr. X. told me that it is illegal to cross here, and there is a police officer at the corner," his fear will be overcome by convincing him that his informant misled him and that it is lawful to cross. In the latter instance, that which was the immediate stimulus to anxiety—the idea of breaking the law in the presence of a policeman—has not lost its power to evoke anxiety—nor is it desirable that it should, for it is quite adaptive.

But although the correcting of misconceptions is not in itself psychotherapeutic in our sense, it is often an essential precondition to psychotherapeutic success. A man may fear to touch pine trees because of a belief drummed into him in childhood that their bark secretes a deadly poison. Suppose that when the therapist has convinced him of the error of his belief he *continues* to have an automatic fear reaction to pine trees. This reaction can now be removed by reciprocal inhibition techniques which would not have been possible while he regarded the trees as *really* poisonous.

A clinical illustration of the importance of preliminary clarifications of meaning may be found in the account of the treatment of paranoid obsessions in Case 9.

B. THOUGHT STOPPING

In certain patients a great deal of anxiety is due to insistent trains of thought that are disturbing out of all proportion to the realities involved. For example, a person may think constantly of the consequences of his business collapsing even though there is no objective threat of this. It is clearly not unreasonable that thoughts of this kind should generate anxiety; but the very persistence of a useless thought is itself unadaptive. The desirability of suppressing such thoughts was pointed out by Dollard and Miller (1950, pp. 445–59), but no method was given other than suggesting that the patient be told to keep his thoughts on the tasks of the day—which very few patients can do merely in obedience to a prescription.

Not long ago a surprisingly simple method for freeing patients from useless thoughts was devised by J. G. Taylor (1955) of the University of Cape Town. The patient is asked to shut his eyes and to verbalize a typical unadaptive thought sequence. Suddenly the therapist shouts, "Stop!" All this is repeated several times, and attention is drawn to the fact that the thoughts actually do stop each time. The patient is then told that he him-self can stop his thoughts equally successfully by saying "stop" subvocally. The thoughts of course soon return, but after repeated stopping, they return less readily and become progressively easier to stop. With assiduous practice some patients become largely or entirely free of these futile thoughts within a week or so.

For patients on whom this procedure fails I have adopted a modification that usually has the desired effect. A buzzer activated by pressure on a telegraph key is placed on the desk between us. The patient is told to try to keep his mind on pleasant thoughts, about the objects around him or anything else. If, however, any disturbing thought intrudes, he is at once to depress the knob of the telegraph key. Upon the buzzer sounding I instantly shout, "Stop!" Usually during the first two or three minutes, the patient may depress the key between 10 and 20 times per minute, and then the frequency progressively declines so that toward the end of the 15 minutes allowed for this procedure, he depresses it perhaps once every two minutes. Evidently, a habit of inhibiting disturbing thoughts has be-gun to be built up. The patient is enjoined to go on trying at all times to exclude useless thoughts from his mind. This is generally highly successful except in the case of chronic, well-defined obsessional ideas, and even with these, worth-while amelioration is sometimes obtained.

Like the correcting of misconceptions this method is not directly thera-peutic in the sense of detaching neurotic responses from stimuli. But its lowering of the general level of anxiety both alleviates the patient's suffer-ing and makes for easier therapeutic reciprocal inhibition of the anxieties aroused by specific stimuli. Of course, there may be cases whose neurosis consists basically of a habit of thinking disturbing thoughts. One case treated by Taylor was apparently of this character, for a long-standing chronic anxiety state with insomnia was very largely overcome by this method in four interviews. This person has maintained her improvement for two years.

C. THE USE OF DRUGS

What concerns us here is not the use of drugs for temporary relief of symptoms but the possibility of employing them for enhancing fundamental psychotherapeutic effects. Theoretically, a drug could exert a favorable influence either by depressing anxiety responses so that these are the more easily inhibited by antagonistic responses, or it could augment antago-nistic responses, with the same result. It is not to be expected, however, that *every* drug that diminishes anxiety will give a therapeutic advantage to the antagonistic responses. The drug must have a locus of action that affects the anxiety in whatever part of the central nervous system the an-tagonistic response has its inhibitory action. Thus, a drug like tetraethylammonium chloride that acts on sympathetic ganglia would not be useful for this purpose (except perhaps in a few cases where anxiety response–produced stimuli were themselves specially conditioned to produce other neurotic responses).

There is some evidence of beneficial effects of drugs in experimental neuroses. The first to report this was Pavlov (1927, p. 300; 1928, p. 375; 1941, pp. 95–97). Neurotic dogs of the excitatory type were usually brought back to normal in the course of a week or two by the use of large doses of sodium or potassium bromide. Pavlov found the drugs useless in the inhibitory type of neurosis. However, Petrova (1938) found that if, in these cases, the bromide was administered in *small* doses, the recovery of the animal was aided. Dworkin, Raginsky, and Bourne (1937) also studied the action of bromides on neurotic dogs, and of other sedative drugs as well. Sodium amytal, nembutal, avertin, and alcohol all had a marked effect on the animals, but this seldom lasted for more than 24 hours. With bromides, on the other hand, no effect was observed after one injection or several single injections. But when administration was continued for ten successive days, signs of recovery were noted in six to seven days, and were very definite after ten days. Thereafter, despite discontinuance of the drug, recovery was maintained for weeks or months. Masserman and Yum (1946) observed improvement in neurotic cats given daily doses of alcohol for a week or two. They state that in the experimental cage "neurotic animals, while mildly intoxicated, became sufficiently disinhibited to reexplore the problem situation, try to work the switch, answer signals and seek food, and thus dissipate their neurotic phobias, aversions and aberrations."

In clinical therapy of the neuroses the use of drugs is still a virtually unexplored field. It is true that Soviet psychiatrists (e.g., Vaynburg and Birman, 1935) have claimed lasting beneficial effects from the use of bromides in neuroses, but satisfactory substantiating evidence of this is difficult to obtain. Nobody seems to have recommended alcohol as an adjuvant to fundamental psychotherapy, for obvious reasons, but it may well turn out to have its uses under properly controlled conditions. The therapeutic effects of chemical enhancement of a drive antagonistic to anxiety are evident in a case in which psychic impotence was overcome by the use of male sex hormones, reported by Miller, Hubert, and Hamilton (1938).

I have experimented to a small extent with codeine as an aid to psychotherapy. In a few of the cases in whom desensitization procedures could not be successfully applied because of poor relaxation, the difficulty was overcome by the patient taking codeine (½ to 1 grain) an hour before the time of the interview.

Occasionally, I have tried to diminish a patient's sensitivity to a recurring fearful situation by prescribing codeine an hour before each expected exposure to the situation. The only case in which this measure was clearly successful was a man who had a marked phobia toward all kinds of bodily deformities in others. This had become more important recently because it had become necessary for him to have discussions several times monthly with a business colleague suffering from advanced Parkinsonism. Codeine phosphate (one grain) an hour before each meeting abolished all awareness of anxiety. After the sixth meeting the dose was reduced to ¾ grain, after the ninth to ½ grain, and after the eleventh to ¼ grain. Thereafter the patient needed no drug to meet his business colleague without anxiety.

A most striking instance of the overcoming of fears by the systematic use of drugs has recently been brought to my notice by S. Rachman (1957) of the University of the Witwatersrand. The patient, a severe and intricate case of agoraphobia of five years' standing, had become worse during two years of psychoanalysis and then made considerable progress after about 18 months of hypnotic desensitization combined with graduated tasks, so that whereas at first he could not venture in space beyond the bounds of his house and his shop next door, he was now able to travel without disturbance about two miles from home by car. But progress was slow, and he was eager to return to Australia, the land of his birth. Thereupon, Rachman, in collaboration with the patient's general practitioner, embarked upon a course of treatment which he describes as follows:

On January 18, half an hour after a subcutaneous injection of Pethidine (Demerol) 100 mg. and Scopolamine gr. 1/200, he went on a drive in his car in the company of his family physician. They travelled about 6 miles from home and remained away 1½ hours. In the course of this time, he felt marked relaxation, dryness of his mouth, and sleepiness, but not the slightest fear, despite the presence of apprehensive thoughts. The experiment was repeated on January 24, with the use this time of only 75 mg. of Pethidine, and was again completely successful. On January 27, having been given 50 mg. of Pethidine and Scopolamine, gr. 1/200 (a dose which was constant for all injections), the patient took the wheel and went on a long drive with his wife and me, again feeling completely relaxed throughout. He was given several more treatments of this kind, during which the dose of Pethidine was brought down first to 50 mg. and then to 25 mg. Altogether he had 9 treatments in the course of 2½ months, and the range of his excursions progressively increased. Finally, on March 18, he left Johannesburg with his family for Durban en route for Australia. They travelled by car and before they set out he was given a last injection containing 25 mg. of Pethidine. He arrived in Durban without mishap and without anxiety. I received a letter from him written from the ship on arrival in Australia, saying that he was feeling fine and eating enormously.

14 | Evaluation of

Reciprocal Inhibition Methods

The only valid measure of the value of any system of psychotherapy is its success in bringing about lasting remission of the undesirable reactions that distress and disable neurotic patients. Success is the yardstick by which alone comparison can be made with other modes of psychotherapy. Two outstanding sources of variability tend to discredit comparisons—selection of patients and the difficulties involved in categorizing degrees of improvement. Future investigations will no doubt standardize both of these matters as much as possible. In the meantime we must make do with the data that we have, and assume (*a*) that the varieties of patients treated in consulting rooms are, by and large, similar everywhere in the Western world, and (*b*) that most psychiatrists would usually agree when a case is "cured" or "much improved" even though their opinions might differ widely regarding lesser degrees of change.

On previous occasions, I have presented the results of treatment on the reciprocal inhibition principle of two series of patients making up a total of 122 (Wolpe, 1952*d*, 1954). To these a further 88 cases are now added. The patients of all three series have been mainly South Africans of European descent, with a small sprinkling of Indians and visitors from other countries. Of the present series 67 per cent were referred to me by medical practitioners including psychiatrists and 5.8 per cent by psychologists; the remaining 27.2 per cent came directly, either on the recommendation of earlier patients or through various personal contacts.

It is important to realize, regarding any statistical survey of patients which examines the results of therapy, that *there are two stages at which selection occurs*. The first is at the time of the initial interviews, when the therapist has to decide whether he will treat or reject a given patient. The second occurs when the therapist with the list of treated patients before him has to consider if there are any who should be excluded. With respect to initial selection, my only criterion has been a diagnosis of *neurosis*.

Every patient so diagnosed has been accepted, no matter how long-lasting or severe his case, and irrespective of whether or not he has had treatment previously. Psychotics and psychopaths have not been accepted for treatment, unless through an error of diagnosis.

Patients are eligible for inclusion in the series only if they have had an "adequate" amount of therapy. Therapy is naturally regarded as adequate in every patient who is either apparently cured or much improved. In those who have benefited less, it is regarded as adequate if a reasonable trial has been given to each of the reciprocal inhibition techniques that seem applicable to the case. In an unsuccessful case it is usually possible to state within about 40 sessions, and often much earlier, that the techniques have been given a fair trial. The issues involved in a few cases whose status was doubtful were discussed with Dr. David A. Hamburg. It was decided, regarding those for whom the doubt was not resolved, to exclude them from the series but append a note for each.

Evaluation of Change

Effectiveness of treatment has been estimated as far as possible by reference to the five criteria suggested by Knight (1945)—symptomatic improvement, increased productiveness, improved adjustment and pleasure in sex, improved interpersonal relationships, and ability to handle ordinary psychological conflicts and reasonable reality stresses. There are many cases, of course, in which not all of these criteria are relevant—for example, when sexual adjustment or productiveness or both were normal when therapy began. The only criterion that is an absolute *sine qua non* is *symptomatic improvement.** But symptomatic improvement can be regarded as significant only if it is evident in stimulus situations that would previously have evoked symptoms. Improvement attributable to such causes as removal from the environment of anxiety-evoking stimuli (see Chapter 6) does not constitute evidence of change. In addition to the use of Knight's criteria, I have tried to make it a rule to administer the Willoughby questionnaire so as to compare the score with that registered before formal treatment began. I have frequently not readministered it when the initial score was low, and too often also not when it was high, for various reasons, usually because the patient terminated therapy although some of his sensitivities still remained, and I had expected to go on with their treatment. Successful therapy is accompanied by a marked drop in the Wil-

---

* It is odd that those who pour scorn on "mere" symptomatic change on the supposition that "real" change requires something "deeper" so often fail to achieve even symptomatic change.

loughby score where the range of the questionnaire coincides substantially with major areas of the patient's neurosis. (See Table 6.)

Categories of Change

Again following Knight's suggestions, patients have been subdivided into five groups—(1) apparently cured, (2) much improved, (3) moderately improved, (4) slightly improved, and (5) unimproved.

"Apparently cured" patients are those who either have no symptoms at all even when exposed to the most severe conditions that could in the past have produced symptoms, or have occasional slight and transient symptoms during such exposure. These patients will be expected to have Willoughby scores that are within "normal" limits (p. 111) although there could be satisfactory exceptions to this. For example, Patient 17 in Table 1 came for treatment of a severe claustrophobia because a very necessary operation for a chronic dislocation of a shoulder joint was being prevented by his dread of the prospect of bandages around his chest. Desensitization overcame the claustrophobia completely and enabled him to undergo the operation without a qualm. It seems legitimate to categorize this as "apparently cured," despite the fact that if the Willoughby had been repeated the score would almost certainly still have been higher than 20, for the patient had a stutter related to social situations but did not feel it serious enough to justify treatment with his meager financial resources.

"Much improved" patients have very marked symptomatic improvement estimated at not less than 80 per cent, but their symptoms are still more than negligible. They function well in all areas, but perhaps suboptimally in some. Their Willoughby scores, if initially raised, have dropped markedly, but not usually below 20.

In the light of the foregoing, the categories "moderately improved," "slightly improved," and "unimproved" speak for themselves. Cases falling into these three categories are regarded as failures.

A Problem in the Categorizing of Results and a Suggested Solution

The above method of categorizing results is of value for comparative purposes, only if the groups of patients studied by the various therapists are at least roughly comparable. But there could well be variations in the distribution of "easy" and "difficult" cases. The cure of some patients certainly involves much more than the cure of others. For example, a patient with a phobia in a single dimension that is fully disposed of in a few sessions would be very properly listed as "apparently cured"; while another patient with widely ramified disturbances who, saved perhaps from a leucotomy, becomes a reasonably effective citizen but continues to have considerable neurotic reactivity would be regarded as "moderately improved." Yet much more change has been wrought in the second of these two patients than in the first.

A way of avoiding such anomalies as exemplified by the above, and of obtaining at the same time greater uniformity in future comparative studies of therapy, would consist of two steps: (1) break down each case into its "neurotic reactivity areas" (corresponding more or less to the hierarchy themes described in Chapter 9), and (2) assign to each area an intensity dimension, based on the judgment of the therapist.* Thus, at a relatively early stage it will be possible to state in quantitative language how much change is required and, subsequently, how much has been achieved in each area. Though this method is susceptible to errors and omissions, it would unquestionably provide more information for making comparisons than do the customary diagnostic subdivisions (anxiety state, reactive depression, etc.).

Statistical Data on the Results of Therapy

Table 1 gives basic information about each one of the patients in the present series.

A classification of cases according to the usual subdivisions is given in Table 2. This is mainly of value insofar as it indicates how many hysterical and obsessive cases there were, for these often present special problems in therapy. Phobias and cases of impotence are classed among the anxiety states, and so are the so-called "character neuroses." When the last-named are studied from the standpoint adopted in this book, they are found to consist of anxiety reactions to more or less intricate stimulus hierarchies usually with a social basis. A typical example is Patient 27 (Table 1). She had been regarded as a character neurosis case by five psychoanalysts from whom she had almost unbroken treatment without effect for nine years. I found that she had tremendous anxiety to anything suggesting rejection and desensitized her by the use of hierarchies on this theme (Chapter 9).

It may be noted that the expression "conversion reactions," suggested by the American Psychiatric Association, has not been adopted here as a substitute for "hysteria" since it implies acceptance of a hypothesis about hysteria that is inconsistent with the approach of this book.

---

* An objective measure would of course be preferable, but we are far from possessing one of sufficiently wide applicability at present.

TABLE 1

Patient No.	Sex	Age	Salient Clinical Features	Therapeutic Methods, Comments	Therapeutic Time Span (Months)	No. of Interviews
			GROUP I: APPARENTLY CURED			
1	F	24	Marked inferiority feelings; situational and interpersonal anxiety W.46	Assertion; desensitization	3	14
2	F	42	Hysterical paresthesia and coldness, left hand (Case 15) W.10	No active treatment	1	4
3	M	32	Severe anxious depression; homosexual W.52	Assertion (after cure of neurosis became completely heterosexual [2-year follow-up])	3	21
4	M	42	Interpersonal and situational anxiety; reactive drinking W.41	Assertion; some relaxation	3	12
5	F	24	Agoraphobia; interpersonal anxiety (Case 11) W.61	Assertion; relaxation; conditioned motor response	46	185
6	F	22	Interpersonal anxiety; phobias W.43	Assertion; desensitization	2	18
7	M	53	Impotence; phobias W.38	Use of sexual response; desensitization	12	22
8	F	36	Interpersonal anxiety; some inferiority feelings W.33	Relaxation in life situation; desensitization	4	14
9	F	46	Severe interpersonal anxieties; peptic ulcer (Case 7) W.56	Desensitization	10	25
10	M	39	Interpersonal anxiety W.24	Assertion; relaxation	1	12
11	M	11	Interpersonal anxiety; ticlike movements W.24	Desensitization	1	8

12	M	31	Impotence (Case 4) W.?	Use of sexual responses	1	1
13	M	25	Exhibitionism associated with marked interpersonal anxieties W.61	Assertion; desensitization; cure became complete after marriage	20	116
14	F	35	Severe lifelong situational and interpersonal anxiety with depressive spells W.44	Assertion; relaxation	3	22
15	M	22	Insomnia five years; chronic "guilt"; situational anxiety W.15	Abreactions under hypnosis	2	16
16	M	40	Impotence (Case 5) W.17	Use of sexual responses	3	15
17	M	23	Claustrophobia W.44	Desensitization	3	16
18	F	30	Atypical interpersonal anxiety; peptic ulcer W.23	Assertion; desensitization	27	101
19	M	22	Impotence based on injury phobia (Case 8) W.26	Desensitization	3	23
20	M	46	Impotence W.25	Use of sexual responses	3	11
21	M	28	Paranoid obsessions (Case 9) W.34	Desensitization	41	124
22	M	36	Hypochondriacal and other phobias W.31	Desensitization	2	17
23	F	40	Interpersonal anxieties; phobias; atopic dermatitis W.29	Assertion; desensitization	6	29
24	F	21	Interpersonal anxieties; dysphonia W.54	Assertion; relaxation	2	15
25	F	36	Atypical social anxieties; depression W.25	Assertion; desensitization	17	61
26	F	54	Hysterical spasms (Case 16) W.20	Atarax	1	1
27	F	36	Interpersonal anxieties W.38	Assertion; desensitization	4	30
28	F	49	Interpersonal anxieties; widespread phobias W.59	Assertion; desensitization	11	60

TABLE 1—(Continued)

Patient No.	Sex	Age	Salient Clinical Features	Therapeutic Methods, Comments	Therapeutic Time Span (Months)	No. of Interviews
			GROUP II: MUCH IMPROVED			
29	M	52	Situational anxiety; migraine W.38	Assertion	2	21
30	M	35	Severe inferiority feelings W.29	Assertion; relaxation; desensitization	21	55
31	M	42	Situational anxiety; migraine W.21	Assertion; carbon dioxide	1	8
32	F	21	Interpersonal anxiety; inferiority W.72	Assertion; "psychodrama"	3	12
33	M	57	Situational anxiety; asthma W.12	Assertion; some relaxation	1	9
34	F	24	Interpersonal anxiety; partial frigidity W.28	Use of sexual responses; desensitization	5	19
35	M	40	Reactive depression W.45	Desensitization	3	17
36	M	41	Interpersonal anxiety; marked stutter W.39	Assertion; desensitization	23	80
37	M	41	Situational and interpersonal anxiety; pervasive anxiety W.59	Assertion; desensitization; carbon dioxide	24	75
38	M	30	"Looking" phobia; interpersonal anxieties (Case 17) (See Note) W.49	No formal treatment	1	5
39	M	44	Atypical interpersonal anxiety W.22	Assertion; relaxation	1	8
40	M	46	Interpersonal anxiety; impotence W.40	Assertion; desensitization; use of sexual responses	10	41
41	F	31	Interpersonal anxiety; multiple phobias; severe obsessional state W.46	Assertion; desensitization	75	246
42	M	40	Interpersonal anxiety; "Writer's cramp"; voyeurism W.56	Assertion; desensitization	6	47
43	M	26	Phobias on death theme; interpersonal anxiety W.62	Desensitization	7	23
44	F	48	Interpersonal anxiety W.37	Assertion; desensitization	4	17

			Multiple phobias; interpersonal anxieties W.47	Desensitization	4	51
46	M	27	Severe inferiority feelings; interpersonal anxiety; multiple phobias W.39	Assertion; desensitization; abreaction (Case 18)	46	263
47	F	30	Situational and interpersonal anxiety W.35	Assertion; some relaxation	2	18
48	M	68	Situational anxiety W.28	Assertion; relaxation	1	5
49	F	21	Phobia; interpersonal anxiety W.35	Assertion; desensitization	2	8
50	M	28	Interpersonal and situational anxiety; inferiority with "overcompensation" W.33	Assertion; desensitization	12	54
51	F	25	Interpersonal anxiety W.53	Assertion; relaxation	1	6
52	F	33	Interpersonal anxiety; multiple phobias; hysterical symptoms W.61	Desensitization; some assertion; saved from leucotomy	10	42
53	M	24	Obsessional ideas; phobia W.19	Desensitization	2	12
54	F	21	Interpersonal anxiety; fear of marriage W.52	Desensitization	2	16
55	F	24	Interpersonal anxiety; claustrophobia W.44	Assertion; desensitization	41	145
56	F	21	Interpersonal anxiety; obsession W.39	Assertion; desensitization	10	32
57	M	28	Interpersonal and situational anxiety W.69	Assertion; desensitization	9	32
58	F	25	Situational anxiety; phobias W.36	Desensitization	7	28
59	M	20	Interpersonal anxiety; kleptomania W.70	Assertion; desensitization	14	62
60	M	40	Interpersonal anxiety; impotence W.62	Assertion; desensitization; use of sexual responses	6	23
61	F	29	Interpersonal and situational anxiety; reactive depressions W.61	Assertion; desensitization	13	39

TABLE 1—(Continued)

Patient No.	Sex	Age	Salient Clinical Features	Therapeutic Methods, Comments	Therapeutic Time Span (Months)	No. of Interviews
62	M	30	Inferiority feelings, severe social inadequacy, and interpersonal anxiety W.74	Assertion; instruction in techniques of living; desensitization	50	212
63	M	37	Atypical interpersonal and situational anxieties; inhibited sexual feelings W.29	Assertion; desensitization	19	48
64	F	31	Interpersonal and situational anxieties W.73	Some assertion; desensitization	4	23
65	M	41	Interpersonal anxiety; impotence W.63	Assertion; desensitization; use of sexual response	40	109
66	M	27	Interpersonal anxiety W.50	Assertion; some relaxation	6	18
67	F	24	Phobia; interpersonal anxiety W.30	Correction of misconceptions; relaxation	1	12
68	M	43	Phobia with atypical anxiety reaction; interpersonal anxiety W.37	Desensitization	15	17
69	M	34	Interpersonal anxiety; peptic ulcer W.54	Assertion; desensitization	3	14
70	M	25	Hypochondriacal phobias; interpersonal anxiety W.41	Relaxation	3	9
71	M	35	Phobias; pervasive atypical anxiety W.7	Desensitization; carbon dioxide	5	22
72	F	22	Claustrophobia and other phobias; interpersonal anxieties W.44	Assertion; desensitization	5	46
73	M	25	Severe inferiority; interpersonal anxieties W.69	Assertion; desensitization	24	73
74	F	20	Interpersonal anxiety W.59	Assertion; desensitization	11	42
75	F	34	Interpersonal anxiety; agoraphobia W.58	Assertion and desensitization	15	117

76	M	27	Interpersonal anxiety; inferiority W.61	Assertion; desensitization	4	11
77	M	36	Interpersonal anxiety; severe inferiority W.52	Assertion; desensitization	10	61
78	M	29	Interpersonal anxiety; inferiority; multiple phobias; marked pervasive anxiety (Case 10) W.68	Assertion; desensitization; carbon dioxide	34	86
GROUP III: MODERATELY IMPROVED, SLIGHTLY IMPROVED, AND UNIMPROVED						
79	M	14	Severe stammer due to respiratory spasm W.19	Relaxation; retraining of breathing; slightly improved (see Note)	13	50
80	M	67	Obsessions W.37	Desensitization; avoidance conditioning; moderately improved (see Note)	15	47
81	F	28	Severe agoraphobia; interpersonal anxiety W.43	Assertion; desensitization; 5 sessions of conditioned motor response; slightly improved (see Note)	5	39
82	F	50	Interpersonal anxiety; multiple phobias and minor compulsions W.73	Assertion; desensitization; slightly improved (see Note)	6	42
83	F	32	Severe interpersonal anxiety; phobias; pervasive anxiety W.99	Assertion; desensitization; carbon dioxide; slightly improved (see Note)	50	205
84	M	37	Pervasive anxiety W.31	Relaxation; "anxiety relief"; carbon dioxide; unimproved (see Note)	4	18
85	F	33	Interpersonal anxiety; sexual anxiety; inferior feelings; phobias; pervasive anxiety W.42	Assertion; relaxation; desensitization; moderately improved (see Note)	4	57
86	M	47	Severe obsessions W.55	Avoidance conditioning; unimproved (see Note)	1	10
87	M	40	Interpersonal anxiety; writer's cramp W.24	Assertion; desensitization; interpersonal anxiety much improved; writer's cramp unimproved	2	25
88	F	41	Reactive depression W.31	Assertion; relaxation; unimproved (see Note)	3	17

213

1. Notes on Some Patients Listed

Patient 38. The doubt about listing this patient was quelled on the ground that the complaint for which he desired treatment was completely overcome. There was some evidence that as a result of this his interpersonal anxiety was beginning to decline generally.

Patient 79. During the fourth month of treatment this patient made a very notable improvement in response to training in speech with forced exhalation. Two months later, while showing him off to the speech therapist who had previously treated him, I applied some pressure when he faltered. This resulted in a marked relapse which persistent treatment only partly counteracted.

Patient 80. This was a long-standing obsession about the possibility of having left objects like razor blades and needles lying about so that children might find them and injure themselves. It was improved to a considerable extent by desensitization, and later improved further by three avoidance-conditioning sessions just before I left for overseas.

Patient 81. This girl became impatient about the treatment after five months. There was indeed little to show for so much treatment, but I did feel that more substantial headway was about to be made.

Patient 82. A period of marked optimism and improvement in symptoms for about four months was followed by relapse. It transpired that she *had never reacted with anxiety* to the imagined hierarchy items. The improvement was evidently due to a pervasive feeling of authoritative support, which dissolved when my departure overseas became imminent.

Patient 83. With assertion and desensitization this patient improved in six months from an almost entirely helpless state to take up employment as a shorthand typist; she continued working for three years, during which she made slow progress while coming for treatment very irregularly. In December 1955, against my emphatic advice, she exposed herself to a situation that would inevitably evoke great anxiety and, in consequence, had a marked relapse. In attempting to obtain abreaction in the hope of accelerating recovery I merely evoked more anxiety and made her worse still, though not as bad as she had been in the beginning. After this I could do nothing with her. Carbon dioxide was of no use for her pervasive anxiety, apparently because of anxiety related to the "suffocation" feeling.

Patient 84. This ex-soldier had suffered from nervousness, irritability, and insomnia ever since a near-miss by a bomb 11 years before. No specific anxiety-evoking stimulations were found related to the pervasive anxiety. I was unable to obtain reciprocal inhibition of his anxiety by any of the means at my disposal.

Patient 85. A very severe neurosis had been precipitated ten years previously by a marriage to a man toward whom the patient came to feel increasing repugnance—with good reason. The first need was to get her out of this distressing situation, and as a result of my intervention she managed to take action leading to divorce. After this she was about 50 per cent improved, but I had to abandon further therapy because my presence in relation to some severe predivorce crises had made me a conditioned stimulus to anxiety.

Patient 86. After his girl friend unexpectedly wed another man three years previously, this patient, who had always been "nervous and faddy," began to be plagued by unwelcome thoughts.

214

He had had psychoanalysis and then ECT, but instead of improving had become steadily worse, so that when I saw him he could not perform simple movements such as sitting down unless "favorable thoughts" were in his mind. There was no response to the measures I used, and I did not persist, feeling sure I could not help him.

Patient 88. The reactive depression was caused by a frustrating love affair. After I taught the patient how to handle it effectually, she felt much better, but her lover was soon shown up to be a scoundrel and the affair came to an end. But then, as she had no other close personal ties of any kind, she became depressed again, though less than she had been at first, and refused further treatment.

2. Notes on Some Omitted Patients

Patient 89. A man of 36, who presented as a very severe war neurosis with numerous phobias, turned out to be a psychopathic personality given to elaborate pathological lying. Though there undoubtedly were neurotic reactions too, and much treatment was given, the whole picture was utterly confused by his lies.

Patient 90. A woman of 24 with congenital ichthyosis was sent for psychotherapy by a physician because the skin was always better when she was unusually relaxed, particularly when on holiday. In the course of eight sessions I taught her relaxation. This did not improve the ichthyosis, but occipital headaches that had afflicted her daily during the past two years completely disappeared.

Patient 91. A woman of 36 was seen in a state of severe tension because she was seven months pregnant with a child conceived during an extramarital affair. Her husband knew all about it, and was very understanding and willing to accept the child as his own; but this did not alleviate her emotional state. After 24 interviews in the course of a month, devoted mainly to rationalizing the situation, and to some relaxation and desensitization she was somewhat improved. Thereafter she went to a psychiatrist who gave her ECT which, it seems, had a dulling effect that enabled her to withstand the crisis.

Patient 92. A woman of 37 gave a history of lifelong swinging moods without apparent outward cause. But besides these presumably endogenous fluctuations, irritation and depression could be set off by apparent hostility from other people even when she was feeling well. She made good progress to a point where she was judged "moderately improved," and then after the 17th interview ceased to attend. A year later it was learned that she was having psychiatric treatment elsewhere.

215

TABLE 2

CONVENTIONAL DIAGNOSTIC CLASSIFICATION OF CASES

	1952 Series	1954 Series	Present Series	Totals
Anxiety state	39	33	63	135
Hysteria	6	3	4	13
Reactive depression	7	3	5	15
Obsessions and compulsions..	5	6	8	19
Neurasthenia	3	0	0	3
Mixed and unclassified......	10	7	8	25
	70	52	88	210

Table 3 gives the results of treatment on reciprocal inhibition principles of the three series of patients. The general average of about 90 per cent of highly favorable outcomes has been maintained. The slight decline in the present series is at least partly attributable to the fact that it contains a considerable number of patients referred by psychiatrists.

TABLE 3

RESULTS OF RECIPROCAL INHIBITION PSYCHOTHERAPY

	No. of Cases	Apparently Cured	Much Improved	Slightly to Moderately Improved	Unimproved
1952 series	70	34	26	7	3
1954 series	52	20	30	1	1
Present series	88	28	50	7	3
Totals	210	82 (39.0%)	106 (50.5%)	15 (7.2%)	7 (3.3%)

Although no systematic follow-up study has been made, follow-up information has been obtained on 45 "apparently cured" and "much improved" patients two to seven years after the end of treatment. Of these a solitary, "much improved" patient relapsed to a moderate extent after about a year, but communication was insufficient to establish the circumstances that led up to this. Every one of the remaining 44 patients either maintained improvement or improved further without any additional formal aid.

These follow-up data are evidence against the psychoanalytic hypothesis that no lasting results can be expected of psychotherapy that does not influence "the repressed." The data tend to refute that hypothesis over the whole range of the neuroses, far beyond the particular case of hysteria

(p. 186 n.). If repression were the essence of neurosis, apparently successful measures that leave "the repressed" untouched would be followed before long by relapse, i.e., the emergence of new symptoms or the recurrence of old ones. If, on the other hand, neurotic symptoms are nothing but conditioned responses, "deconditioning" measures such as described in this book will be all that is needed to eliminate the symptoms permanently; and after thorough extinction of the neurotic responses relapse will not be expected.

Of course, as long as a considerable amount of anxiety conditioning is extant in a person, there is a basis for it to increase and to "spread" to new stimuli, as described in Chapter 6. But if renewed neurotic manifestations should arise in a patient in whom all known anxiety-evoking stimuli have been thoroughly dealt with, it must, according to our hypothesis, be for one of two reasons. Either other stimuli, previously unsuspected, had also been conditioned to neurotic responses, or new stimuli have been freshly conditioned by recent entirely new neurotigenic stresses. I have observed several instances of the first of these possibilities and one instance of the second. "Relapse" probably never occurs in the absence of one or other of these conditions. Symptoms do not simply "well up from the depths."

In Table 4 the 88 patients of the present series are subdivided according to the number of interviews given. It may be noted that 57 of them, very nearly two-thirds, had 40 interviews or fewer.

TABLE 4

DISTRIBUTION OF INTERVIEWS (PRESENT SERIES)

No. of interviews:								Over
1–10	11–20	21–30	31–40	41–50	51–60	61–70	71–80	80
No. of patients:								
13	26	14	4	9	5	3	3	11

Table 5 contains certain averages of duration of therapy in terms of therapeutic time span in months, as well as number of interviews. Both successful and unsuccessful cases spent a mean of something over 10 months in therapy. The mean of 51 interviews for unsuccessful cases is higher than that for successful cases (43.6 interviews), but drops to 33.9 if Patient 83 is omitted (see Notes on Table 1). The over-all mean of 45.6 is strikingly higher than the mean of about 26 recorded for the two earlier series. It is explained partly by the fact that, as a result of the higher turnover of patients since 1951, more long-term cases came to finality in 1955 and 1956, and partly by the already mentioned fact that more presumably "difficult" cases were referred by psychiatrists in the most recent period. The median number of interviews is 23.0, compared with 17.5 in the 1954 series.

TABLE 5

DURATION OF THERAPY (PRESENT SERIES)

	Mean Therapeutic Time Span (Months)	Mean No. of Interviews	Median No. of Interviews
Apparently cured and much improved groups	10.8	43.6	22.0
Slightly to moderately improved and unimproved groups	10.2	51.0	40.5
Whole series	10.7	45.6	23.0

Table 6 compares the Willoughby scores before and after treatment in patients of the "apparently cured" and "much improved" groups. It is disappointing that only 34 comparisons are available, but the change is clear in both groups and greater in the "apparently cured" group whose

TABLE 6

WILLOUGHBY SCORES BEFORE AND AFTER TREATMENT

Apparently Cured Group			Much Improved Group		
Patient	Before Treatment	After Treatment	Patient	Before Treatment	After Treatment
1	46	17	34	28	17
3	52	10	36	39	20
5	61	7	40	40	22
8	33	15	41	46	17
9	56	13	42	56	20
10	24	8	44	37	24
13	61	17	46	39	20
17	44	18	50	33	21
21	34	10	55	44	24
24	54	16	56	39	22
25	25	5	58	36	23
27	38	10	60	63	30
28	59	15	64	73	37
			65	53	31
Mean	45.2	12.2	66	50	14
			69	54	26
			70	41	24
			73	69	46
			67	30	26
			77	52	23
			78	68	30
			Mean	44.8	25.6

posttreatment mean of 12.2 is well within the arbitrary "normal" limit of 20 (p. 111). The mean for the "much improved" group falls 5.6 points short of this limit. In the "moderately improved, slightly improved, and unimproved group" the only comparative scores available are for Patient 82 (73 to 67), Patient 83 (99 to 56), and Patient 87 (24 to 13). (See Notes on Table 1.)

In Table 7 the combined results of our three series are compared with Hamilton and Wall's (1941) New York Hospital Series (as a representative example of conventional therapy other than psychoanalysis), and with the largest reported psychoanalytically treated series—from the Berlin Psychoanalytic Institute (Knight, 1941). That these two are among the most favorable of previously reported series will be evident to the reader who cares to peruse the summary of reports of results compiled by Eysenck (1952). In the case of the Berlin series two figures are given for the total number of cases and for the percentages. The larger total includes those patients who had less than six months of psychoanalysis.

TABLE 7

COMPARATIVE RESULTS

Series	No. of Cases	Apparently Cured or Much Improved	Improvement: Moderate, Slight, or Nil
Berlin Psychoanalytic Institute (Knight, 1941)	263–402*	163* (62–40.5%)	100–239* (38–59.5%)
New York Hospital (Hamilton and Wall, 1941)	100	53 (53%)	47 (47%)
Combined reciprocal inhibition series..	210	188 (89.5%)	22 (10.5%)

* See text.

The most important point about the comparative figures in Table 7 is that nearly 90 per cent of the patients in our series were either apparently cured or much improved, and only about 60 per cent of the cases in the other two series. If the favorable results of the present series are, to the extent of 60 per cent, regarded as due to the nonspecific reciprocal inhibition that would occur in any kind of interview situation, the additional 30 per cent of good results appears to be attributable to the special measures for obtaining reciprocal inhibition described above. Furthermore, the relatively small average number of interviews needed suggests that the use of these special measures early in treatment accelerates the improvement of those patients who would have responded to the nonspecific factors alone.

To obtain a proper perspective on the effects of any therapeutic method it is necessary to know what percentage of patients would get well without therapy. For reasons given earlier (pp. 198–99), many neurotic patients have their anxieties weakened in the normal course of life. But the unsatisfactory statistical position that Eysenck found in 1952 has scarcely improved. Even the Denker (1946) study has very little significance—for two reasons—(1) the "superficial" therapy practiced by general practitioners can by no means be assumed to be without effects (pp. 193–95); and (2) some general practitioners are quite prone to diagnose insurance patients as "psychoneurotic" without sufficient grounds and even when they suspect that the patient is malingering.

The Present Status of Reciprocal Inhibition as the Main Basis of Fundamental Therapy of Human Neuroses

The following are some major facts that support the hypothesis that reciprocal inhibition has a central role in human psychotherapy:

1. In general, it is possible to overcome a habit by forming a new and antagonistic habit in the same stimulus situation (pp. 29–31).

2. Animal neuroses are overcome if feeding can be made to occur in the presence of anxiety-evoking stimuli (pp. 55–59). Under other conditions anxiety inhibits feeding, and presenting anxiety-evoking stimuli in special circumstances can lead to the conditioning of anxiety to food-approach stimuli (pp. 59–60).

3. By deliberately applying responses antagonistic to anxiety responses, neurotic anxiety-response habits can be overcome, and more neurotic patients can be successfully treated, apparently, than by other methods (p. 219).

4. The success of other approaches to therapy is explicable on the reciprocal inhibition principle (pp. 193–94).

5. "Spontaneous" improvement of neuroses in the ordinary course of life is explicable on the reciprocal inhibition principle (pp. 198–99).

It is obvious that if the reciprocal inhibition principle is indeed a master key to the cure of neurosis, a much brighter future lies before the world's victims of neurotic suffering. But in a matter like this, conviction cannot be founded on one man's experience. The proposition must be put to the test by others.

Bibliography

Ades, H. W., F. A. Mettler, and E. A. Culler. (1939) Effect of lesions in the medial geniculate bodies upon hearing in the cat. *Amer. J. Physiol.* 125: 15.

Adrian, E. D. (1928) The Basis of Sensation. London: Christophers.

Adrian, E. D., and D. W. Bronk. (1928) The discharge of impulses in motor nerve fibers. Part I. Impulses in single fibers of the phrenic nerve. *J. Physiol.* 66: 81.

———. (1929) The frequency of discharge in reflex and voluntary contractions. *J. Physiol.* 67: 119.

Anderson, A. C. (1933) Runway time and the goal-gradient. *J. Exper. Psychol.* 16: 423.

Anderson, O. D., and H. S. Liddell. (1935) Observations on experimental neurosis in sheep. *Arch. Neurol. Psychiat.* 34: 330.

Anderson, O. D., and R. Parmenter. (1941) A long term study of the experimental neurosis in the sheep and dog. *Psychosom. Med. Monogr.* 2, Nos. 3 and 4.

Andersson, B. (1953) The effect of the injection of hypertonic solutions in parts of the hypothalamus of goats. *Acta Physiol. Scand.* 28: 188.

Anrep, G. V. (1923) The irradiation of conditioned reflexes. *Proc. Roy. Soc. London* 94B: 404.

Applezweig, M. H. (1951) Response potential as a function of effort. *J. Comp. Physiol. Psychol.* 44: 225.

Arnold, M. B. (1945) The physiological differentiation of emotional states. *Psychol. Rev.* 52: 35.

Ax, A. F. (1953) The physiological differentiation of anger and fear in humans. *Psychosom. Med.* 15: 433.

Babkin, B. P. (1938) Experimental neuroses in animals and their treatment with bromides. *Edinburgh Med. J.* 45: 605.

———. (1946) Antagonistic and synergistic phenomena in autonomic nervous system. *Trans. Roy. Soc. Canada*, Sect. 5, 40: 1.

Bajandurow, B. (1932) Zur Psychologie des Sehenanalysators bei Vogeln. *Z. Vergl. Physiol.* 18: 288. Quoted by S. W. Cook (1939a).

Barlow, J. A. (1952) Secondary motivation through classical conditioning: One trial nonmotor learning in the rat. *Amer. Psychologist* 7: 273.

———. (1956) Secondary motivation through classical conditioning: A reconsideration of the nature of backward conditioning. *Psychol. Rev.* 63: 406.

Barron, F., and T. F. Leary. (1955) Changes in psychoneurotic patients with and without psychotherapy. *J. Consult. Psychol.* 19: 239.

Bass, M. J., and C. L. Hull. (1934) The irradiation of a tactile conditioned reflex in man. *J. Comp. Psychol.* 17: 47.

Beach, F. A. (1941) Female mating behavior shown by male rats after injection of testerone propionate. *Endocrinology* 29: 409.

———. (1942a) Analysis of the factors involved in the arousal, maintenance and manifestation of sexual excitement in male animals. *Psychosom. Med.* 4: 173.

——. (1942b) Effect of testosterone propionate on copulatory behavior of sexually inexperienced male rats. *J. Comp. Psychol.* 33: 227.

——. (1942c) Comparison of copulatory behavior of male rats reared in isolation, cohabitation and segregation. *J. Genet. Psychol.* 60: 121.

——. (1947) A review of physiological and psychological studies of sexual behavior in mammals. *Physiol. Rev.* 27: 240.

Berkun, M. M. (1957) Factors in the recovery from approach-avoidance conflict. *J. Exper. Psychol.* 54: 65.

Berlyne, D. E. (1950) Novelty and curiosity as determinants of exploratory behavior. *Brit. J. Psychol.* 51: 68.

Bernreuter, R. G. (1933) The measurement of self sufficiency. *J. Abnorm. Soc. Psychol.* 28: 291.

Bingham, H. C. (1928) Sex development in apes. *Comp. Psychol. Monogr.* 5: 161.

Bremer, F. (1930) Nouvelle recherches sur la sommation centrale. *Compt. Rend. Soc. Biol. Paris.* 104: 810.

Brogden, W. J. (1939) Sensory pre-conditioning. *J. Exper. Psychol.* 25: 323.

Brogden, W. J., E. A. Lipman, and E. Culler. (1938) The role of incentive in conditioning and extinction. *Amer. J. Psychol.* 51: 109.

Brooks, C. M., and J. C. Eccles. (1948) Inhibition of antidromic responses of motoneurones. *J. Neurophysiol.* 11: 431.

Brush, F., E. S. Brush, and R. L. Solomon. (1955) Traumatic avoidance learning: the effects of CS-US interval with a conditioning procedure. *J. Comp. Physiol. Psychol.* 48: 285.

Bunch, M. E., and M. M. Winston (1936) The relationship between the character of the transfer and retroactive inhibition. *Amer. J. Psychol.* 48: 598.

Calvin, J. S. (1939) Decremental factors in conditioned response learning. Ph.D. thesis, Yale University. Quoted by C. L. Hull (1943).

Cannon, W. B. (1929) Bodily Changes in Pain, Hunger, Fear and Rage. 2d ed. New York, Appleton.

Carmichael, L. (1926) The development of behavior in vertebrates experimentally removed from the influence of external stimulation. *Psychol. Rev.* 33: 51.

——. (1927) A further study in the development of behavior in vertebrates experimentally removed from the influence of external stimulation. *Psychol. Rev.* 34: 34.

Cohen, L. H. (1953) Personal communication.

Coleman, R., M. Greenblatt, and H. C. Solomon. (1956) Physiological evidence of rapport during psychotherapeutic interviews. *Dis. Nerv. System.* 17: 2.

Cook, S. W. (1939a) A survey of methods used to produce "experimental neurosis." *Amer. J. Psychiat.* 95: 1259.

——. (1939b) The production of "experimental neurosis" in the white rat. *Psychosom. Med.* 1: 293.

Coppock, H. W. (1951) Secondary reinforcing effect of a stimulus repeatedly presented after electric shock. *Amer. Psychologist* 6: 277.

Culler, E. (1938) Observations on direct cortical stimulation in the dog. *Psychol. Bull.* 35: 687.

Denker, R. (1946) Results of treatment of psychoneuroses by general practitioners. *New York State J. Med.* 46: 2164.

Dicks, H. V. (1939) Clinical Studies in Psychopathology. Baltimore, Williams & Wilkins.

Di Mascio, A., R. W. Boyd, and M. Greenblatt. (1957) Physiological correlates of tension and antagonism during psychotherapy. *Psychosom. Med.* 19: 99.

Dimmick, F. L., N. Ludlow, and A. Whiteman. (1939) A study of "experimental neurosis" in cats. *J. Comp. Psychol.* 28: 39.

Dollard, J., and N. E. Miller. (1950) Personality and Psychotherapy. New York, McGraw-Hill.

Dumas, G. (1928) Le choc emotionel. *J. Psychol. norm. path.* 25: 130.

Dunlap, K. (1932) Habits: Their Making and Unmaking. New York, Liveright.

Dworkin, S. (1939) Conditioning neuroses in dog and cat. *Psychosom. Med.* 1: 388.

Dworkin, S., J. O. Baxt, and E. Dworkin. (1942) Behavioral disturbances of vomiting and micturition in conditioned cats. *Psychosom. Med.* 4: 75.

Dworkin, S., B. B. Raginsky, and W. Bourne. (1937) Action of anaesthetics and sedatives upon the inhibited nervous system. *Curr. Res. Anaesth.* 16: 238.

Dykman, R. A., and W. H. Gantt. (1956) Relation of experimental tachycardia to amplitude of motor activity and intensity of the motivating stimulus. *Amer. J. Physiol.* 185: 495.

Eccles, J. C. (1931) Studies on the flexor reflex. III. The central effects produced by an antidromic volley. *Proc. Roy. Soc.* 107B: 557.

———. (1937) The discharge of impulses from ganglion cells. *J. Physiol.* 91: 1.

———. (1946) Synaptic potentials of motoneurones. *J. Neurophysiol.* 9: 87.

———. (1953) The Neurophysical Basis of Mind. London, Oxford University Press.

Eccles, J. C., and C. S. Sherrington. (1930) Reflex summation in the ipsilateral spinal flexion reflex. *J. Physiol.* 69: 1.

———. (1931a) Studies on the flexor reflex. II. The reflex response evoked by two centripetal volleys. *Proc. Roy. Soc.* 107B: 535.

———. (1931b) Studies on the flexor reflex. VI. Inhibition. *Proc. Roy. Soc.* 109B: 91.

Eysenck, H. J. (1947) Dimensions of Personality. London, Routledge.

———. (1952) The effects of psychotherapy: An evaluation. *J. Consult. Psychol.* 16: 319.

———. (1953) Uses and Abuses of Psychology. London, Penguin Books.

———. (1955a) A dynamic theory of anxiety and hysteria. *J. Ment. Sci.* 101: 28.

———. (1955b) Cortical inhibition, figural after-effect and theory of personality. *J. Abnorm. Soc. Psychol.* 51: 94.

———. (1956) Personal communication.

———. (1957) The Dynamics of Anxiety and Hysteria. London, Routledge & Kegan Paul.

Farber, I. E. (1948) Response fixation under anxiety and non-anxiety conditions. *J. Exper. Psychol.* 38: 111.

Farrar, C. B. (1957) Psychotherapy. *Amer. J. Psychiat.* 113: 805.

Fenichel, O. (1945) Psychoanalytic Theory of Neurosis. New York, Norton.

Finger, F. W. (1945) Abnormal animal behavior and conflict. *Psychol. Rev.* 52: 230.

Fitts, P. M. (1940) Preseveration of non-rewarded behavior in relation to food deprivation and work requirement. *J. Genet. Psychol.* 57: 165.

Fodor, N. (1946) Hysterical color blindness caused by infantile sexual guilt. *J. Clin. Psychopath.* 8: 279.

Fonberg, E. (1956) On the manifestation of conditioned defensive reactions in stress. *Bull. Soc. Sci. Lettr. Lodz. Class III. Sci. Math. Natur.* 7: 1.

Franks, C. M. (1956) Conditioning and personality: A study of normal and neurotic subjects. *J. Abnorm. Soc. Psychol.* 52: 143.

Freeman, G. L., and J. H. Pathman. (1940) The relation of overt muscular discharge to physiological recovery from experimentally induced displacement. *J. Exper. Psychol.* 30: 161.

Freud, S. (1893) On the psychical mechanism of hysterical phenomena. In Collected Works of Freud, Vol. I. London, Hogarth Press, 1949.

Gantt, W. H. (1938) The nervous secretion of saliva: The relation of the conditioned reflex to the intensity of the unconditioned stimulus. *Amer. J. Physiol.* 123: 714.

――――. (1944) Experimental basis for neurotic behavior. *Psychosom. Med. Monogr.* 3, Nos. 3 and 4.

――――. (1949) Psychosexuality in animals. In Psychosexual Development in Health and Disease. New York, Grune and Stratton.

Gellhorn, E. (1943) Autonomic Regulations. New York, Interscience Publ.

――――. (1953) The Physiological Foundations of Neurology and Psychiatry. Minneapolis, University of Minnesota Press.

Gellhorn, E., and L. Thompson. (1944) Muscular pain, tendon reflexes and muscular co-ordination in man. *Proc. Soc. Exp. Biol. & Med.* 56: 209.

Goodson, F. A., and A. Brownstein. (1955) Secondary reinforcing and motivating properties of stimuli contiguous with shock onset and termination. *J. Comp. Physiol. Psychol.* 48: 381.

Grindley, G. C. (1929) Experiments on the influence of the amount of reward in learning in young chicks. *Brit. J. Psychol.* 20: 173.

Grinker, R. R., and J. P. Spiegel. (1945a) Men Under Stress. London, J. and A. Churchill, Ltd.

――――. (1945b) War Neuroses. Philadelphia, Blakiston.

Grundfest, H., and B. Campbell. (1942) Origin, conduction and termination of impulses in the dorsal spino-cerebellar tract. *J. Neurophysiol.* 5: 275.

Guthrie, E. R. (1935) The Psychology of Human Learning. New York, Harper.

Haggard, E. A., and G. L. Freeman. (1941) Reactions of children to experimentally induced frustration. *Psychol. Bull.* 38: 581.

Hamilton, D. M., and J. H. Wall. (1941) Hospital treatment of patients with psychoneurotic disorders. *Am. J. Psychiat.* 98: 551.

Hamilton, E. L. (1929) The effect of delayed incentive on the hunger drive in the white rat. *Genet. Psychol. Monogr.* 5: 131.

Harris, A. (1954) A comparative study of results in neurotic patients treated by two different methods. *J. Ment. Science* 100: 718.

Hartman, C. G. (1942) Endocrine influences on instinctual processes. *Psychosom. Med.* 4: 206.

Harvey, O. L. (1932) Concerning the Thurstone "Personality Schedule." *J. Soc. Psychol.* 3: 200.

Hebb, D. O. (1947) Spontaneous neurosis in chimpanzees: Theoretical relations with clinical and experimental phenomena. *Psychosom. Med.* 9: 3.

Herzberg, A. (1945) Active Psychotherapy. London, Research Books.

Hess, W. R. (1947) Vegetative Funktionen und Zwischenhirn. Basel, Schwabe. Quoted by E. Gellhorn, 1953.

Hilgard, E. R. (1957) Personal communication.

Hilgard, E. R., and D. G. Marquis. (1940) Conditioning and Learning. New York, Appleton.

Hovland, C. I. (1936) "Inhibition of reinforcement" and phenomena of experimental extinction. *Proc. Natl. Acad. Sci.* 22: 430.

――――. (1937) The generalization of conditioned responses: I. The sensory generalization of conditioned responses with varying frequencies of tone. *J. Gen. Psychol.* 17: 125.

Hudgins, C. V. (1933) Conditioning and the voluntary control of the pupillary light reflex. *J. Gen. Psychol.* 8: 3.

Hull, C. L. (1943) Principles of Behavior. New York, Appleton.

Humphreys, L. G. (1939) Generalization as a function of method of reinforcement. *J. Exper. Psychol.* 25: 361.

Hurwitz, H. B. M. (1956) Conditioned responses in rats reinforced by light. *Brit. J. Animal Behav.* 4: 31.

Ischlondsky, N. E. (1944) Quoted by W. H. Gantt (1944).

Jacobsen, C. F., J. B. Wolfe, and T. A. Jackson. (1935) An experimental analysis of the functions of the frontal association areas in primates. *J. Nerv. Ment. Dis.* 82: 1.

Jacobson, E. (1938) Progressive Relaxation. Chicago, University of Chicago Press.

———. (1939) Variation of blood pressure with skeletal muscle tension and relaxation. *Ann. Int. Med.* 12: 1194.

———. (1940) Variation of pulse rate with skeletal muscle tension and relaxation. *Ann. Int. Med.* 13, 1619.

———. (1956) Personal communication.

James, W. T. (1941) Experimental observations indicating the significance of work on conditioned motor reactions. *J. Comp. Psychol.* 32: 353.

Johnson, H. K. (1948) Psychoanalysis: A critique. *Psychiat. Quart.* 22: 321.

Johnson, L. M. (1933) Similarity of meaning as a factor in retroactive inhibition. *J. Gen. Psychol.* 9: 377.

Jones, E. (1948) Papers on Psychoanalysis. London, Balliere, Tindall and Cox.

Jones, H. G. (1956) The application of conditioning and learning techniques to the treatment of a psychiatric patient. *J. Abnorm. Soc. Psychol.* 52: 414.

Jones, M. C. (1924*a*) Elimination of children's fears. *J. Exper. Psychol.* 7: 382.

———. (1924*b*) A laboratory study of fear. The case of Peter. *J. Genet. Psychol.* 31: 308.

Jung, C. G. (1923) Psychological Types. New York, Harcourt, Brace.

Kagan, J. (1955) Differential reward value of incomplete and complete sexual behavior. *J. Comp. Physiol. Psychol.* 48: 59.

Kamin, L. J. (1954) Traumatic avoidance learning: The effects of CS-US interval with a trace conditioning procedure. *J. Comp. Physiol. Psychol.* 47: 65.

Kappauf, W. E., and H. Schlosberg. (1937) Conditioned responses in the white rat. III. Conditioning as a function of the length of the period of delay. *J. Genet. Psychol.* 50: 27.

Karn, H. W. (1938) A case of experimentally induced neurosis in the cat. *J. Exper. Psychol.* 22: 589.

———. (1940) The experimental study of neurotic behavior in infra-human animals. *J. Gen. Psychol.* 22: 431.

Kawamura, T., and N. Yoshii. (1951) A study on the experimental neurosis of rats. Part I. Behavior patterns. *Med. J. Osaka University* 2: 133.

Kish, G. B. (1955) Learning when the onset of illumination is used as a reinforcing stimulus. *J. Comp. Physiol. Psychol.* 48: 261.

Knight, R. P. (1941) Evaluation of the results of psychoanalytic therapy. *Amer. J. Psychiat.* 98: 434.

Koffka, K. (1930) Some problems of space perception. In C. Murchison, ed., Psychologies of 1930. Worcester, Clark University Press.

Krasnogorski, N. I. (1925) The conditioned reflexes and children's neuroses. *Amer. J. Dis. Child.* 30: 754.

Landis, C. (1937) A statistical evaluation of psychotherapeutic methods. In L. Hinsie, Concepts and Problems of Psychotherapy. New York, Columbia University Press.

Langley, J. N., and H. K. Anderson. (1895) The innervation of the pelvic and adjoining viscera. *J. Physiol.* 19: 71.

Lasswell, H. D. (1935) Verbal references and physiological changes during the psychoanalytic interview. *Psychoanal. Rev.* 22: 10.

———. (1936) Certain prognostic changes during trial interviews. *Psychoanal. Rev.* 23: 241.

La Verne, A. A. (1953) Rapid coma technique of carbon dioxide inhalation therapy. *Dis. Nerv. Syst.* 14: 141.

La Verne, A. A., and M. Herman. (1955) An evaluation of carbon dioxide therapy. *Amer. J. Psychiat.* 112: 107.

Lazarus, A. A., and S. Rachman. (1957) The use of systematic desensitization in psychotherapy. *South African Med. J.* 31: 934.

Leschke, E. (1914) Quoted by J. G. Beebe-Center in The Psychology of Pleasantness and Unpleasantness. New York, Van Nostrand, 1932.

Liddell, H. S. (1944) Conditioned reflex method and experimental neurosis. In J. McV. Hunt, Personality and the Behavior Disorders. New York, Ronald Press.

Liddell, H. S., and T.L. Bayne. (1927) The development of "experimental neurasthenia" in sheep during the formation of difficult conditioned reflexes. *Amer. J. Physiol.* 81: 494.

Lion, K. S. (1952) Oculomotric muscle forces and fatigue. *Illuminat. Engineering* 47: 388.

Lloyd, D. (1941) A direct central inhibitory action of dromically conducted impulses. *J. Neurophysiol.* 4: 184.

———. (1946) Facilitation and inhibition of spinal motoneurones. *J. Neurophysiol.* 9: 421.

Lorente de No, R. (1935a) The refractory period of the motoneurones. *Amer. J. Physiol.* 111: 283.

———. (1935b) The summation of impulses transmitted to motoneurones through different synapses. *Amer. J. Physiol.* 113: 524.

———. (1938a) Synaptic stimulation of motoneurones as a local process. *J. Neurophysiol.* 1: 195.

———. (1938b) Analysis of the activity of the chains of internuncial neurones. *J. Neurophysiol.* 1: 207.

———. (1939) Transmission of impulses through cranial motor nuclei. *J. Neurophysiol.* 2: 402.

Lorenz, K. (1943) Die angeborenen Formen Möglicher Ehrfahrung. *Zs. Tierpsychol.* 5: 235.

Lucas, K. (1909) The "all-or-none" contraction of the amphibian skeletal muscle fiber. *J. Physiol.* 38: 113.

Lundberg, G. A. (1937) Foundations of Sociology. New York, Macmillan.

Maatsch, J. L., H. M. Adelson, and M. R. Denny. (1954) Effort and resistance to extinction of the bar-pressing response. *J. Comp. Physiol. Psychol.* 47: 47.

Maier, N. R. F. (1949) Frustration: The Study of Behavior without a Goal. New York, McGraw-Hill.

Maier, N. R. F., and N. M. Glaser. (1942) Studies of abnormal behavior in the rat.

IX. Factors which influence the occurrence of seizures during auditory stimulation. *J. Comp. Psychol.* 34: 11.

Maier, N. R. F., and J. V. Longhurst. (1947) Studies of abnormal behavior in the
rat. XXI. Conflict and audiogenic seizures. *J. Comp. Psychol.* 40: 397.

Malmo, R. B., J. F. Davis, and S. Barga. (1952) Total hysterical deafness: An
experimental case study. *J. Personal.* 21: 188.

Malmo, R. B., H. Wallerstein, and C. Shagass. (1953) Headache proneness and
mechanisms of motor conflict in psychiatric patients. *J. Personal.* 22: 163.

Marx, M., R. Henderson, and C. Roberts. (1955) Positive reinforcement of the bar-
pressing response by a light stimulus following dark operant pre-tests with no
after effect. *J. Comp. Physiol. Psychol.* 48: 73.

Masserman, J. H. (1943) Behavior and Neurosis. Chicago, University of Chicago
Press.

————. (1946) Principles of Dynamic Psychiatry. Philadelphia, Saunders.

Masserman, J. H., and K. S. Yum. (1946) An analysis of the influence of alcohol
on experimental neuroses in cats. *Psychosom. Med.* 8: 36.

Max, L. W. (1935) Breaking up a homosexual fixation by the conditioned reaction
technique. A case study. *Psychol. Bull.* 32: 734.

May, M. A. (1948) Experimentally acquired drives. *J. Exper. Psychol.* 38: 66.

McGeogh, J. A. (1942) The Psychology of Human Learning. New York, Long-
mans, Green.

McGeogh, J. A., and E. T. McDonald. (1931) Meaningful relation and retroactive
inhibition. *Amer. J. Psychol.* 43: 579.

McGeogh, J. A., F. McKinney, and H. Peters. (1937) Studies in retroactive inhibition. IX. Retroactive inhibition, reproductive inhibition, and reminiscence.
J. Exper. Psychol. 20: 131.

Meduna, L. J. (1947) Carbon Dioxide Therapy. Springfield, Ill., Charles C Thomas.

Meyer, V. (1956) Personal communication.

Mikhailoff, S.. (1933) Expériences réflexologiques, Expériences nouvelles sur Pa-
gurus striatus. *Bull. Inst. Oceanog. Monaco* No. 418, p. 1. Quoted by G. H. S.
Razran, *Psychol. Bull.* 1933, 30: 261.

Mill, J. S. (1898) A System of Logic. Book III, Chap. V, Sec. 3. London, Long-
mans, Green.

————. (1924) Autobiography. New York, Columbia University Press.

Miller, L. H. (1956) Table of percentage points of Kolmogorov statistics. *J. Amer.
Statist. Assn.* 51: 111.

Miller, N. E. (1944) Experimental studies of conflict. In J. McV. Hunt, ed., Personality and the Behavior Disorders. New York, Ronald Press.

————. (1948) Studies of fear as an acquirable drive. I. Fear as motivation and
fear-reduction as reinforcement in the learning of new responses. *J. Exper.
Psychol.* 38: 89.

————. (1950) Learnable drives and rewards. In S. S. Stevens, Handbook of Experimental Psychology. New York, Wiley.

Miller, N. E., and J. Dollard. (1941) Social Learning and Imitation. New Haven,
Yale Univ. Press.

Miller, N. E., E. Hubert, and J. Hamilton. (1938) Mental and behavioral changes
following male hormone treatment of adult castration hypogonadism and psychic impotence. *Proc. Soc. Exp. Biol. & Med.* 38: 538.

Moehlig, R. C. (1940) Castration in the male. *Endocrinology* 27: 743.

Mowrer, O. H. (1940) Anxiety-reduction and learning. *J. Exper. Psychol.* 27: 497.

————. (1947) On the dual nature of learning—a re-interpretation of "condition-ing" and "problem-solving." *Harvard Educ. Rev.* 17: 102.

Mowrer, O. H., and E. G. Aiken. (1954) Contiguity vs. drive-reduction in condi-tioned fear: Variations in conditioned and unconditioned stimuli. *Amer. J. Psychol.* 67: 26.

Mowrer, O. H., and H. M. Jones. (1943) Extinction and behavior variability as a function of effortfulness of task. *J. Exper. Psychol.* 33: 369.

Mowrer, O. H., and L. N. Solomon. (1954) Contiguity vs. drive-reduction in condi-tioned fear: The proximity and abruptness of drive-reduction. *Amer. J. Psy-chol.* 67: 15.

Mowrer, O. H., and P. Viek. (1948) Experimental analogue of fear from a sense of helplessness. *J. Abnorm. Soc. Psychol.* 43: 193.

Olds, J., and P. Milner. (1954) Positive reinforcement produced by electrical stimulation of septal area and other regions of rat brain. *J. Comp. Physiol. Psychol.* 47: 419.

Osgood, C. E. (1946) Meaningful similarity and interference in learning. *J. Exper. Psychol.* 36: 227.

————. (1948) An investigation into the causes of retroactive inhibition. *J. Exper. Psychol.* 38: 132.

Pack, G. (1923) New experiments on the nature of the sensation of thirst. *Amer. J. Physiol.* 65: 346.

Pavlov, I. P. (1927) Conditioned Reflexes. Translated by G. V. Anrep. London, Oxford University Press.

————. (1928) Lectures on Conditioned Reflexes. Trans. by W. H. Gantt. New York, Liveright.

————. (1941) Conditioned Reflexes and Psychiatry. Trans. by W. H. Gantt. New York, International Publ.

Penfield, W. (1954) Studies of the cerebral cortex of man—a review and an inte-gration. In J. Delafresnaye, ed., Brain Mechanisms and Consciousness. Spring-field, Ill., Charles C Thomas.

Penfield, W., and T. Rasmussen. (1950) The Cerebral Cortex of Man. New York, Macmillan.

Perin, C. T. (1942) Behavior potentiality as a joint function of the amount of training and degree of hunger at the time of extinction. *J. Exper. Psychol.* 30: 93.

Petrova, M. K. (1935) New data concerning the mechanisms of the action of bro-mides on the higher nervous activity. Quoted by B. P. Babkin (1938).

Pollitt, J. (1957) Natural history of obsessional states: A study of 150 cases. *Brit. Med. J.* 1: 194.

Popper, K. R. (1957) Philosophy of Science: A Personal Report, in British Phi-losophy in the Mid-Century, ed., C. A. Mace. London, Allen and Unwin.

Prosser, C. L., and W. S. Hunter. (1936) The extinction of startle responses and spinal reflexes in the white rat. *Amer. J. Physiol.* 117: 609.

Rachman, S. (1957) Personal communication.

Raymond, M. J. (1956) Case of fetishism treated by aversion therapy. *Brit. Med. J.* 2: 854.

Renshaw, B. (1941) Influence of discharge of motoneurones upon excitation of neighbouring motoneurones. *J. Neurophysiol.* 4: 167.

————. (1942) Reflex discharges in branches of the crural nerve. *J. Neurophysiol.* 5: 487.

Reyna, L. J. (1946) Experimental extinction as a function of the interval between extinction trials. Unpublished Ph.D. dissertation, University of Iowa, 1946.

Reynolds, B. (1945) A repetition of the Blodgett experiment on latent learning. *J. Exper. Psychol.* 35: 504.

Richter, C. P. (1927) Animal behavior and internal drives. *Quart. Rev. Biol.* 2: 307.

Rohrer, J. H. (1947) Experimental extinction as a function of the distribution of extinction trials and response strength. *J. Exper. Psychol.* 37: 473.

Roule, L. (1933) Fishes: Their Journeys and Migrations. New York, Norton.

Rowan, W. (1931) The Riddle of Migration. Baltimore, Williams & Wilkins.

Sainsbury, P., and J. G. Gibson. (1954) Symptoms of anxiety and tension and the accompanying physiological changes in the muscular system. *J. Neurol. Neurosurg. Psychiat.* 17: 216.

Salter, A. (1949) Conditioned Reflex Therapy. New York, Creative Age Press.

———. (1952) The Case Against Psychoanalysis. New York, Holt.

Sargant, W., and E. Slater. (1947) Treatment by insulin in sub-shock doses. *J. Nerv. Ment. Dis.* 105: 493.

Schaffer, H. R. (1954) Behavior under stress: A neurophysiological hypothesis. *Psychol. Rev.* 61: 323.

Schlosberg, H. (1934) Conditioned responses in the white rat. *J. Genet. Psychol.* 45: 303.

Sears, R. R., and L. H. Cohen. (1933) Hysterical anaesthesia, analgesia and astereognosis. *Arch. Neurol. Psychiat.* 29: 260.

Seitz, P. F. D. (1953) Dynamically oriented brief psychotherapy: Psychocutaneous excoriation syndrome. *Psychosom. Med.* 15: 200.

Shapiro, H. A. (1937) Effects of testosterone propionate on mating. *Nature* 139: 588.

Sheffield, F. D., and T. B. Roby. (1950) Reward value of a non-nutritive sweet taste. *J. Comp. Physiol. Psychol.* 43: 471.

Sherrington, C. S. (1906) Integrative Action of the Nervous System. New Haven, Yale University Press.

———. (1924) The problems of muscular receptivity. *Nature* 113: 929.

———. (1947) The Integrative Action of the Central Nervous System. Cambridge, Cambridge University Press.

Shirley, M. M. (1933) The First Two Years. Vol. III. Personality Manifestations. Inst. Child Welfare Monogr. No. 8. Minneapolis, University of Minnesota Press.

Shurrager, P. S., and E. Culler. (1940) Conditioning in the spinal dog. *J. Exper. Psychol.* 26: 133.

Shurrager, P. S., and M. C. Shurrager. (1946) The rate of learning measured at a single synapse. *J. Exper. Psychol.* 36: 347.

Siegel, S. (1956) Non-parametric Statistics. New York, McGraw-Hill.

Skinner, B. F. (1938) The Behavior of Organisms. New York, Appleton.

Smith, M. P., and G. Buchanan. (1954) Acquisition of secondary reward by cues associated with shock reduction. *J. Exper. Psychol.* 48: 123.

Sollman, T. (1942) A Manual of Pharmacology. 6th ed. Philadelphia, Saunders.

Solomon, R. L. (1948) Effort and extinction rate: A confirmation. *J. Comp. Physiol. Psychol.* 41: 93.

Solomon, R. L., and E. S. Brush. (1956) Experimentally derived conceptions of anxiety and aversion. Nebraska Symposium on Motivation. Ed., M. R. Jones.

Solomon, R. L., and L. C. Wynne. (1954) Traumatic avoidance learning: The principles of anxiety conservation and partial irreversibility. *Psychol. Rev.* 61; 353.

Stevens, S. S., H. Davis, and M. Lurie. (1935) The localization of pitch perception on the basilar membrane. *J. Gen. Psychol.* 13: 297.

Stone, D. R. (1955) Responses to imagined auditory stimuli as compared to recorded sounds. *J. Consult. Psychol.* 19: 254.

Switzer, S. A. (1930) Backward conditioning of the lid reflex. *J. Exper. Psychol.* 13: 76.

Sylvester, J. D., and L. A. Leversedge. (1955) Conditioning techniques in the treatment of writer's cramp. *Lancet* 1: 1147.

Taylor, J. G. (1950) Reaction latency as a function of reaction potential and behavior oscillation. *Psychol. Rev.* 57: 375.

———. (1955) Personal communication.

Teitelbaum, H. A., C. S. Hoekstra, D. N. Goldstein, I. D. Harris, R. M. Woods, and D. Cohen. (1946) Treatment of psychiatric disorders due to combat by means of a group therapy program and insulin in sub-shock doses. *J. Nerv. Ment. Dis.* 104: 123.

Thorndike, E. L. (1932) Reward and punishment in animal learning. *Comp. Psychol. Monogr.* 8, No. 39.

Tinbergen, N. (1951) The Study of Instinct. London, Oxford University Press.

Tolman, E. C. (1932) Purposive Behavior in Animals and Men. New York, Appleton.

Vaynburg, I. S., and B. N. Birman. (1935) Application of small doses of bromide in neuroses. *Sovet. Vrach. Gaz.* P1093.

Wang, G. H., C. P. Richter, and A. F. Guttmacher. (1925) Activity studies in male castrated rats with ovarian transplants, and the correlation of the activity with the histology of the grafts. *Amer. J. Physiol.* 73: 581.

Washco, A. (1933) The Effects of Music upon Pulse Rate, Blood-Pressure and Respiration. Philadelphia, Temple University Press.

Watson, J. B., and P. Rayner. (1920) Conditioned emotional reactions. *J. Exper. Psychol.* 3: 1.

Wendt, G. R. (1936) An interpretation of inhibition of conditioned reflexes as competition between reaction systems. *Psychol. Rev.* 43: 258.

Wilder, J. (1945) Facts and figures on psychotherapy. *J. Clin. Psychopath.* 7: 311.

Wilhelmi, A. E. (1946) Energy transformations in muscle. Chap. III of Howell's Textbook of Physiology. 15th ed. Ed., J. E. Fulton. Philadelphia, Saunders.

Williams, S. B. (1938) Resistance to extinction as a function of the number of reinforcements. *J. Exper. Psychol.* 23: 506.

Willoughby, R. R. (1932) Some properties of the Thurstone Personality Schedule and a suggested revision. *J. Soc. Psychol.* 3: 401.

———. (1934) Norms for the Clarke-Thurstone Inventory. *J. Soc. Psychol.* 5: 91.

Wohlgemuth, A. (1923) A Critical Examination of Psychoanalysis. London, Allen and Unwin.

Wolberg, L. R. (1948) Medical Hypnosis. New York, Grune and Stratton.

Wolf, S., and H. G. Wolff. (1947) Human Gastric Functions. New York, Oxford University Press.

Wolfe, J. B. (1934) The effect of delayed reward on learning in the white rat. *J. Comp. Psychol.* 17: 1.

Wolfe, J. B., and M. D. Kaplon. (1941) Effect of amount of reward and consummation activity on learning in chickens. *J. Comp. Psychol.* 31: 353.

Wolff, H. G. (1950) Life stress and cardiovascular disorders. *Circulation* 1: 187.

Wolfle, H. M. (1932) Conditioning as a function of the interval between the conditioned and the original stimulus. *J. Gen. Psychol.* 7: 80.

Wolpe, J. (1948) An approach to the problem of neurosis based on the conditioned response. Unpublished M.D. Thesis, University of the Witwatersrand.

———. (1949) An interpretation of the effects of combinations of stimuli (patterns) based on current neurophysiology. *Psychol. Rev.* 56: 277.

———. (1950) Need-reduction, drive-reduction, and reinforcement: A neurophysiological view. *Psychol. Rev.* 57: 19.

———. (1952a) Experimental neurosis as learned behavior. *Brit. J. Psychol.* 43: 243.

———. (1952b) The formation of negative habits: A neurophysiological view. *Psychol. Rev.* 59: 290.

———. (1952c) The neurophysiology of learning and delayed reward learning. *Psychol. Rev.* 59: 192.

———. (1952d) Objective psychotherapy of the neuroses. *South African Med. J.* 26: 825.

———. (1952e) Primary stimulus generalization: A neurophysiological view. *Psychol. Rev.* 59: 8.

———. (1953a) Learning theory and "abnormal fixations." *Psychol. Rev.* 60: 111.

———. (1953b) Theory construction for Blodgett's latent learning. *Psychol. Rev.* 60: 340.

———. (1954) Reciprocal inhibition as the main basis of psychotherapeutic effects. *Arch. Neurol. Psychiat.* 72: 205.

———. (1956) Learning versus lesions as the basis of neurotic behavior. *Amer. J. Psychiat.* 112: 923.

Woodbury, C. B. (1943) The learning of stimulus patterns by dogs. *J. Comp. Psychol.* 35: 29.

Woolsey, C. N., and E. M. Walze. (1942) Topical projection of nerve fibres from local regions of the cochlea to the cerebral cortex of the cat. *Bull. Johns Hopkins Hosp.* 31: 315.

Yates, A. J. (1957) The application of learning theory to the treatment of tics. *J. Abnorm. Soc. Psychol.* (in press).

Yerkes, R. M. (1939) Sexual behavior in the chimpanzee. *Human Biol.* 2: 78.

Zbrozyna, A. W. (1953) Phenomenon of non-identification of a stimulus operating against different physiological backgrounds in dogs. *Lodzkie Towarzystwo Naukowe* 3, No. 26 (in Polish with English summary).

———. (1957) The conditioned cessation of eating. *Bull. Acad. Polonaise Sci.* 5: 261.

Index

85; correcting misconceptions, 106;
danger of increasing sensitization,
193; desensitization based on relaxation (q.v.), 139–65; fortuitous therapy, 198–99; fundamental psychotherapy, 106, 200; history-taking,
105–7; interview-induced responses,
182–85; interview procedure, 105–14;
introductory statement to patients,
111; Jacobson's differential relaxation,
135–38; list of responses utilized, 113;
permissiveness of therapist, 106; records of interviews, 105; responses used
in life situation, 114–38; results of,
207–19; sexual responses (q.v.), 130–
35; use of conditioned motor response,
174–80

Rachman, S., 203,
Raginsky, B. B., 40, 202
Rasmussen, T., 16
Raymond, M. J., 182
Rayner, P., 48
Reactive inhibition, 24–26, 27–28; in ex-
traverts, 88; low level in autonomic
responses, 66, 71; in therapy, 71
Reciprocal inhibition: applications in
therapy, 113; between motor and autonomic responses, 65; demonstrated in
experimental neurosis, 60; desensitization by, 139–65; evaluation of methods, 205–20; in the life situation, 114–
38; mechanism of cure, 67; present
status of, 220; response-eliminating
mechanism, 29–31; as therapeutic
principle, 71–75
Reflexes, 17–19
Reinforcement: definition, 20; effect of
distribution, 22; effect of number, 21;
role of drive reduction, 22–24; time
relations in, 21
Relapse, modes of, 217
Relaxation: autonomic effects of, 72;
Jacobson's method, 135–38; method of
training, 136–37; systematic desensitization by (q.v.), 139–65
Renshaw, B., 11
Repression, 94
Repression theory, ix, 33; evidence
against, 186, 216–17

Resentment, 114–15, 117
Respiratory responses in therapy, 74,
166–72
Response, definition, 3–4
Results of therapy, 207–19
Retroactive inhibition, 30
Reyna, L. J., 25
Reynolds, B., 22
Richter, C. P., 7
Roberts, C., 24
Roby, T. B., 24
Rohrer, J. H., 25
Roule, L., 19
Rowan, W., 18

Sainsbury, P., 36
Salter, A., ix, 107, 111, 114, 119
Sargant, W., x
Schaffer, H. R., 70
Schlosberg, H., 20, 22
Sears, R. R., 184
Seitz, P. F. D., 120
Selection of patients, 205–6
Self-sufficiency, 107
Sexual responses: autonomic effects, 72;
inhibited by anxiety, 36; use in ther-
apy, 130–35
Shagass, C., 36
Shapiro, H. A., 6, 7
Sheffield, F. D., 24
Sherrington, C. S., 11, 12, 26, 27, 29
Shirley, M. M., 76
Shurrager, M. C., 21
Shurrager, P. S., 21
Siegel, S., 108
Skinner, B. F., ix, 7, 22, 23
Slater, E., x
Smith, M. P., 180
Sollman, T., 10
Solomon, H. C., 194
Solomon, L. N., 23
Solomon, R. L., 21, 23, 26, 69–70
Space constriction in neurosis produc-
tion, 65, 68, 80, 81
Spiegel, J. P., 196
"Spontaneous" therapy, 198–99
Statistical data on results, 207–19
Stevens, S. S., 12
Stimulus: ambivalent stimuli, 38; defi-
nition of, 4; effects of compound stimu-